STUDENT ACTIVITIES IN

LIFE SCIENCE

for Christian Schools

SECOND EDITION

William S. Pinkston Jr. and David Anderson

TEACHER'S EDITION

Bob Jones University Press, Greenville, South Carolina 29614

This textbook was written by members of the faculty and staff of Bob Jones University. Standing for the "old-time religion" and the absolute authority of the Bible since 1927, Bob Jones University is the world's leading Fundamentalist Christian university. The staff of the University is devoted to educating Christian men and women to be servants of Jesus Christ in all walks of life.

Providing unparalleled academic excellence, Bob Jones University prepares its students through its offering of over one hundred majors, while its fervent spiritual emphasis prepares their minds and hearts for service and devotion to the Lord Jesus Christ.

Photograph Credits:
Cover: Unusual Films

NOTE:
The fact that materials produced by other publishers may be referred to in this volume does not constitute an endorsement by Bob Jones University Press of the content or theological position of materials produced by such publishers. The position of the Bob Jones University Press, and the University itself, is well known. Any references and ancillary materials are listed as an aid to the student or the teacher and in an attempt to maintain the accepted academic standards of the publishing industry.

Student Activities in LIFE SCIENCE for Christian Schools® Teacher's Edition
Second Edition

William S. Pinkston Jr., M.Ed.

Revised by
David Anderson, Ph.D.

Editor David Harris
Designer Brian Johnson
Composition Ted Rich

Produced in cooperation with the Bob Jones University College of Arts and Science, Bob Jones Academy, and Bob Jones Junior High School.

for Christian Schools is a registered trademark of Bob Jones University Press.

ISBN 0-89084-943-9

15 14 13 12 11 10 9 8 7

Part of the study of life science involves your learning various observations that others have made. It would be impossible for you to reobserve in your entire life all that men have observed and learned about God's physical creation. Thus, if you are to make wise decisions about using the physical world around you, you must learn about some of these observations.

The study of life science, however, is more than learning about observations that others have made. Life science also involves your making observations and drawing your own conclusions about them. In this way you can learn not only how to investigate the physical world but also how much you can trust even the best observations of others.

This book, *Student Activities in* LIFE SCIENCE *for Christian Schools*®, Second Edition, was developed to help your study of life science in both areas: learning of others' observations and making your own observations.

Ideas and Investigations

There are two types of activities in this book: *Ideas* and *Investigations.*

Ideas

Ideas are designed to help you learn the information in LIFE SCIENCE *for Christian Schools*®. These exercises should help you build your vocabulary, extend your understanding, and remember the important material that is found in your text. Your teacher will assign various Ideas sections when you have covered the material in your reading or in class. Some of the exercises are very simple; others are designed to make you think and are not so easy. Many of them are designed so that you can check yourself to make sure that you have the right answer.

How much the Ideas sections help you will depend upon *your* attitude toward them. If you approach them as something that you need to finish as quickly as possible so that you can do something else, you will gain little from them. If you race through the exercises quickly, you will learn almost nothing as you do them. Try to *learn* as you do the Ideas sections. Do not be satisfied just with getting the right answer and racing on to the next question. Make sure that you know and understand what you do in the exercises so that if the same or similar questions appear on a quiz or a test, you will be able to answer them correctly. If your teacher were to give you a blank copy of an Ideas section as a quiz the day after you did it as homework, you should be able to get 100 percent on it. If you are not working the Ideas sections that carefully, you are not using them wisely.

Investigations

Investigations sections are designed to help you learn more about life science by doing something. You may perform an experiment, make observations, do library research, or do various other activities. There are several different types of Investigations.

Class Investigations

Class Investigations are designed to be done in class by the entire class. Often a Class Investigation involves your performing an experiment. Usually there are observations to be made and analyzed in a Class Investigation. Some Class Investigations will be performed individually, others will be performed by groups, and some will be done as a demonstration by your teacher while you and your classmates observe.

Research Investigations

A Research Investigation usually involves your finding information in other books. Sometimes it involves talking with a person to find out what he does or knows about something. In the Research Investigations you are given some information about a topic and are told how to find out more about it. Often you are asked to make an oral or written report about your findings.

Field Investigations

A Field Investigation involves your finding out what something is like. It may involve going into your back yard to look at something, or it may involve taking a trip to a zoo, the woods, or somewhere else to make various observations. In Field Investigations you are told what you are looking for and where you can find it. Often you are asked to make an oral or written report about your findings.

Personal Investigations

A Personal Investigation is something that you can do on your own, often at home. Personal Investigations usually involve making an oral or written report about your findings.

Safety

Sometimes you will be asked to use materials that could be dangerous if used improperly. For this reason you are never to *play* with any of the equipment used in this class. **Never use equipment for any purpose other than the purpose for which it is intended.** In this way neither you, your friends, nor the equipment will be hurt. The directions in the Investigations include safety symbols to alert you to possible danger. The safety symbols are explained below. When you see a particular symbol in an assigned Investigation, your teacher should explain to you what the danger is and how to protect yourself.

Animals: Animals that you are to observe, collect, or encounter may inflict dangerous stings or bites (bees or fire ants).

Body protection: Chemicals, stains, or other materials could damage your skin or clothes. You should wear a laboratory apron and/or latex gloves.

Chemical fumes: Chemical fumes may present a danger. Use a chemical fume hood or a well-ventilated area.

Electricity: An electrical device (hot plate, lamp, or microscope) will be used. Use the device with care.

Eye protection: There is possible danger to the eyes from chemicals or other materials. Wear safety goggles.

Fire: A heat source or open flame is to be used. Be careful to avoid skin burns and ignition of combustible materials.

Gas: Improper use of gas can result in burns, explosion, or suffocation. Be careful to check that the gas is turned off when you are finished.

Plants: Plants that you are to observe, collect, or encounter may have sharp thorns or spines, or they may cause contact dermatitis (such as poison ivy).

Pathogen: Organisms encountered in the Investigation could cause human disease (water- and soil-borne organisms, saliva).

Poison: A substance in the Investigation could be poisonous if ingested.

Sharp objects: Cuts are possible from broken glassware (broken test tubes, thermometers, microscope slides) or sharp instruments (scalpels, razor blades, knives).

Policies and Procedures

You will notice that the pages in this book are perforated so that they can be easily removed. In order for your teacher to look over your work, grade it, and help you do better work in the future, you may be asked to turn in various pages of this book. Be sure that you have your name and the other requested information written at the top of the page before you hand in the paper. When it is returned, you should put it into a loose-leaf notebook so that you do not lose it. Some of the Investigations ask you to hand in a written report. You will do these reports on your own paper and will not need to turn in a page from this book. When your reports are returned, you should also place them in your notebook. Your teacher may wish to collect your notebook periodically in order to review your work. Keep it neat and safe.

You will often be given various pieces of equipment to work with in class. To help you identify pieces of equipment you may be unfamiliar with see Appendix A. You are expected to be careful with this equipment. Do not damage it. If your equipment is damaged when you get it, show it to your teacher immediately. If you damage a piece of equipment, report it to your teacher immediately.

Do your own work. It is often easy to ask a friend what his answer was for a particular question. That, however, is cheating. If you have difficulties with a section or a specific question, ask your teacher about it. Of course, if you are working together as a group on a particular project, it is not cheating for you and other members of the group to discuss what you are doing. Cheating involves your getting from someone else an answer that you were to supply yourself. When you cheat, you are saying, "I have found this answer, and I deserve credit for it," when actually you did not find the answer and, therefore, do not deserve credit for it. Cheating is lying to your teacher, to yourself, and to God.

It is the prayer of the author and those who have worked with him in preparing this book that you may "grow in grace, and in the knowledge of our Lord and Saviour Jesus Christ" as you use this book to study life science.

To the Teacher

As a teacher, you desire to transmit knowledge to students by many different teaching methods. A list of such learning methods includes lectures, drill, question and answer, discussion, storytelling, objects (visual aids), demonstrations, projects, experiments, and reports. The last four items of this list (demonstrations, projects, experiments, and reports) can be generally referred to as *activities.* They are the methods that allow the students to be *actively* involved in the process of learning. For this reason, the major portion of this book is a collection of activities under the title *Investigations.*

This book covers more Investigations than the average traditional class can do in one school year. The intention for this is to provide you with a selection from which you can choose the Investigations best suited to your students' needs. The teaching schedule and marginal notes in the teacher's edition of the text offer suggestions about how and when to use each Investigation.

The first portion of each chapter in this book includes a collection of worksheets under the title *Ideas.* This section of the chapter will help students understand the basic material and concepts in *LIFE SCIENCE for Christian Schools*®. The Ideas sections reinforce concepts, stress vocabulary, require reasoning or memory, or incorporate combinations of these skills. You will probably want the students to do the Ideas sections for the parts of the text you cover.

At the back of this book you will find a list of materials required for the Investigations. Some of them you can purchase locally (coded *L*); others you will need to order from a scientific supply house (coded *SH*). Go over this list carefully before school begins to determine what you will need to purchase for the year. Submit your "shopping list" to your school authorities early so that your orders can be processed in time. It is wise to order supplies for the entire school year at the same time since some supply houses discount the prices of bulk orders. As your supplies arrive and you make local purchases, develop an inventory list that will help you keep track of your needs.

A decision that teachers commonly face is how much credit to give for class activities. Most states require that 20 percent of the classroom time in high-school science courses be devoted to hands-on activities. If your state makes a requirement like this for junior high schools, then the Investigations should compose about one-fifth of the students' final grades. To facilitate grading the Investigations and the Ideas sections, the students should remove an entire chapter from the book at one time. This chapter should be stored in a notebook until you have finished the chapter. Then the students should turn in their notebooks so that you can grade the entire chapter at once.

Name ______________________________

Date ____________ Hour ______________

1–Life and Science

Ideas 1a

Searching for the Truth

Directions: Read each of the statements about the great auk carefully. Then decide which of the following categories best describes each statement. Place the letter of the proper category in the blank in front of the statement. You may use each category more than once.

The great auk is pictured and discussed on page 366 of the text. Students should not need this information to answer these questions. Encourage students to be sure that they understand each of the categories before they try to determine the answers. You may wish to review characteristics of the categories before giving the assignment.

Categories

a. Historical fact based on physical evidence

b. Historical fact based on recorded evidence

c. Scientific fact based on observations

d. Universal statement

e. Value judgment

*d*______ 1. There are no great auks alive today.

*e*______ 2. The great auk was a beautiful bird.

*a*______ 3. By examining preserved specimens in various museums, scientists have determined that the great auks stood about 75 cm high.

*b*______ 4. The journals of many sailors tell of great auks that nested on islands in the Atlantic Ocean off the coast of North America.

*c*______ 5. Today common murre, smaller birds that can fly, live on the islands where the great auks once lived.

*b*______ 6. According to many ship logs, ships stopped at these islands to stock up on meat.

*e*______ 7. The meat of the great auk was very tasty.

*d*______ 8. Although the great auks could not fly, they were all excellent swimmers.

*a*______ 9. The eggs preserved in museums show that great-auk eggs were mottled brown and white.

*c*______10. The little auk, which is 8 inches long, nests in Greenland and in Iceland.

Ideas 1b

Biblical Truth

Directions: Listed below are five evidences that the Bible is the Word of God. Complete each evidence by choosing the correct word from the choices and then writing it in the blank.

accurate	claim	descriptions	history
includes	prophecy	refuses	testimony

1. The Bible's ___claim___ to be the Word of God
2. Fulfilled ___prophecy___
3. ___Accurate___ history
4. Accurate ___descriptions___ of the physical world
5. Inner ___testimony___ of the believer

Ideas 1c

The Scientific Method

Directions: Select the proper terms from the list to complete the paragraph below. Write your answers on the lines to the left of the paragraph. You may use each term only once.

hypothesis	observations	analyze	control group
predict	problem	chose	experiment
scientific method	survey	data	experimental variable
verify	workable	bias	experimental group

___scientific method___ 1.
___problem___ 2.
___hypothesis___ 3.
___experiment___ 4.
___control group___ 5.
___experimental group___ 6.
___experimental variable___ 7.
___observations___ 8.
___data___ 9.
___analyze___ 10.
___chose___ 11.
___verify___ 12.

John's science teacher said that seeds do not need light in order to sprout. John had always heard that plants need light. He decided to use the __1__ to determine which was correct. His __2__ was, "Do plant seeds need light in order to sprout?" John's __3__ was that plant seeds do need light in order to sprout. To begin his __4__, he obtained four small cups and filled each one with soil. He then put three seeds in each cup. John placed two of these cups inside a dark cabinet and used them as his __5__. He put the other two cups on a sunny window ledge and used them as his __6__. Every other day he added the same amount of water to each of the cups. In this experiment John planned to have light as the __7__. Every day John recorded his __8__ of the seeds. Once a seed sprouted, John used a ruler to measure the plant's daily growth. He also wrote notes about the color of the sprouts. All of these notes would serve as his __9__. After two weeks John made a chart of the results of his experiment. He made the chart to help him __10__ the data. After looking at the chart, John __11__ an answer. Based on his observations, John decided that his hypothesis was wrong, since seeds sprouted as well in the dark as in the light. However, from his data he also concluded that soon after the seeds sprouted, differences developed in the two groups. John doubted the results of his experiment. Since he had used only bean seeds, he decided that he would need to perform additional experiments in order to __12__ the results of this experiment.

Name ______________________
Date __________ Hour __________

Ideas 1d

Review

Part 1

If pressed for time, assign only one part.

Directions: Use the definitions to help unscramble the terms.

1. absi *bias* What a person wants to believe
2. daat *data* Pieces of information
3. sfscyali *classify* To arrange data so that relationships can be seen
4. ecicsne *science* Man's observations of the physical world
5. lekaborw *workable* Usable
6. iifdeevr *verified* Known to be correct
7. laveu tnudjgem *value judgment* Decision about whether something is right or wrong
8. bvrsieotaosn *observation* What we can tell about our surroundings by using our senses

Part 2

Directions: Read the following statements. In the space provided, write *True* if the statement is true and *False* if the statement is false and draw a line through the word or words that make the statement false. In the space in the margin, write the word or words necessary to make the statement true. There are five true and five false statements.

never — *False* 1. True science will ~~sometimes~~ contradict the Word of God.

True 2. A newspaper is an example of recorded evidence.

True 3. Good scientific observations must be measurable or repeatable.

survey — *False* 4. To find out how many students who live in the state of Arizona are taking life science this year, you would conduct a ~~scientific experiment~~.

True 5. Science cannot be used to make value judgments.

fulfilled — *False* 6. The ~~unfulfilled~~ prophecies in the Bible help to demonstrate that the Bible is the Word of God.

True 7. A photograph would be recorded evidence of a historical event.

control — *False* 8. An experiment is made up of two groups: the experimental group and the ~~survey~~ group.

True 9. After a person analyzes all the available data, he can choose the best answer to a problem.

hypothesis — *False* 10. A ~~factor~~ is a guess about the solution to a problem.

Name ______________________________
Date ______________ Hour ______________

Class Investigation 1a

Is Measuring Accurate?

Goals

- Recognize the inaccuracy of measurements made by humans.
- Practice measuring.

Materials

Experiment 1: yarn, ruler

Experiment 2: cross section of a woody stem

Experiment 3: sand, tablespoon, paper (13 cm or 5 in. square), balance

Experiment 4: meter stick or yardstick, ruler

Procedures

Experiment 1: *How long is this piece of yarn?*

- Lay the yarn flat on your desk in as straight a line as possible.
- Lay the ruler next to the yarn and determine the length of the yarn.
- Record your observation on the data chart.

Experiment 2: *How many growth rings are visible in this cross section of a tree trunk or branch?*

- Count the growth rings from the center of the cross section and work your way to the outside.
- Record your observation on the data chart.

Experiment 3: *How much does 5 tablespoons of sand weigh?*

- Place one square of paper on the balance.
- Using the tablespoon measure, place 5 tablespoons of sand on the square of paper.
- Using the method described by your teacher, determine the weight of the sand.
- Carefully dump the sand back into the container and discard the square of paper.
- Record your observation on the data chart.

Experiment 4: *How tall is* ______________________________*?*

- Your class will choose one person whose height will be measured. Write that person's name in the blank above.
- Measure the person's height.
- Record your observations on the data chart.

Individual Data Chart	
Experiment #	**Observation**
1	Length of yarn =
2	Number of growth rings =
3	Weight of sand =
4	Height of person =

Give the students little, if any, help in measurement techniques. The main goal is to demonstrate that human measurements vary in their accuracy. Ensure variation in the following ways.

In Experiment 1 have only 30.5 cm (12 in.) rulers and yarn that is about 33 to 38 cm (13 to 15 in.) long. You should use yarn because it can stretch easily.

In Experiment 2 do not tell the students whether they should count the bark.

In Experiment 3 have each student supply his own square of paper, which would then be a variable. Do not tell the students whether to use level or unlevel tablespoonfuls. Consider having a spoon that they cannot level.

Technically, mass *and* weight *are not the same. However, in common usage they are sometimes considered to be the same. Such is the case in this book.*

Experiment 3 probably takes the most time and should be avoided if you are rushed or have a large class.

Methods of speeding up the exercise: Divide the class in halves, thirds, or fourths, depending upon the size, and have each group complete the exercise as instructed. Have more than one balance available for weighing sand.

In Experiment 4 offer the student a meter stick (or yardstick) and an area of the wall that has something sticking out of it (such as the chalk tray or a bulletin-board frame) so that the meter stick will be difficult to position against the wall.

Have the equipment available to do several of these exercises and then let the students choose the experiment that they want to do.

Mention that it is possible to be both precise and inaccurate at the same time. Precision is the state of being clearly expressed or delineated. Accuracy is to have no errors, or at least to be within the allowed variation. For example, if an object truly weighs 5.8 g and student A reports it as 5.4902 g while student B reports it as 5.79 g, student A is more precise, but is precisely wrong.

Observations

On the charts below record the names of your class members and the data they obtained. Be sure to record the units for each observation of the data.

Experiment # ____________________

No.	Name	Data	No.	Name	Data	No.	Name	Data
1.			12.			23.		
2.			13.			24.		
3.			14.			25.		
4.			15.			26.		
5.			16.			27.		
6.			17.			28.		
7.			18.			29.		
8.			19.			30.		
9.			20.			31.		
10.			21.			32.		
11.			22.			33.		

Experiment # ____________________

No.	Name	Data	No.	Name	Data	No.	Name	Data
1.			12.			23.		
2.			13.			24.		
3.			14.			25.		
4.			15.			26.		
5.			16.			27.		
6.			17.			28.		
7.			18.			29.		
8.			19.			30.		
9.			20.			31.		
10.			21.			32.		
11.			22.			33.		

Name ____________________

Date __________ Hour __________

Experiment # ____________

No.	Name	Data	No.	Name	Data	No.	Name	Data
1.			12.			23.		
2.			13.			24.		
3.			14.			25.		
4.			15.			26.		
5.			16.			27.		
6.			17.			28.		
7.			18.			29.		
8.			19.			30.		
9.			20.			31.		
10.			21.			32.		
11.			22.			33.		

Experiment # ____________

No.	Name	Data	No.	Name	Data	No.	Name	Data
1.			12.			23.		
2.			13.			24.		
3.			14.			25.		
4.			15.			26.		
5.			16.			27.		
6.			17.			28.		
7.			18.			29.		
8.			19.			30.		
9.			20.			31.		
10.			21.			32.		
11.			22.			33.		

The answers in the Summing Up section will vary, depending upon the exercise and the data obtained. Look for careful thought in the students' answers. We suggest that you assign the Summing Up section as homework. After you collect it, discuss the answers in class. You may need to counsel those students who do poorly on this exercise. If they lack understanding, encourage them to try harder. If they lack drive and desire to put forth the effort, challenge them. If the condition persists in later exercises, parental conferences may be needed.

Summing up

1. Did every member of your class report the same measurement?

   ☐ Yes ☐ No

2. Did every member of your class report his values in the same unit (e.g., feet, inches, meters)? ☐ Yes ☐ No

   If not, convert all the values to the unit that most of the students used to report these measurements.

   Why is it important that everyone report his data in the same unit? ***to facilitate calculations and comparisons***

3. Calculate the average value of all the measurements reported. (Add all the measurements and divide the total by the number of measurements.) Be sure to include the units. The average measurement is __________ .

   Did any student actually report this average value as his measurement?

   ☐ Yes ☐ No

   Would this average value be a good answer for your experiment?

   ☐ Yes ☐ No Why ? ***Answers will vary. A few abnormal measurements could make the average value less meaningful.***

4. Which value did most students report as their measurement? __________

   Is this value the same as the average? ☐ Yes ☐ No

   Would this value be a good answer for your experiment?

   ☐ Yes ☐ No Why ? ***Answers will vary. A few measurements in agreement may or may not reflect the overall meaning of the data.***

5. What value would you choose for the answer to the experiment? __________

   Why? ***Answers will vary.***

6. What was the smallest measurement reported? __________

7. What was the largest measurement reported? __________

8. Is either of these values unreasonable? ☐ Yes ☐ No If so, which one and why? __________

9. Why were so many different values reported for the measurement of the same thing? Give as many reasons as you can. ***Answers will vary. (human error, stretching (of yarn), differences in measurement techniques, variation of measured objects, defective/inaccurate measuring devices, and so forth)***

10. If your class were to do the project again, how could you make more accurate measurements? ***Answers will vary, but should include elimination of the problems stated in question 9.***

Name ______________________

Date ____________ Hour ____________

Class Investigation 1b

Popcorn Science

This investigation should be highly teacher directed. There are many avenues of inquiry that the students could follow. Lead the students to answer the questions below with answers similar to those given.

Goal

- Use a scientific method.

Materials

popcorn kernels of various *natural* colors, hot plate, popcorn popper

White and yellow popcorn is available in grocery stores. Natural red, blue, black, and multicolored are available as autumn decorations. They are also available in specialty food stores all year.

Procedures and observations

In this investigation you will use the steps of a scientific method. Answer the questions below in complete sentences. Your teacher will guide you with helpful hints, but the answers must be your own.

Establish the problem

1. Your teacher will show you some unpopped popcorn kernels. Describe the kernels. ***Students should note the differences in the coat color and possibly other differences.***

2. What color do you think the popcorn will be after it is popped? ***Answers will vary.***

   Do you know for sure? ***no***

3. Write a question about popcorn color that could be answered by using a scientific method. ***Though there are many correct possibilities, direct the students to ask the question "Is popped popcorn the same color as the unpopped kernel color?"***

Form a hypothesis

Though you may not be certain of the answer to your question, you have probably popped and eaten popcorn before. Thus, you probably have an idea about what the answer to the problem should be. How do you think unpopped kernel color and popped kernel color are related? (This statement is your hypothesis; write it as a statement, not as a question.)
Students should state that coat color and popped color are either the same or different.

Experiment

1. On the lines below explain an experiment you could do that would determine if your hypothesis is correct or incorrect. ***Students should suggest popping the various colors of kernels to reveal what color of popped corn will result. The control group would be some of each color of kernels kept unpopped for comparison.***

Use the hot plate to pop individual kernels (just one of each color). They should pop in less than a minute if placed on a hot surface such as a hot plate burner.

2. Your teacher will perform the experiment.

Classify and analyze the data

In the space below make a chart that organizes the data of the experiment.

You may need to help some students decide how to organize the data.

Color of unpopped kernel:	Color of popped popcorn:
yellow	*white*
white	*white*
red	*white*
blue	*white*
black	*white*

Choose an answer

Was your hypothesis right or wrong? ***Answers will vary.***

Verify the answer

1. Is it possible that something could have gone wrong in the experiment to give incorrect results? ***Yes***
2. List one thing that could have caused you to get incorrect results. ***Answers will vary but could include that the kernels were not representative of all such kernels, that kernels were accidentally switched, or that the unusual manner of popping (single kernel on a hot surface) affected the color.***
3. What could be done to make it more likely that the experiment's results are free of errors? ***Students should suggest repeating the experiment or popping more kernels.***
4. Your teacher will help you verify the answer.

Separately pop a bowl full of each kernel color of popcorn. Allow the students to eat it.

Use the answer to predict outcomes

Suppose another color of popcorn kernel were available. Based on the results of this experiment, what color would it pop? ***white***

You may wish to reserve one color of popcorn kernel for this last question. Or you might want to try some of the dyed specialty popcorn which are not naturally the dyed color.

Supplementary reading

"Popcorn and Popcorn Poppers." *Consumer Reports,* June 1989, pp. 355-62.

Name ____________________
Date __________ Hour __________

2–Classifying Living Things

Ideas 2a

The Modern Classification System

Directions: Listed among the following terms are the seven basic levels of classification. Write them in the correct order on the vertical lines below. In the boxes above the lines write the letter choice corresponding to each classification level. When you complete the exercise, the letter choices will spell a word that relates to the classification system.

U - genus	T - variety	S - species
I - phylum	E - family	N - class
F - group	L - kingdom	R - tribe
W - kind		A - order

Most general (largest group)

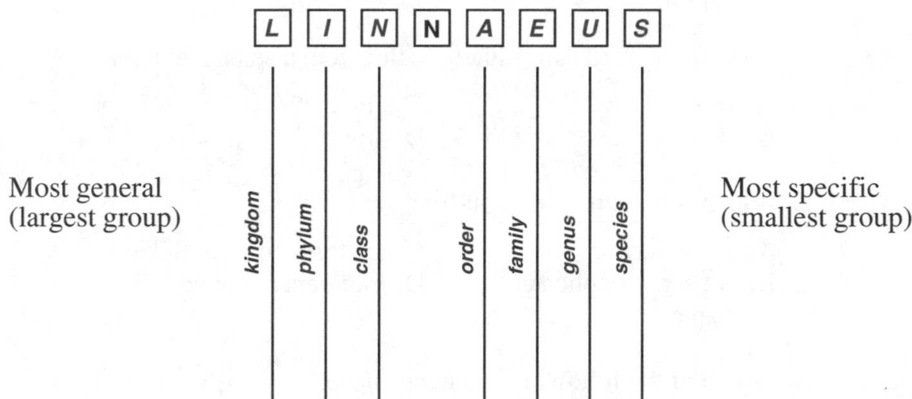

Most specific (smallest group)

How does the word that solves the puzzle relate to the classification system? *Linnaeus is the man who proposed the classification system used today.*

Scientific Names

Directions: Choose the best completion answer for each of the following statements and record your choice in the blank by the number. Then use the letters of your answer (*A, B, C,* or *D*) with the key below to plot a trail on the map on page 13. If all your answers are correct and you correctly plot the trail, your trail will end in the country which answers the question below the map.

If the answer to a statement is *A,* draw a line 5° northward from your last stopping point.

If the answer to a statement is *B,* draw a line 5° southward from your last stopping point.

If the answer to a statement is *C,* draw a line 5° eastward from your last stopping point.

If the answer to a statement is *D,* draw a line 5° westward from your last stopping point.

B ______ 1. How many words are usually included in a scientific name?

A. one
B. two
C. three
D. four

D ______ 2. Which is *not* a requirement for a scientific name?

A. Latin form
B. must not duplicate a name
C. underlined or italicized
D. can never change

A ______ 3. Which of the following is a genus name?

A. *Canis*
B. *familaris*
C. German
D. shepherd

A ______ 4. Which of the following is a scientific name?

A. *Pisum sativa*
B. Pisum sativa
C. Pisum Sativa
D. *Pisum Sativa*

C ______ 5. A scientific name is sometimes called the

A. German name.
B. common name.
C. genus-species name.
D. prime name.

A ______ 6. What language form is used in a scientific name?

A. Latin
B. German
C. English
D. Spanish

Name ______________________

Date ____________ Hour ____________

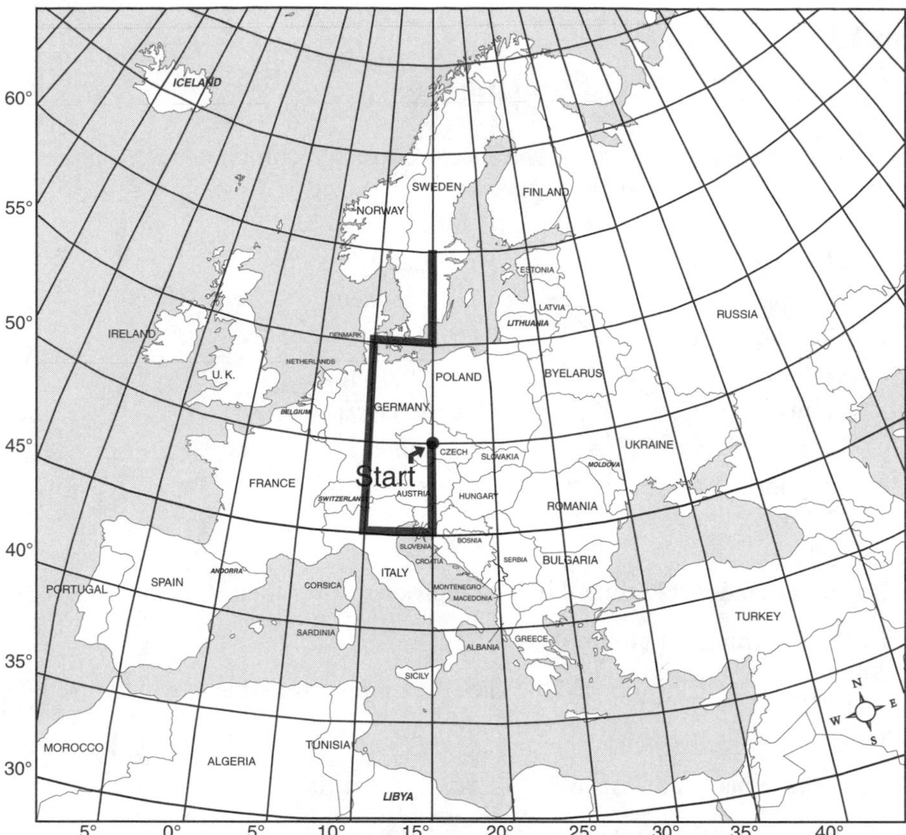

Which country was Carolus Linnaeus's homeland? *Sweden*

Ideas 2c

Classification of Some Organisms

Directions: List two or three characteristics of the organisms in each of the kingdoms. Then list at least two examples of organisms in each kingdom.

1. Monera ***unicellular or colonial; lack membranes around their nuclei; microscopic; examples: bacteria, blue-green algae***

2. Protista ***no true tissues; unicellular or colonial; examples: paramecium, amoeba, algae, diatoms***

3. Fungi ***unicellular or colonial; no true stems, roots, or leaves; lack chlorophyll; examples: mushrooms, mold, yeast***

4. Plantae ***have tissues; most are green; have cell walls containing cellulose; examples: moss, ferns, pines, cedars***

5. Animalia ***no cell walls around cells; obtain food from other organisms; examples: jellyfish, coral, sponge, fish, amphibians, reptiles, birds, mammals***

Ideas 2d

Review

Directions: Choose a word from the list to correctly complete each sentence below. A word may be used only once.

classify	Latin
common	Linnaeus
English	one
Galileo	phylum
genus	scientific
kind	three
kingdom	two

1. God commanded all living things to reproduce after their ___*kind*___
2. To arrange things in groups is to ___*classify*___
3. ___*Linnaeus*___ proposed the classification system that is widely used today.
4. A scientific name consists of ___*two*___ words.
5. A scientific name follows the language form of ___*Latin*___.
6. An organism may have many ___*common*___ names.
7. The largest category in the modern classification system is the ___*kingdom*___.

Name ______________________

Date ____________ Hour ____________

Field Investigation 2a

Grouping Plants by Characteristics

This investigation is best done as a class activity. You may want to collect the specimens yourself, or you could ask the students each to bring in a specimen of a particular type (for example, oak branches). Compiling the lists of characteristics as a class may be a profitable exercise.

Goal

- Identify and observe plant traits that could be used to classify them.

Materials

plant specimens

Procedures and observations

To many people, plants are plants. They consist of trees, shrubs, flowers, and that's about it. If, however, you take the time to look carefully at them, they will reveal many differences.

For some plants (oaks, pines) students will collect different species of a single genus. For other plants (roses, marigolds, mums) students will collect different varieties of a single species. Give clear instructions to the students so they know the kinds of plants you want them to collect.

1. Make a collection of several different types of the same kind of plant. Be sure your collection is of only one kind of plant. For example, you can collect branches of several different types of oaks, maples, pines, roses, or azaleas. Various types of marigolds, philodendrons, mums, ferns, or similar plants would also be good specimens to collect. If the plant is small, you may collect the entire plant. If the plant is a large shrub or a tree, collect only a portion of a stem.
2. Carefully observe the plants you have collected. Note the similarities between them. Note the differences between them. Compile lists that describe the similarities and differences between the various specimens.

You should become familiar with the various types of oaks (or whatever plant you are using in your class) that are common in your area. You can then point out the differences and similarities that scientists use to classify these organisms.

Kind of plant: *will vary depending on teacher instructions*

List up to 10 similarities shown by your specimens.

1. *Answers will vary.*
2. ______
3. ______
4. ______
5. ______
6. ______
7. ______
8. ______
9. ______
10. ______

Make sure that students use or bring in large enough specimens. A single oak leaf or even a small section of stem will not provide as many identifiable characteristics as a section of stem that is a foot or two long.

You may want to combine this investigation with Investigation 2b.

Home School Tip

If you do not combine this investigation with Investigation 2b, then do not bother to bring the collected plant specimens home. Make the observations requested while on a hike or field trip. If you do combine this with Investigation 2b, then follow the instructions as written.

List up to 10 differences shown by your specimens.

1. ***Answers will vary.***
2.
3.
4.
5.
6.
7.
8.
9.
10.

Name ____________________
Date __________ Hour ____________

Field Investigation 2b

Plant Names

Goal

- Use plant traits to identify and name specific plants.

Materials

gardening books, seed catalogs, or reference books

Procedures and observations

You probably know the names of almost everyone who lives near your home. You probably also know the names of any animals that you would commonly see in your yard. But what about the plants? Do you know them by name?

1. Make a bird's-eye-view drawing of your house and yard. If you do not have a yard that you can draw, draw your school grounds, a friend's yard, or even a section of a park. Indicate the location of all the major plants that are in the area you are drawing.
2. Using gardening books and seed catalogs, identify the plants in your yard. You may also take trips to a plant nursery to ask questions about the plants you are identifying. Discussions with gardeners or with the people who planted the yard may also be helpful. Try to find out the scientific names of all the plants in your yard. Often you will be able to find the varieties of these plants as well.
3. Using coded symbols, mark the plants on your diagram. Prepare a short description of the different plants you labeled on your diagram. Include various facts that you discovered about the plants while you were looking for the plants' names. You may also include drawings or photographs of the plants.

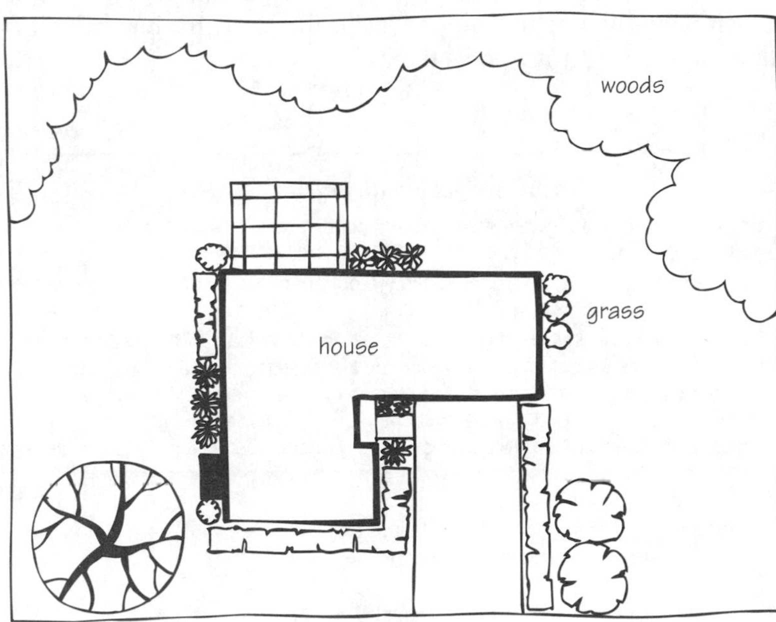

Quercus nigra (pin oak)
Cornus florida (dogwood)
Pinus alba (white pine)
Ilex opacq fosterii (holly)
Rhododendron choral bell (azalea)
Althaea rosea (hollyhock)

Consider doing this as a class project, with all the students working on a single area (such as the school grounds, a nicely planted yard, or a park). If possible, each student could then be responsible for a particular plant. He could write a report and be responsible for finding it in the yard.

Good resource books for this investigation include gardening handbooks, plant and seed catalogs, and the specialized keys of cultivated plants that are available in libraries. Have available some of the classification keys to native plants in your area.

Make sure that the students choose a planted area rather than a native area. The plants in a planted and maintained area are usually quite easy to identify. Often they are the same in most yards that are in the same section of the country.

Discourage students from attempting areas that include large beds of perennials or annuals. You may want to have students do only the trees and shrubs.

You may want to have students prepare herbarium mounts of the various plants they identify. This will work well if you are doing this as a class project. Simple herbariums require only pressing and mounting of the dried specimens on paper with glue or tape. Instructions for making good herbarium mounts can be found in various books, and the materials are available through biological supply companies.

You may want to combine this investigation with Investigation 2a.

Home School Tip
This investigation is perfect for a home school.

Students should begin this activity at the first of the school year. Establish the date that the collection will be due. It is suggested that the students work on this project for three to five weeks.

Home School Tip

If it is necessary for you to document your student's work to the authorities, the collection (or a photo of it) can be included with other submitted materials (since the collection is a major project). Save your student's insect collection in a sealed box with mothballs. If the collection has many moths or butterflies, put these in a separate box because they are more likely to become messy.

Consider purchasing an insect collecting kit that includes most of the materials listed here.

At the beginning of the assignment, discuss killing jars and their safe use. Encourage the students to begin immediately.

The non-acetone type of fingernail polish remover contains ethyl acetate. If you use this source of ethyl acetate, use a brand that has as few other ingredients as possible.

Establish the number of mounted, correctly identified insects that students will need in order to earn each particular grade. Fifty different insects for an A and twenty for a D is not unreasonable.

If possible, have sample insect collections for the students to view as they begin their projects. Having sample collections will help the students to understand what is being discussed in the exercise.

After assigning the project, you may wish to check weekly the progress of your students. Ask each student to turn in a sheet of paper with his name on it and an indication of how many insects he has collected and how many he has identified. You may want to speak with any students who lag behind.

Field Investigation 2c

Making an Insect Collection

Goals

- Use a classification key to identify organisms.
- Gain experience in collecting organisms.
- Become familiar with orders of insects.

Materials

box to hold collected insects temporarily, ethyl or isopropyl alcohol, clear fingernail polish, killing jar (made from a large-mouth jar with a screw lid or a coffee can with a plastic lid, cotton or a sponge, newspaper, cardboard, ethyl acetate), hand lens, materials for displaying insects, mothballs, paper triangles, straight pins

Procedures

1. Catch as many different adult insects as you can without damaging them. Immature insects, such as nymphs and larvae (grubs, caterpillars, and the like) of insects, are sometimes difficult to identify and often require special killing-and-mounting procedures. Do not collect these forms. See page 20 for some suggestions on where to look for insects.
2. Kill the insects you catch.
   - Make a killing jar by following the directions below. You can kill many insects by placing them in your killing jar as soon as you catch them. Leave them in the killing jar until they are dead.
   - You can kill beetles easily by dropping them into a small jar of ethyl or isopropyl alcohol (70-80%). Beetles sometimes survive in killing jars for long periods of time.
   - Do not place butterflies and moths into your killing jar. They may ruin their wings by flapping around inside the jar. Kill a butterfly or moth by squeezing firmly on its thorax.

How to Make a Killing Jar

Use a large-mouth jar with a screw lid or a coffee can with a plastic lid. Make several jars of various sizes if you plan to catch several insects at one time.

Place a half-inch-thick layer of cotton in the bottom of the jar or can. (You may use a sponge instead of cotton.)

Pour ethyl acetate on the cotton or sponge. Keep the killing jar tightly closed as much of the time as possible. The more you keep the jar covered, the fewer times you will have to add ethyl acetate to the cotton or sponge. If the sponge or cotton becomes too dry, add more ethyl acetate. (Professionals often use sodium cyanide, a solid chemical that releases a very poisonous gas. The gas is poisonous to humans as well as insects. Great care must be taken if you use sodium cyanide in your killing jar.)

Cover the cotton or sponge with cardboard that has holes punched in it and that has been cut to fit the bottom of the container.

NOTE: Keep killing jars away from small children and pets.

Name ______________________

Date ____________ Hour ______________

3. Mount the Insects
    - You can mount most insects by sticking pins through the thorax and into a piece of cardboard. Make sure that the insects are suspended in the air on the pins and are not tacked against the cardboard. Be **sure** that an insect is **dead** before you mount it.
    - To mount beetles (order Coleoptera), place the pin through the right wing and abdomen, not through the thorax.
    - Mount tiny insects (such as mosquitoes, gnats, and fruit flies) onto small triangles of stiff paper. Touch a triangle of paper to a small drop of clear fingernail polish; then touch the polish on the paper to the insect. Pin the paper triangles to the cardboard.
4. Protect your mounted insects.
    - Children and friends may want to handle your specimens. Keep your collection away from children and allow friends to look but not to touch. Some insects are very fragile.
    - For temporary storage of your insects, glue a piece of thick, corrugated cardboard to the bottom of a box. (A shoe box works well.) Stick the pins with insects on them into the cardboard.
    - Protect your dead insects from hungry live insects by attaching mothballs inside the collection box. Loose mothballs may damage insects; therefore, put holes in a tiny box filled with mothballs, tape the box shut, and tape it into the corner of the storage box.
5. Identify your insects.
    - Use the classification key on pages 21-23 to determine the correct order for each of your specimens. If your specimen does not exactly fit the limited descriptions given in the key, choose the descriptions that you think fit your specimen the best.
    - Once you have determined the order to which an insect belongs, use books on insects to identify the specimen by common name. Field guides to insects are helpful. Your teacher may be able to suggest specific books to help you.
6. Label and display your insects.
    - Print on a 5x8 cm (2x3 in.) piece of paper the information that applies to each insect. See the example below.

Order: Orthoptera
Common name: red-legged grasshopper
Collector: Beth Anderson
Date collected: September, 1997
Place collected: field, Murry, Ky.

Special insect mounting pins are available from science supply companies. For most students, ordinary pins are fine for pinning larger insects.

The paper triangles can be cut from index cards. In professional collections the triangles are this size:

Encourage students to be creative with the displays of their insect collections. Displaying different orders on leaf-shaped pieces of cardboard to make various insect "trees" can add interest for some students. Few students will keep their insect collections, so mounting the insects in a nice collection box may be a wasted expense.

You may want to start a continuing collection. Consider giving students a date by which they must remove their insect collection from the classroom. If they do not remove their collections, you can then add the insects to a school insect collection.

You may want to have "insect days" during the time the students are collecting insects. "Insect days" are times when, either in class, during a recess or break, or after school, you will be available to help students identify the insects with which they are having problems.

During the time you are discussing Chapter 2, you might want to distribute preserved insects to your class and have the students use the key and various field guides to identify the insects. This is a good method of teaching them how to use these tools and can save you a lot of individual explanations. After this exercise, students should require your help only with the more difficult insects. Be careful not to give them too much help.

After a little practice they should be able to identify common insects by their correct orders.

- Attach the label for each specimen under that specimen by pinning it to the cardboard with the same pin that goes through the specimen.
- Devise a method to display your insect collection. You may display your insects temporarily on a piece of cardboard, or you may display them in a collection box.
- Be sure to arrange your specimens by order when placing them in your display.

Ideas for Catching Insects

1. Look under stones and boards.
2. Collect mushrooms and put them in a closed jar. As the mushrooms dry, insects that were inside will come out.
3. Dig up and turn over a shovelful of earth. Watch it closely and capture the insects that scurry away.
4. Check around outdoor lights at night.
5. At night put a light over a tub of water with a spoonful of kerosene in it. In the morning gather the insects from the tub.
6. Collect caterpillars and grubs. When they become adults, kill and identify them.
7. Leave an open sandwich outside for an hour or two. Insects will be attracted to the food.
8. Attach an insect net to an automobile and drive along at dusk at about 25 to 30 mph. The net will trap many flying insects. This method works very well along country roads.
9. Use an insect net to capture flying insects. Disturbing bushes and tall grass will often arouse many flying insects.

Name ____________________

Date __________ Hour __________

Key to Identification of Common Insect Orders

Several insect orders have been split into additional orders in recent years. For example, what you may have learned years ago as Orthoptera is now Orthoptera, Mantodea, Blattaria, and Grylloblattaria.

Only the most common orders are included in the classification key.

1. Does the organism have six legs?	**Yes** **No**	Go to Number 2. Either this organism is not an insect or it is a larval form (like a caterpillar), which cannot be identified with this key.	
2. Does the insect have wings? (NOTE: Typical membranous wings may be hidden under an outer, thick, hard pair of wings.)	**Yes** **No**	Go to number 3. Go to number 16.	 **unicorn beetle** **(wings open)**
3. Does the insect have two pairs of wings? (NOTE: One pair of covering structures counts as a pair of wings.)	**Yes** **No**	Go to number 4. order *Diptera* (flies, mosquitoes, gnats)	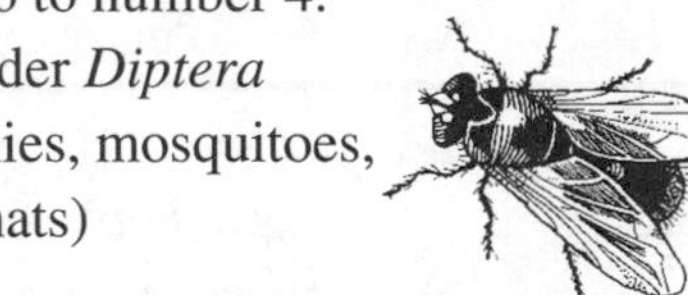 **bluebottle fly** 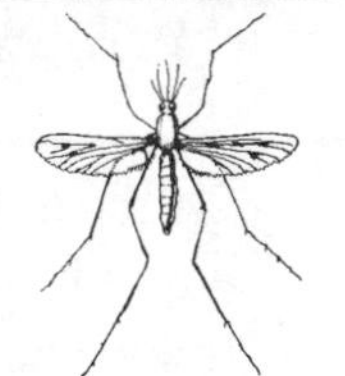 **mosquito**
4. Are both pairs of wings made of the same substance, and are they about the same thickness?	**Yes** **No**	Go to number 10. Go to number 5.	
5. Are the outer wings hard, and do they meet in a straight line in the center of the insect's back?	**Yes** **No**	Go to number 6. Go to number 7.	
6. Does the insect have obvious pincerlike structures extending from its abdomen?	**Yes** **No**	order *Dermaptera* (earwigs) order *Coleoptera* (beetles)	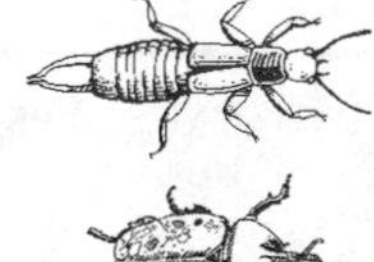 **earwig** **unicorn beetle**
7. Does the outer pair of wings have a leathery section next to the body and membranous tips that overlap when the insect is at rest?	**Yes** **No**	order *Hemiptera* (chinch bugs, squash bugs, stink bugs) Go to number 8.	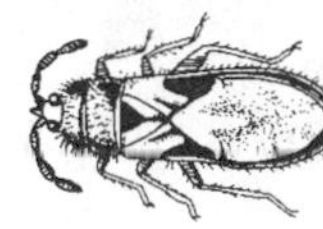 **chinch bug**

Key to Identification of Common Insect Orders

8. Are the hind legs enlarged for jumping?	**Yes**	order *Orthoptera* (grasshoppers, crickets, katydids)	**grasshopper** **cricket**
	No	Go to number 9.	
9. Are the front legs used for grasping prey?	**Yes**	order *Mantodea* (mantids)	**praying mantis** **cockroach**
	No	order *Blattaria* (cockroaches)	
10. Are the insect's wings covered with scales that rub off easily?	**Yes**	order *Lepidoptera* (moths, butterflies)	**moth** **butterfly**
	No	Go to number 11.	
11. Do the insect's wings slope down from its body when it is at rest?	**Yes**	order *Homoptera* (cicadas, aphids, treehoppers, leafhoppers)	**cicada** **leafhopper**
	No	Go to number 12.	
12. Do the insect's wings have very few vertical crossveins?	**Yes**	order *Hymenoptera* (bees, wasps, also ants. Males and females have wings early in life. Members of this order may have wings that look like one pair instead of two pairs because they are hooked together by rows of tiny hooks.)	**ant** (early in life) **hornet**
	No	Go to number 13.	
13. Are there two or three long threadlike tails extending from the insect's abdomen?	**Yes**	order *Ephemeroptera* (mayflies)	**mayfly**
	No	Go to number 14.	
14. Are the insect's antennae short and not obvious?	**Yes**	order *Odonata* (dragonflies)	**dragonfly**
	No	Go to number 15.	

Name ______________________

Date __________ Hour __________

Key to Identification of Common Insect Orders

	Question		Answer	Illustrations
15.	Do the insect's wings have distinctly lined veins?	**Yes**	order *Neuroptera* (ant lions, lace-wings, dobson flies)	**dobson fly**
		No	order *Isoptera* (termites)	**termites** (winged)
16.	Is the insect narrow-waisted (pinched in between the thorax and abdomen)?	**Yes**	order *Hymenoptera* (ants, bees, wasps)	**ant** (no wings)
		No	Go to number 17.	
17.	Does the insect have two short tails extending from its abdomen?	**Yes**	order *Homoptera* (aphids, scale insects, leafhoppers)	**aphid** (no wings); **San Jose scale**
		No	Go to number 18.	
18.	Is the insect small with a soft, plump body and a small head?	**Yes**	order *Isoptera* (termites, white ants in some stages)	**termite** (no wings)
		No	Go to number 19.	
19.	Is the insect tiny with a narrow body flattened on the sides, and is it able to jump with its hind legs?	**Yes**	order *Siphonaptera* (fleas)	**flea**
		No	Go to number 20.	
20.	Does the insect have a very delicate body with long, jointed threadlike tails and antennae?	**Yes**	order *Thysanura* (silverfish, bristletails)	**silverfish**
		No	Go to number 21.	
21.	Does the insect have a stick or twig-shaped body?	**Yes**	order *Phasmida* (walking sticks)	**walking stick**
		No	order *Orthoptera* (certain grasshoppers or crickets in adult and/or nymph stages)	**wingless grasshopper**

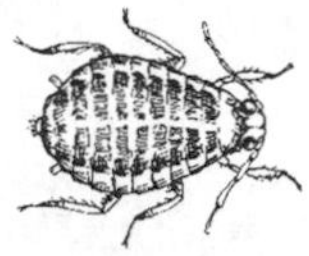

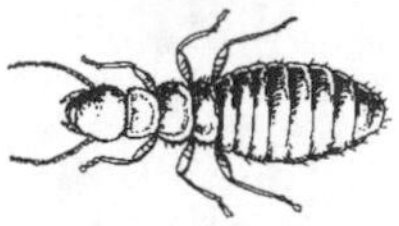

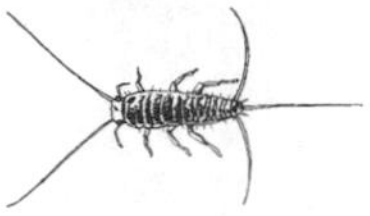

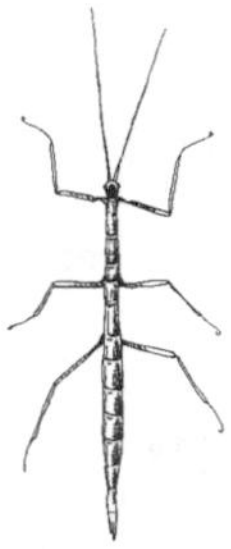

Name ______________________
Date __________ Hour __________

The Living Kingdoms

Directions: Fill in the blanks on the left with the proper name from the modern classification system. Then find and circle that name in the word puzzle on page 28. List examples of that group in the blanks on the right. You need to find only as many examples as there are blanks. In the word puzzle the words may appear horizontally, vertically, or diagonally and may be forward or backward. Only names from the first column appear in the word puzzle.

Kingdom	Description	Examples
1. *Monera*	Kingdom whose members are unicellular or colonial and lack some cellular parts.	*bacteria, blue-green algae*
2. *Animalia*	Kingdom whose members have tissues but lack chlorophyll and cell walls.	*ant, rabbit, cow, dog, worm*
3. *Fungi*	Kingdom whose members are unicellular or colonial; lack chlorophyll; obtain food by secreting enzymes.	*mushroom, mold, rust, yeast*
4. *Protista*	Kingdom whose members are unicellular or colonial and lack tissues; may have chlorophyll.	*algae, protozoans, ciliates, amoeba*
5. *Plantae*	Kingdom whose members have tissues, chlorophyll, and cell walls containing cellulose.	*pine, fern, rose, lily*

Examples answers may vary.

Phylum	Description	Examples
6. *Bryophyta*	Plant phylum whose members lack water-conducting tissues.	*moss, liverwort*
7. *Cnidaria*	Animal phylum whose members live in water and have stinging cells to paralyze and capture prey.	*jellyfish, coral*
8. *Echinodermata*	Animal phylum whose members have spiny skins.	*starfish, sea urchin*
9. *Arthropoda*	Animal phylum whose members have an exoskeleton.	*crab, beetle, lobster, moth*
10. *Anthophyta*	Plant phylum whose members have flowers.	*apple, grass, iris, orchid*
11. *Annelida*	Animal phylum whose members have soft bodies that are divided into segments.	*leech, earthworm*
12. *Chordata*	Animal phylum whose members have backbones.	*fish, bird, snake, rat*
13. *Platyhelminthes*	Animal phylum whose members are flattened worms.	*planarian, tapeworm*
14. *Mollusca*	Animal phylum whose members have soft bodies and, quite often, shells.	*clam, snail*

Name ____________________
Date __________ Hour __________

	Class	Description	Examples
15.	*Mammalia*	Vertebrate class whose members have fur or hair.	*rat, cat, deer, seal*
16.	*Insecta*	Class whose members are the six-legged arthropods.	*butterfly, bee, ant, flea*
17.	*Amphibia*	Class of smooth-skinned vertebrates whose immature forms breathe with gills and whose mature forms breathe with lungs.	*frog, toad, salamander*
18.	*Reptilia*	Vertebrate class whose members have scales and lungs.	*snake, turtle, lizard, alligator*
19.	*Osteichthyes*	Vertebrate class whose members have gills and bony skeletons and are covered by scales.	*trout, eel, perch, seahorse*
20.	*Aves*	Vertebrate class whose members have light, hollow bones.	*eagle, swan, robin, wren*

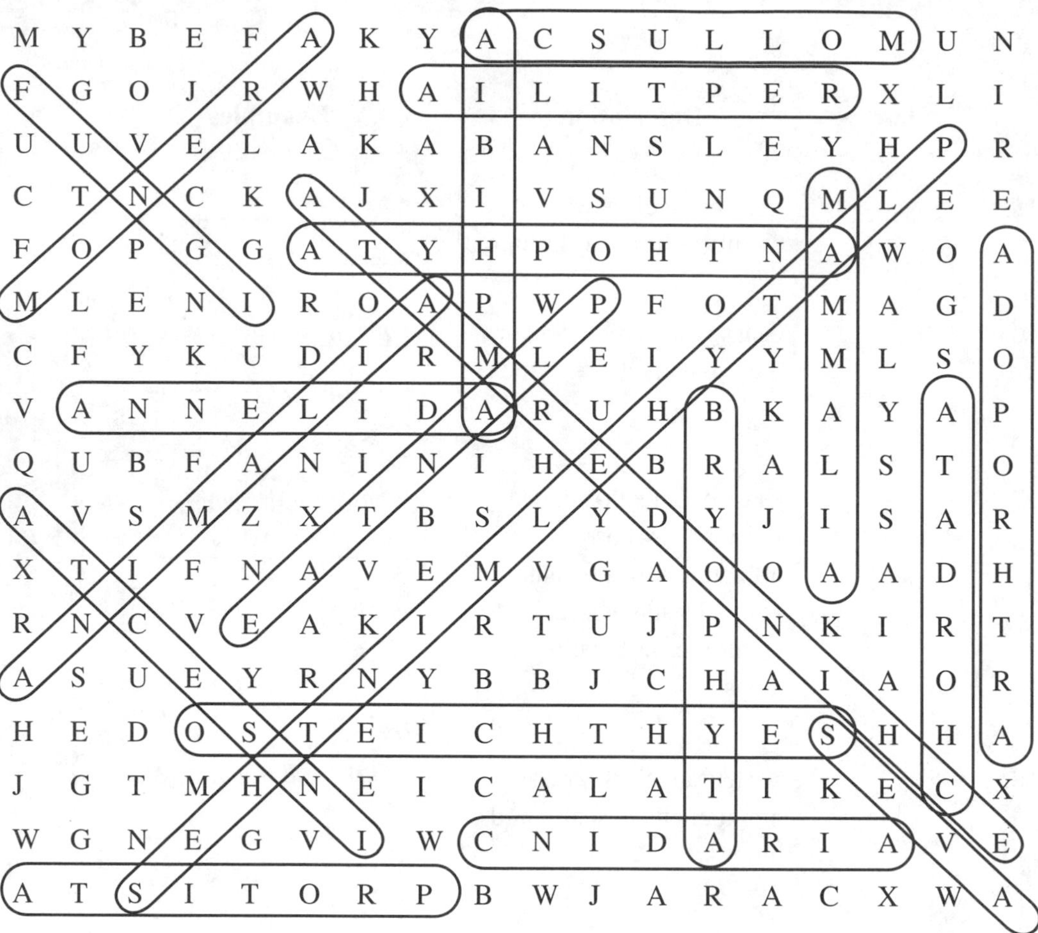

Name ____________________

Date ____________ Hour ____________

Personal Investigation—The Living Kingdoms

Scrapbook of the Living Kingdoms of the World

Collect pictures of living organisms from old magazines and other sources. If you know or can find the names of the organisms, record them in your scrapbook. If the pictures you find are of organisms that are in kingdoms Monera, Fungi, or Protista, group them in sections of your scrapbook labeled for these kingdoms. If your pictures are of organisms that are in kingdom Plantae or kingdom Animalia, arrange them in sections labeled for these kingdoms and also within sections that are labeled for the phyla the organisms are in.

If your pictures are of arthropods, tell what classes the organisms are in and place them in appropriate sections of your scrapbook. If your pictures are of insects, you should tell what orders they are in. If your pictures are of vertebrate animals, tell what classes they are in and group them in appropriate sections of your scrapbook.

You will be awarded points based on the following scale for the pictures you obtain. Try to earn fifty points.

Consider doing this as a class project with the students' bringing in the pictures and your placing them on a bulletin board in groups according to their classification. Each student can then try to earn a certain number of points by bringing in pictures. Since many students will have access to the same magazines, you may want to say that the first person to bring in a picture of a particular organism will be the only one to earn points for that picture.

Home School Tip

Do this investigation only if your student has access to several magazines; finding enough pictures will be difficult otherwise.

Kingdom Monera—5 points each (max. 10 points)
Kingdom Protista—3 points each (max. 9 points)
Kingdom Fungi—3 points each (max. 9 points)
Kingdom Plantae (max. 15 points)
- Phylum Bryophyta—4 points each
- Phylum Pterophyta—3 points each
- Phylum Coniferophyta—3 points each
- Phylum Anthophyta—1 point each (max. 5 points)

Kingdom Animalia—1 point each (max. 20 points)

You can earn no more than ten points in kingdom Monera, nine points in kingdom Protista, and nine points in kingdom Fungi. You can earn no more than fifteen points in kingdom Plantae, of which only five points can be in the phylum Anthophyta. You can earn no more than twenty points in kingdom Animalia, of which only six points can be from insects and only six points can be from phylum Chordata.

Name ______________________

Date __________ Hour __________

3–Life and Cells

Ideas 3a

Being Alive

Directions: Match the following statements with the correct characteristics of life. You may use each characteristic twice.

a. growth
b. movement
c. reproduction
d. energy needs
e. response

d ______ 1. Mushrooms have no chlorophyll and thus cannot produce their own sugar. They must receive their nutrition from decaying material.

e ______ 2. After being watered, a wilted plant becomes stiff again.

a ______ 3. This process occurs when an organism builds more substance than it uses.

b ______ 4. This process is demonstrated by blood circulating inside an organism's body.

a ______ 5. This process may result in one's having to change to a larger shoe size.

c ______ 6. An organism produces other organisms similar to itself.

b ______ 7. This process allows a worm to inch along the ground.

e ______ 8. Nightfall signals a plant to close its flowers.

c ______ 9. Small new plantlets may form from the sides of a plant.

d ______ 10. Most plants depend on chloroplasts to capture sunlight in order to make sugar.

Ideas 3b

The Cell Theory

As an alternative, instruct the students to make two lists. On the first they should include all the organisms shown that are made of cells. On the second, they should list all the organisms that are not made of cells. Since all living organisms are made of cells, there should be nothing on the second list.

Directions: Study the drawing below. Then on the numbered lines, list all the things in the drawing that are made of cells.

1. ***birds/geese***
2. ***trees***
3. ***flowers***
4. ***grass***
5. ***ferns***
6. ***deer***
7. ***squirrel***
8. ***mushrooms***
9. ***fish***
10. ***butterfly***
11. __________
12. __________

Name ______________________
Date __________ Hour __________

Ideas 3c

Cellular Functions

Part 1

Directions: In the blanks below list the four main functions of cells.

Cellular functions:
1. *using energy*
2. *manufacturing*
3. *responding*
4. *reproducing*

Part 2

Directions: Below is a list of cells or organisms performing various activities. In the spaces provided indicate which of the four cellular functions each activity illustrates best.

reproducing 1. A bacterium dividing

responding 2. A person jerking his hand from a hot stove

manufacturing 3. Cells of the stomach making digestive juices

responding 4. A fish swimming away from light and toward shadows

manufacturing 5. A plant cell forming a cell wall

using energy 6. Muscles of your leg working as you run

reproducing 7. A fruit forming seeds

responding 8. A person smelling cookies baking

using energy 9. A bee flying to its hive

manufacturing 10. A bird growing a new feather to replace a lost one

Ideas 3d

Molecules and Life

Directions: In each of the following statements draw a circle around the correct choice in the parentheses. On the lines below each statement, explain why the incorrect choice is not acceptable.

1. Sugar and (starch / enzymes) are important carbohydrates. ***Enzymes are proteins.***

2. Carbohydrates consist of carbon, oxygen, and (nitrogen / hydrogen). ***Carbohydrates consist of only carbon, oxygen, and hydrogen; nitrogen is not found in carbohydrates.***

3. (Enzymes / Nucleic acids) are made of proteins. ***Nucleic acids are made of nucleotides.***

4. Proteins are made of (glucose molecules / amino acids). ***Glucose is a carbohydrate.***

5. The arrangement of nucleotides in (DNA / fat) is a code. ***Fat (lipid) is not composed of nucleotides.***

6. Fat and (carbohydrate / lipid) are the same thing. ***Carbohydrate is a separate category.***

7. RNA is a (nucleic acid / nucleotide). ***A nucleotide is a smaller molecule of which RNA is made.***

Name ______________________
Date ____________ Hour ____________

Ideas 3e

Review

Directions: Complete the crossword puzzle on the back of this page.

ACROSS

3. God is a living ____________.
4. A complete living thing
7. An organism made of a single cell
9. A tiny unit of living material surrounded by a thin membrane
11. Number of unsaved sinners in heaven
12. Organic ____________ are substances that have carbon in them.
13. An organism made of many cells
15. The building blocks of protein are ____________ acids.
17. Cell membranes are made largely of ____________.
19. A small particle of a substance
20. The ability to do work
22. Smaller molecules that compose nucleic acids
23. Robert ____________ called the boxlike structures he saw in cork, *cells.*

DOWN

1. Groups of similar cells working together
2. Will you be able to remember all this for the ____________ examination?
5. Birth, growth, reproduction, and death are all parts of the life ____________.
6. Thick substance contained by cells
8. The living material of a cell
9. Life is the ____________ of being alive.
10. ____________ are a type of protein.
12. Made of many similar cells
14. Made of only carbon, hydrogen, and oxygen
16. The arrangement of nucleotides in DNA is a ____________.
18. Food storage molecules, antibodies, and enzymes
21. Source from which plants directly receive their energy

1 TISSUE
2 FINAL
3 SPIRIT
4 ORGANISM
5 CYCLE
6 PROTOPLASM
7 UNICELLULAR
8 CYTOPLASM
9 CELL
9 CONDITION
10 ENZYMES
11 ZERO
12 COMPOUNDS
12 COLONIAL
13 MULTICELLULAR
14 CARBOHYDRATE
15 AMINO
16 CODE
17 LIPIDS
18 PROTEIN
19 MOLECULE
20 ENERGY
21 SUN
22 NUCLEOTIDES
23 HOOKE

Name ____________________

Date __________ Hour __________

Class Investigation 3a

The pH of Life Substances

Goals

- Measure the pH of common substances.
- Recognize that many substances produced by living things are acids and bases.

Materials    

pH meter, pH paper, materials to be tested (See table below.)

It is not necessary to use both the pH meter and pH paper. However, if you have access to both, it is worthwhile to use both. You may also use litmus paper, but it will indicate only if a substance is an acid or base, not its pH.

Procedures and observations

1. Obtain each of the materials to be tested that are listed in the table below and on the next page. Those that are not a liquid should be dissolved or mixed in a small amount of water. Those that come in small volumes, such as bee venom, should be touched to the pH paper directly. Do not use the pH meter for these.
2. Determine the pH of each material by dipping one piece of pH paper in each material and observing the color change. Match the color with the color scale on the pH paper container. You should determine a number value for the pH. Values less than 7 are acidic, values greater than 7 are basic, and 7 is neutral. Record your results.
3. Your teacher will explain how to use the pH meter. Use the pH meter to determine the pH of each of the materials. Record your results.
4. Based on your measurements, decide whether each substance is an acid or base and record your decisions in the last column of the table.

Home School Tip

Use pH paper (it costs about $1 per hundred pieces). A single student can easily test half of the listed substances. Consider doing both the investigation as written and the alternative described in the marginal notes at the end of this investigation. Use vinegar as the acid and diluted bleach, ammonia, or hydroxide-type drain cleaner as the base. Use caution when preparing the base.

Material	pH paper	pH meter	Acid or base?
aloe	*5*		*acid*
apple juice	*3-5*	*2.9-5.0*	*acid*
banana	*4-5*	*4.6*	*acid*
bee venom	*4-5*		*acid*
coconut milk	*6*	*6.0*	*acid*
coffee (black)	*5-6*	*5.0-6.0*	*acid*
egg white	*8*	*7.6-8.0*	*base*
egg yolk	*7-8*	*7.6-8.0*	*base*
honey	*5*	*5.0*	*acid*
lemon juice	*2-3*	*2.0-2.4*	*acid*
milk	*6-7*	*6.3-6.8*	*neutral or acid*
pine sap	*5*		*acid*
rainwater	*4-6*	*4.3-5.7*	*acid*
saliva	*6-8*	*6.5-7.5*	*acid, base, or neutral*

You need not test all the substances listed here. Half would be enough.

Material	pH paper	pH meter	Acid or base?
canned salmon	*6*	*6.1-6.3*	*acid*
soil	*4-6*	*4.0-6.0*	*acid*
sweat	*4-6*		*acid*
canned tuna	*6*	*5.9-6.1*	*acid*
vegetable oil	*5*		*acid*
vinegar	*2-3*	*2.4-3.4*	*acid*

An alternative to this investigation is to make homemade pH indicator solution. Use a blender to blend ¼ to ½ of a head of red/purple cabbage in water. Filter the solids out of the solution. Add small amounts of acid or base to samples of the cabbage extract. Brilliant color changes will occur with the pH changes.

Summing up

1. How many of the substances tested were acids? ***Answers will vary.***

2. Which gave the most precise pH measurement—pH paper or the pH meter? ***pH meter***

3. Do you think acids and bases are found in living things? Why or why not?
Yes, some of the substances tested in this investigation came from living things and were acids and bases.

4. If you wanted to find the pH of cytoplasm, how would you do it? ***Answers will vary but may include crushing cells to release cytoplasm for testing or the use of micro-electrodes to insert into individual cells.***

Name ______________________________

Date ______________ Hour ____________________

Class Investigation 3b

Protein in Life Substances

Goal

- Determine which common substances contain protein.

Materials

Biuret solution, materials to be tested (see table below), test tubes, test tube rack, goggles, 100 ml graduated cylinder, 10 ml graduated cylinder.

Procedures and observations

1. Obtain each of the materials to be tested that are listed in the table below. Those that are not a liquid should be ground, mixed, or dissolved in a small amount of water.
2. Determine whether each material contains protein by mixing 3 ml of the material with 1 ml of Biuret solution in a test tube. If the material contains protein it will turn pink (or violet).

Material	Color after adding Biuret solution (pink/no change)	Is protein present? (yes/no)
apple juice		
banana		
beans (boiled)		
coconut milk		
egg white		
egg yolk		
flour		
gelatin		
honey		
lemon juice		
milk		
rainwater		
saliva		
canned salmon		
starch		
sugar		
syrup		
tuna (canned)		
vegetable oil		
vinegar		

You may purchase Biuret solution or you may prepare it yourself. It is made by dissolving 2.5 g of copper sulfate pentahydrate (or 1.6 g of anhydrous copper sulfate) in 1 L of water. In another container dissolve 4 g of sodium hydroxide (caution: caustic) in 100 ml of water. Before class, add 2.5 ml of the copper sulfate solution to 100 ml of the sodium hydroxide solution.

As an alternative or as a way to save the leftover solutions, add the copper sulfate solution to the sodium hydroxide solution a drop at a time until it is a deep blue color. Soak filter paper in this final solution and allow it to dry. Cut the filter paper into strips and use it as Biuret test strips. This method will avoid some potential spills by students but takes more advance preparation on your part.

Home School Tip

You need not test all of the substances listed here. Half would be enough. You could also test rennin (from Investigation 3c) and enzymatic contact lens cleaner (since enzymes are proteins). Be sure to provide materials with protein and without protein.

Summing up

1. How many of the substances that were tested contained proteins? *Answers will vary.*

2. Do you think proteins are found in living things? Why or why not? *Yes, some of the substances tested in this investigation came from living things and contained proteins.*

Name ______________________

Date ____________ Hour ______________

Class Investigation 3c

The Action of Enzymes

Goal

- Observe the action of enzymes.

Materials

hot plate, measuring cup, measuring spoons, milk, mixing bowls, rennet tablets, spoons, sugar, thermometer, vanilla

Procedures

1. Label one mixing bowl *A* and another *B*.
2. Heat 0.95 L (4 c.) of milk until lukewarm (about 45°C, 110°F).
3. In each bowl combine 0.47 L (2 c.) of milk, 45 ml (3 tbsp.) of sugar, and 15 ml (1 tbsp.) of vanilla.
4. In a small bowl crush one rennet tablet and mix it with 15 ml (1 tbsp.) of cold water until it is dissolved.
5. Add the dissolved rennet tablet to bowl A and stir the solution for about ten seconds.
6. Cover both bowls and allow them to sit undisturbed for ten minutes.

Observations

After ten minutes uncover the bowls and compare the contents. Note such differences and similarities as color, consistency, taste, and smell.

Bowl A: ***The contents in bowl A should have a pudding consistency. Some students may notice a cream-cheese taste.***

Bowl B: ***The contents in bowl B should have a consistency like that of milk. The flavor of the contents is primarily vanilla.***

For variety, you can substitute flavorings other than vanilla. You may need to experiment to determine the amount that you should add. Mint, for example, requires only about ½ tbsp.

You can do this investigation as a demonstration. Supply plastic spoons for tasting the rennet custard and the milk-sugar-vanilla mixture.

If there are more than twenty students in your class, you may need to increase the recipe.

Immediately after you have stirred the substances, you may place them in individual containers. Be sure they are marked A and B as the bowls are. We recommend that you use small paper cups so that each student will have his own samples to taste and compare.

Rennet tablets are marketed under the brand name Junket by Salada Foods, a subsidiary of the Kellogg Company. There are other manufacturers who serve different areas of the country. Their rennet tablets can be found in grocery stores. Rennet tablets are often used to thicken homemade ice cream or to make rennet custard. They are sometimes found with gelatin, ice cream toppings, spices, or gourmet and diet foods. They presently cost about $1.40 for 12 tablets.

The enzyme rennin catalyzes the curdling of the milk. Rennin is used to make cottage cheese and many other cheeses. Rennin is found in the human stomach and in the stomachs of mammals and a few other animals. In the stomach, milk curdles into the semisolid state like the curdles formed in the rennet custard made in this experiment.

The smell that most students will notice during the manufacturing and eating of the custard is the vanilla. The rennin itself does not give off a significant odor.

Rennet custard tastes best after it has been chilled. If your class period is long enough, you may want to have the students observe their custard but not taste it until you have chilled it. Do not chill the custard until it has set.

Home School Tip

Your small class size gives you the ability to do a little extra in this investigation. Do this investigation as written and also do some of the alternatives suggested below.

An alternative to this investigation would be to demonstrate the action of proteolytic (protein-breaking) enzymes. Use hard-boiled egg white as the protein source. Add pieces of egg white to separate solutions of the following enzymes and let them sit overnight. Be sure to keep an untreated control group in water. With some enzymes, the egg white may appear to dissolve. With other enzymes the degradation will cause changes in texture and may not be noticeable until the egg white is touched.

Bromelin—*health food stores and fresh pineapple juice*
Chymotrypsin—*health food stores*
Enzymatic contact lens cleaner—*department stores*
Papain—*health food stores, some meat tenderizers, and papaya*
Pepsin—*health food stores*
Trypsin—*health food stores*

Powdered or pill forms should be dissolved in water. Most of these enzymes have a pH optimum of between 4 and 8. Pepsin's optimal pH is 1.5 (i.e., you will need to acidify the pepsin solution.)

Summing up

1. Rennet tablets contain an enzyme called rennin. What is an enzyme? ***An enzyme is a catalyst that is made of protein and is found in living organisms.***

2. The sugar and the vanilla were flavorings in the experiment. The rennin acted on the milk. What did it do to the milk? ***It caused the milk to become a solid.***

Name ______________
Date ________ Hour ________

4–Cell Structure

Ideas 4a

Membranes and Their Important Properties

Directions: Match the statements below with the terms. Place the letter of the term on the blank of the appropriate statement. Enter the number of the statement in the corresponding lettered hexagon in the figure below. If you complete the figure correctly, you will find that each diagonal and vertical row of three hexagons will total the same number. Write the number in the blank at the bottom.

a. lipid
b. active transport
c. osmosis
d. selective permeability
e. passive transport
f. diffusion
g. fluid mosaic

__d__ 1. Allows some molecules through but not others

__f__ 2. Movement away from an area of high concentration

__e__ 3. Does not require extra energy to pass through the membrane

__b__ 4. Requires the use of extra energy

__c__ 5. Movement of water through the membrane without requiring extra energy

__a__ 6. Together with protein, accounts for the molecules that compose membranes

__g__ 7. Describes the current membrane model

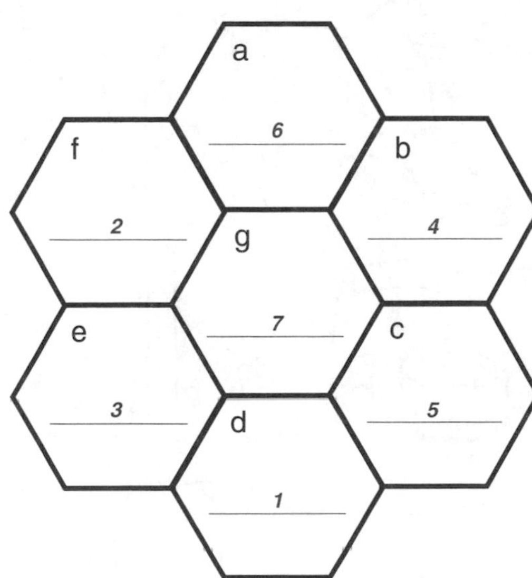

The common total is __14__.

Ideas 4b

The Compound Light Microscope

Home School Tip

Do Ideas 4b even if you do not have a microscope. Your student needs to be as familiar with microscopes as possible.

Directions: Match the terms below with their definitions by writing the proper letter choices in the blanks provided. Then label the diagram using the list of terms.

a. arm
b. base
c. body tube
d. diaphragm
e. compound light microscope
f. coarse adjustment knob
g. eyepiece (ocular)
h. fine adjustment knob
i. mirror or light source
j. objectives
k. specimen
l. stage

g _____ 1. Contains the lens(es) that you look into

k _____ 2. Object viewed through a microscope

e _____ 3. Uses two sets of lenses to produce an enlarged image

l _____ 4. Where the slide is placed

j _____ 5. The lenses nearest the object being viewed

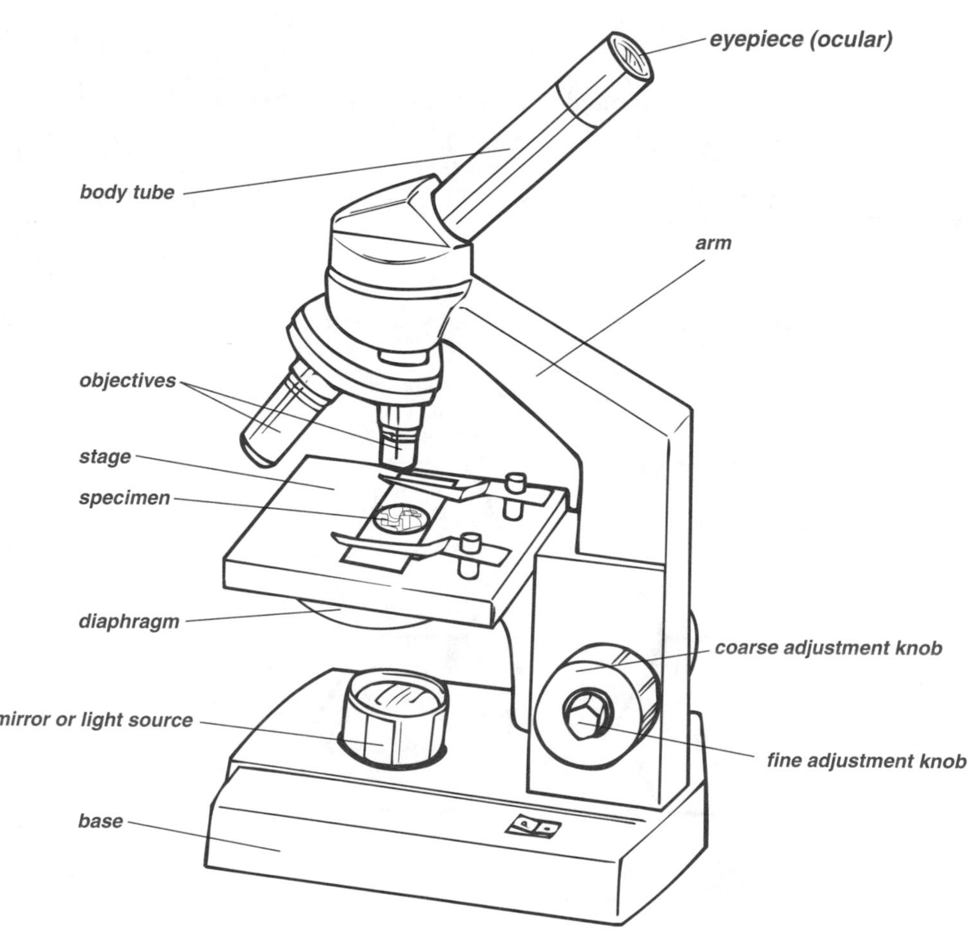

Ideas 4c

Typical Parts of Cells

Directions: The cell membrane has been drawn and labeled for you. Other cellular structures are described under the blanks beside the cell. In each blank, write the name of the structure that is being described; then draw the structure in the cell diagram. Draw a line from the name of the structure to your drawing of the structure.

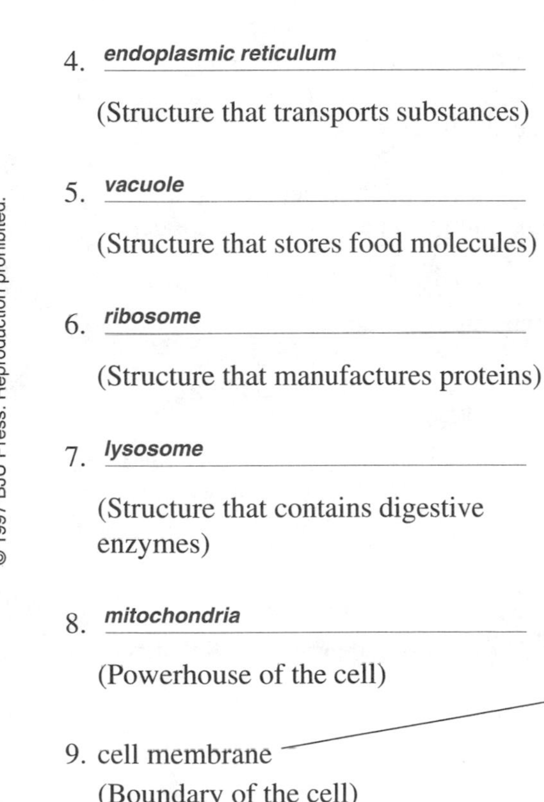

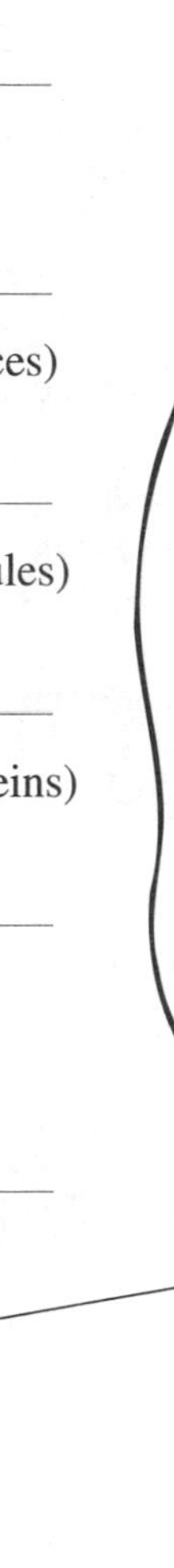

1. *cell wall*

   (Protective coating manufactured by the cell)

2. *Golgi body*

   (Structure that packages substances inside the cell)

3. *nucleus*

   (Control center of the cell)

4. *endoplasmic reticulum*

   (Structure that transports substances)

5. *vacuole*

   (Structure that stores food molecules)

6. *ribosome*

   (Structure that manufactures proteins)

7. *lysosome*

   (Structure that contains digestive enzymes)

8. *mitochondria*

   (Powerhouse of the cell)

9. cell membrane

   (Boundary of the cell)

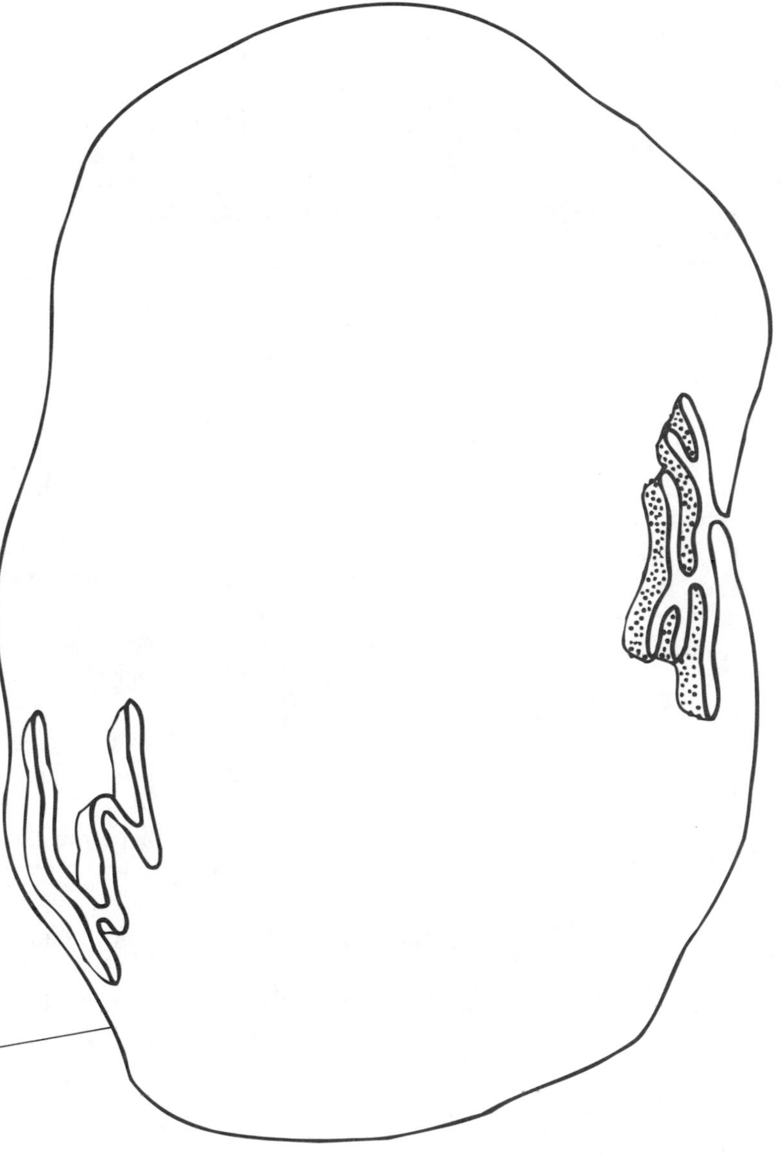

Ideas 4d

Review

Directions: Read the following statements. In the space provided, write *True* if the statement is true and *False* if the statement is false and draw a line through the word or words that make the statement false. In the space in the margin, write the word or words necessary to make the statement true.

True 1. Some cells may completely lack some organelles.

longer *False* 2. Flagella are usually ~~shorter~~ than cilia.

True 3. Lysosomes contain enzymes that dissolve other substances.

True 4. The cell membrane is a fluid mosaic.

True 5. Most cells are too small to be seen without a microscope.

True 6. Golgi bodies collect and package materials from the cytoplasm.

True 7. The nuclear membrane has pores.

water *False* 8. In osmosis, ~~salt~~ molecules diffuse through a membrane.

True 9. DNA contains coded messages that determine the characteristics of a cell.

True 10. Vacuoles may contain food, water, fats, wastes, or chemicals.

DNA *False* 11. Chromosomes are made of the chemical ~~RNA~~.

True 12. When molecules diffuse through a cell membrane, they move from an area of higher concentration to an area of lower concentration.

outside *False* 13. A cell wall is located ~~inside~~ the cell membrane.

True 14. Chloroplasts are organelles that contain the chemical chlorophyll, which is used in photosynthesis.

True 15. A selectively permeable membrane allows certain molecules to pass through it.

Active *False* 16. ~~Passive~~ transport requires energy.

True 17. Organs are groups of tissues that work together to accomplish a particular function.

Name ____________________
Date __________ Hour ______________

Class Investigation 4a

Diffusion Rates

This simple exercise can be done as a demonstration, or it can be done by groups of students in the class. If you are doing the activity as a demonstration, you may wish to use larger containers and larger amounts of water and ink. Plan on doing something else during the time that the ink is diffusing. You may want to do Parts 1 and 2 simultaneously.

Goals

- Observe diffusion.
- Measure different rates of diffusion.
- Determine how certain factors affect diffusion rates.

Materials

250 ml beakers, water (hot and cold), ink (or dark food coloring), measuring spoons, stirring rod or spoon, stopwatch or a clock with a second hand

Part 1: Moving vs. Still Water

Procedures and observations

1. Fill two clean glass beakers each with about 235 ml (1 c.) of water.
2. Place the two beakers next to each other and wait for the water to become still.
3. Measure two identical amounts of ink (about 5 ml or 1 tsp.).
4. Using a stirring rod or a spoon, stir the water in one beaker. Pour one portion of ink into the beaker of moving water and the other portion of ink into the beaker of still water. Be sure to pour both portions of ink at the same time.
5. Record the time required for each beaker to complete diffusion. (Diffusion is complete when all the water in the beaker is the same color; no streaks or currents will be visible.)

   Moving water: ________ minutes ________ seconds

   Still water: ________ minutes ________ seconds

Home School Tip

Substitute clear bowls or measuring cups for the beakers.

Some inks may require only one drop. You should test this ahead of time to find out how much ink to use and how long diffusion will take. Our tests took up to fifteen minutes.

Summing up

1. What is diffusion? ***Diffusion is the random movement of molecules from a place of higher concentration to a place of lower concentration.***
2. In which beaker did diffusion take place more rapidly?

   ☒ stirred ☐ unstirred
3. Explain why diffusion took place more rapidly in one beaker. ***The molecules moved more quickly due to the stirring.***

Part 2: Hot vs. Cold Water

Procedures and observations

You can use boiling water from an automatic coffee-maker and cold water from a refrigerator or a refrigerated drinking fountain.

The hot-water/cold-water demonstration (Part 2) may require several minutes to complete.

1. Set up two beakers of water as you did in Part A. This time, however, one beaker should contain very hot water, and the other beaker should contain very cold water.
2. Prepare two identical amounts of ink as before. Do not stir the water in either beaker.
3. Pour one portion of ink into each beaker and start timing. Be sure to pour both portions of ink at the same time.
4. Record the time it takes for each beaker to reach complete diffusion.

Hot water: ________ minutes ________ seconds

Cold water: ________ minutes ________ seconds

Summing up

1. In which beaker did diffusion take place more rapidly?

   ☒ hot water ☐ cold water

2. Explain why diffusion took place more rapidly in that beaker. ***The molecules were moving more rapidly in the hot water than in the cold water.***

Name ______________________
Date ____________ Hour ______________

Class Investigation 4b

Osmosis

This activity can be done as a demonstration.

Goal

- Demonstrate and observe osmosis.

Materials

thistle tube, rubber bands or string, selectively permeable membrane, clear corn syrup, 500 ml beaker, water, ring stand, clamp

You can purchase selectively permeable membranes (dialysis tubing) from biological supply houses. You may be able to substitute sausage skins.

Setting up

1. Put your finger over the narrow end of the thistle tube; then pour syrup into the thistle-shaped bulb. The syrup should fill the bulb and go down the tube a couple of centimeters (about an inch). (The tube should not be filled with syrup.)
2. Keeping your finger over the end of the tube, have another student place the membrane over the open end of the bulb. Secure the membrane with a string or rubber band so that no syrup can leak out when the bulb is turned downward.
3. Turn the thistle tube so that the bulb is pointed down and remove your finger from the end of the tube. Allow the syrup to settle.

Various biological supply houses have inexpensive, reusable, ready-made osmometers that can be filled with syrup and used for this activity. The membranes on some of these osmometers, if properly cared for, can last several years.

You can make your own syrup by dissolving sugar (sucrose or fructose) in water. Fructose is available in grocery stores. Honey can also be substituted. Molasses can be substituted, but it does not work as well. You may wish to add a drop of food coloring to your syrup. This will help you to detect leaks.

Procedures and observations

1. Place the thistle tube bulb in a beaker of water as shown in the diagram.
2. Using a wax pencil or a piece of tape, mark the level of syrup in the tube.

   Record the time: ______________________

3. Every ten minutes, record the level of syrup in the tube. Continue these observations as long as your class hour lasts.

   10 minutes: ____________ 30 minutes: ____________
   20 minutes: ____________ 40 minutes: ____________

4. If possible, leave the apparatus set up overnight and observe the results the next day.
5. Observations after twenty-four hours: ______________________

Home School Tip

Instead of an osmometer you can make "sausages" from the dialysis tubing by tying each end of a 5 in. section. Fill one sausage with syrup before tying the second end. Similarly fill another with water. The one with syrup will become more turgid as water enters it by osmosis. The one containing water should remain unchanged.

Summing up

1. What is osmosis? ***Osmosis is the diffusion of water molecules through a selectively permeable membrane.***

2. What caused the level of syrup to rise in the tube? ***Osmosis caused the syrup to rise. The water molecules moved from the water into the syrup, causing it to rise.***

3. Why do syrup molecules remain in the tube and not pass from the tube into the beaker of water? ***The syrup molecules are too large and will not pass through the membrane.***

The last question is not covered in the text. It will be difficult for most students to answer. You may wish to discuss this question in class.

4. If you left this apparatus set up for a long period of time, would the action you observed ☐ continue indefinitely or ☒ come to a stop?
   Why? ***Gravity would soon equal the push that the water molecules have, and osmosis would stop.***

Name ______________________

Date __________ Hour ____________

Class Investigation 4c

How to Use a Microscope

Goal

- Practice using a compound light microscope.

Materials

coverslips, eyedropper, glass slides, microscope, newspaper or other printed materials

Setting up

Follow the instructions on page 54 to obtain and set up your microscope.

1. Compute the powers available on your microscope. On pages 72-73 of your text, you will find instructions for determining the powers available on a microscope.
2. Fill in the chart below regarding your microscope. Your microscope may have only two or three objectives. If so, use only the first two or three lines of the chart.

	Objective power		Eyepiece power		Total magnification
Objective 1	_____x	times	_____x	equals	_____x
Objective 2	_____x	times	_____x	equals	_____x
Objective 3	_____x	times	_____x	equals	_____x
Objective 4	_____x	times	_____x	equals	_____x

3. In this book, the term *low power* refers to a total magnification of about 100x. The term *high power* refers to a total magnification of about 400x.

Procedures and observations

Prepare your microscope for viewing.

1. Open the diaphragm on your microscope to its largest setting.
2. If your microscope has an electric light, plug it in and turn it on.
3. If your microscope has a mirror, adjust it until you are able to see a bright light through the eyepiece (ocular). You should try to use the brightest light source available, but you should not use direct sunlight.

Prepare a microscope slide for viewing.

1. Carefully clean and dry a glass slide and a coverslip. Once you have cleaned them, handle the slide and coverslip only by the edges. This will prevent your viewing fingerprints by mistake.
2. Place a single drop of water on the center of your slide.
3. Cut a letter *e* from a piece of newspaper and place it on the drop of water.
4. Carefully place the coverslip on top of the drop of water. If air bubbles appear near the piece of paper, tap the coverslip with a pencil. If too many bubbles remain, take the slide apart and start over.

Home School Tip

It is best to have a microscope in Life Science. It is essential in Biology. If you are planning on teaching Biology at home, you might consider obtaining and using a microscope in Life Science. Remember to order slides too.

Ideally, one microscope should be provided for every two to four students. Most of the exercises in this book can be accomplished with one microscope for every five to eight students, although the students will accomplish considerably less per unit of time.

The typical school microscope is equipped with 4x, 10x, and 40x objectives and a 10x eyepiece (resulting in magnifications of 40x, 100x, and 400x). The 4x objective is called the scanning lens and is used for centering the specimen on the microscope. The 10x objective is referred to as "low power" and the 40x objective as "high power."

Some microscopes have a 100x objective (1000x total magnification) or an oil immersion lens. The activities in this book do not require this lens or magnification.

Microscopes with these recommended magnifications are available inexpensively at toy stores; however, these microscopes are **not** *recommended. They are not built to take the wear and tear of school use. A more significant problem is their poor resolution (ability to see detail). Better microscopes are sturdy and give good lens resolution. Used microscopes are sometimes available at optical instrument repair shops. (See the Yellow Pages under "Microscopes" in medium- to large-sized cities.) Often schools that are replacing their microscopes sell their old ones to such establishments, which then overhaul them and sell them at prices below retail.*

About every two to five years, depending upon their use, microscopes should be taken to an optical repair shop for cleaning and adjustment. This preventative service will help to protect your investment.

This exercise will work well if there is a microscope for every two to five students. If you have fewer microscopes than this, you may wish to do this exercise as a demonstration and have the students observe the newspaper after you have set up the microscopes.

You may wish to use a prepared microscope slide rather than a newspaper. You may want to combine Investigations 4c and 4d.

If your microscopes are not parfocal, you will need to give your students additional instructions for focusing their microscopes on high power.

You will need to show students how to hold a slide and a coverslip by the edges so that they do not get fingerprints on them.

You may also want to demonstrate how to set these items on the edges of a book or desk to make them easy to pick up.

Use plastic coverslips. They are much safer than glass.

5. Place the slide on the stage of your microscope and position it so that the piece of newspaper is in the middle of the opening in the stage. Clip the slide in place.

Focus the microscope on low power.

1. Position the low-power objective so it is directly under the body tube of your microscope. On some microscopes the objectives will click into place.
2. While looking at the side of your microscope, turn the coarse adjustment knob until the objective *almost* touches the coverslip.
3. Look through the objective and *slowly* turn the coarse adjustment knob so that the body tube goes *up* (or the stage goes *down*) until you are able to see the newspaper.

   NOTE: Never turn the coarse adjustment knob so that the body tube goes down (or the stage goes up) while you are looking through the eyepiece! You could cause the objective to push into the slide and break it.
4. If you have raised the objective more than an inch from the coverslip, you have raised it too far. Look at the side of your microscope and turn the coarse adjustment knob until the objective almost touches the coverslip. Then look through the eyepiece and start raising the body tube again.
5. If you are still unable to see the newspaper, try the following:
   - Adjust the diaphragm to a slightly smaller setting and then try to focus the microscope again.
   - Check to make sure the newspaper is directly above the center of the opening in the stage and directly under the objective.
6. If you still cannot see the newspaper, ask your teacher for help.
7. Once you have found the newspaper by using the coarse adjustment knob, use the fine adjustment knob to obtain a clear image. You can adjust the fine adjustment knob either direction, but you should never have to turn it more than a full turn in either direction.
8. Often you will need to readjust your fine adjustment knob while you are viewing something through the microscope.

Note what happens when you move your slide.

1. While looking through the objective, move your slide slightly to the left. What happens to the image that you are viewing? ***It moves to the right.***
2. Move your slide slightly to the right. What happens to the image that you are viewing? ***It moves to the left.***
3. Move your slide so that it goes away from you slightly. What happens to the image when you do this? ***It moves toward you.***
4. Move your slide so that it comes toward you slightly. What happens to the image when you do this? ***It moves away from you.***

Name ______________________

Date __________ Hour __________

5. Describe what the newspaper and the printed *e* look like under the low power of a microscope. ***Answers will vary.***

Focus your microscope on high power.

1. Move your slide so that an edge of the newspaper crosses the center of the area you see through the microscope. Be sure this is in the very center!
2. Carefully rotate the objectives so that the high-power objective is directly below the body tube.
3. Adjust the fine adjustment knob. The image should be in focus when you turn the knob less than a full turn.
4. If necessary, adjust the amount of light coming through the diaphragm.
5. If you cannot see a good image through your microscope, return to low power and focus again. Make sure that your newspaper is in the center of the area you are viewing through the microscope. Try to focus on high power again. If you still have problems, ask your teacher for help.
6. Move the slide around and observe the newspaper and the letter *e* on high power.
7. What is the difference between the image you see under low power and the image you see under high power? ***Answers will vary. Students may indicate that under high power they noticed some aspect of the paper or ink that they did not notice before, that they were able to see less of the newspaper than they saw before, that the image appeared larger, or that the field of viewing was dimmer.***
8. Make slides of printed letter *e*s from magazines and other sources. Typed letters are interesting. What differences do you notice between different kinds of paper and between different forms of printing? ***Answers will vary.***

Rules for Using Microscopes

Carry the microscope properly. Excessive jarring and bumping may bring the lenses out of adjustment. To avoid damaging the microscope, observe the following rules:

1. When taking a microscope out of the cabinet or cupboard, be careful not to bang the microscope against the sides of the cabinet.
2. Carry the microscope with one hand under the base and the other on the arm of the microscope.
3. Be sure to keep the microscope close to your body in an upright position so that the eyepiece does not slip out of the body tube.
4. Place the microscope gently on the table and position it about 8 cm (3 in.) from the edge.

Prepare the microscope properly. You may need to clean your microscope before you begin to use it. Observe these rules while you clean it.

1. Use only lens paper to clean the lens surfaces and the mirror. Wipe the lenses in one direction across the diameter of each lens.
2. Consult your instructor if any material remains on your eyepiece or objectives.
3. Under no circumstances should you attempt to take your microscope apart.

Return the microscope properly. When you have finished using a microscope, you should observe the following rules:

1. Make sure the body tube is straight up and down.
2. Position the lowest power objective directly under the body tube.
3. Adjust the body tube to its lowest position.
4. Carefully return the microscope to the place where you obtained it.

Name ____________________
Date __________ Hour __________

Class Investigation 4d

Observing Cells with a Microscope

Select prepared slides of various types of cells. Protozoans, human tissues, plant tissues, and algae would be good to use. Prepare several fresh wet mounts for the students. Geranium leaf epidermis, stained onion skin, flower petal epidermis, slices of cork, edges of elodea leaves, a live protozoan (amoebas are good), cheek epithelial cells, banana cells, tomato skin, and others are possible.

Goal

- Observe and compare cells.

Materials

cork, coverslips, elodea, eyedropper, flower, geranium leaf, glass slides, microscope, onion, potato, prepared slides of various cells, protozoan specimen, methylene blue, iodine solution, single-edged razor blades, toothpicks

Procedures and observations

Observe through a microscope several prepared slides (slides that have dead cells permanently mounted on them) that your teacher has chosen.

Before the students observe the slides, tell them the name of the cell they will be observing and discuss how the cell was prepared. Students can record this information in their charts before they observe the cell.

1. Prepared slides usually have specimens that have been stained for easier viewing.
2. Observe through a microscope several slides of fresh specimens that your teacher has prepared. Some fresh specimens must be stained to be seen clearly; other specimens have natural color and do not need to be stained.
3. On the chart below, list the names of the cells you observed and record your observations and descriptions.

Tell the students to have in mind specific structures that they are to look for as they observe the cells. Then they can write their descriptions as other students are looking at the specimens.

Name of cell	Observations and description of cell*

*Describe the size, shape, color, and number of cells seen and list any cellular parts that you can see.

Elodea is also used in other investigations. See the Materials lists in this activities manual.

To make the iodine solution, dissolve 10 g of potassium iodine in 100 ml of water. Add 5 g of iodine. This solution is used to test for starch. It causes materials that contain starch to become dark blue or black. The solution may be diluted if necessary and should be stored in darkness. Iodine solutions may also be purchased ready-made. Tincture of iodine, which is available in drugstores, can be used as the iodine solution.

Summing up

1. Based on your observation, what conclusions can you draw regarding the differences between plant and animal cells? *Answers will vary. Plants have cell walls and plastids.*
2. Which two or three cellular structures did you see most often? *Answers will vary.*

To save time you may want to prepare the wet mounts before class begins and then explain to the students how you prepared the slides. You may also want to have the microscopes already set up, focused, and ready for observations. If time and the number of microscopes permit, you may give students the slides (some preserved, some fresh) and have them focus the microscopes. After students have observed their own slides, they can then move to other microscopes and look at other specimens.

If you have a large class or few microscopes, you should probably focus the microscopes, permit students to observe the specimens, and then change the slides.

Have the students do the Summing Up section as homework; then discuss the answers after you have collected the work.

3. Did you see anything moving inside the fresh cells? If you did, what cells were they and what do you think was moving? ***Answers will vary but may indicate cytoplasmic streaming.***

4. What other observations did you make regarding cells? ***Answers will vary.***

Name ______________________
Date ____________ Hour ____________

5–Activities of Cells

Ideas 5a

Order Among Cells

Directions: Write your responses in the spaces provided.

1. What is meant by "division of labor"? Give two examples of division of labor. (Give examples that are not spoken of in Chapter 5.) *Answers will vary. Certain members of a group carry on necessary functions that are not carried on by other members of that group. Examples will vary.*

2. Read Romans 12:4-8 and I Corinthians 12:12-25. Describe the division of labor in the body of Christ. Be sure to discuss the benefits and responsibilities of members in the body of Christ. Are you a member of the body of Christ? *Students should make the following points in their answers: (1) members have different gifts (functions); (2) no part (member) should think himself more important or less important than any other part; (3) benefit comes from other members using their gifts (functioning); (4) each part is responsible to use his gift(s). Hopefully, your students will truthfully answer that they are a member of the body of Christ. This question is an opportunity to discuss salvation.*

Ideas 5b

Respiration

Directions: Use the definitions to help unscramble the terms.

1.	ragus	*sugar*	Most common energy source in cellular respiration
2.	tacmlyosp	*cytoplasm*	Where the first part of cellular respiration occurs
3.	rebcaio	*aerobic*	Type of cellular respiration that requires oxygen
4.	ticcla	*lactic*	Acid produced in muscles during anaerobic respiration
5.	ayctlast	*catalyst*	Characteristic that makes enzymes reusable
6.	ithmodoraicn	*mitochondria*	Organelles associated with cellular respiration
7.	mentfatrenoi	*fermentation*	Alcoholic is one example of this type of respiration.

Name ______________________
Date ____________ Hour ____________

Ideas 5c

Photosynthesis

Directions: Below are several groups of words. In each group three of the four words (or phrases) are related to one another. Draw a line through the unrelated word and then write a sentence using the remaining related words. Your sentence should show how the words are related. You may slightly change the form of the word in your sentence (for example, product to products, stored to storage).

The answers given here are the most logical. Students, however, may devise other good sentences that involve three of the four words in each group. The day after assigning this exercise, you may wish to work half of it in class and then grade the rest when you collect the assignment.

1. photosynthesis / ~~cellulose~~ / sugar / oxygen ***Sugar and oxygen are products of photosynthesis.***
2. light energy / ~~consumer~~ / photosynthesis / chemical energy ***Photosynthesis is a process that changes light energy into chemical energy.***
3. ~~consumer~~ / photosynthesis / chlorophyll / pigment ***Chlorophyll is a pigment used in photosynthesis.***
4. chlorophyll / chloroplasts / ~~light~~ / organelles ***Chlorophyll is found in tiny organelles called chloroplasts.***
5. ~~sugar~~ / light / carbon dioxide / water ***Carbon dioxide, light, and water are starting materials for photosynthesis.***
6. sugar / oxygen / ~~pigments~~ / products ***Sugar and oxygen are products of photosynthesis.***
7. sugar / cellulose / cell walls / ~~oxygen~~ ***Cellulose found in cell walls is made of many sugar molecules.***
8. producers / food / photosynthesis / ~~respiration~~ ***Producers make their own food through photosynthesis.***
9. ~~sugar~~ / light / pigments / absorb ***Pigments absorb light energy.***
10. membrane / ~~mitochondria~~ / chloroplast / chlorophyll ***Chlorophyll is located in the inner chloroplast membrane.***

Ideas 5d

Review

Students may need to rework each category a few times to obtain the correct answers.

Directions: Choose the correct set of words to complete the following statements about *photosynthesis, aerobic cellular respiration,* and *anaerobic cellular respiration.* You may use each answer only once. Each category has its own list of answers.

Photosynthesis

a. carbon dioxide
b. chloroplasts
c. sugar
d. oxygen
e. cells
f. photosynthesis
g. cellulose
h. water

1. __*b*__ are located in the __*e*__.
2. __*a*__ is combined with __*h*__.
3. __*g*__ is made from __*c*__.
4. __*f*__ produces sugar and releases __*d*__.

Aerobic Cellular Respiration

a. aerobic
b. catalysts
c. cellular respiration
d. energy
e. enzymes
f. sugar
g. mitochondria
h. with

1. __*f*__ is broken down to release __*d*__.
2. __*c*__ occurs in the cell's __*g*__.
3. __*a*__ respiration occurs __*h*__ oxygen.
4. The __*b*__ of aerobic cellular respiration are __*e*__.

Anaerobic Cellular Respiration

a. alcoholic
b. anaerobic
c. carbon dioxide
d. fermentation
e. lactic acid
f. muscles
g. without
h. yeast

1. __*b*__ cellular respiration occurs __*g*__ oxygen.
2. __*a*__ fermentation occurs in __*h*__.
3. __*e*__ fermentation may occur in human __*f*__.
4. __*c*__ is a gas produced in alcoholic __*d*__.

Name ______________________
Date ____________ Hour ____________

Class Investigation 5a

Turgor Pressure

We suggest that you not do this activity as a demonstration. Have enough dishes, salt water, fresh water, and potatoes so that the class can be divided into groups of two to four students.

Goals

- Observe the effects of salt water on plant cells.
- Demonstrate turgor pressure.

Materials

dishes, knife, potato, salt water, water

You may want to cut the potatoes for the students. Potato carving is not the objective of this activity and can waste a great deal of class time. You can cut the potatoes a few hours before class begins and keep them in cold water. Just before class time drain them. Students do not need to know that the potatoes have been in cold water for a period of time. Keeping the potatoes like this will not affect the outcome of the activity.

Setting up

1. Place about 5 cm (about 2 in.) of water in a dish. Label the dish "plain water."
2. Place the same amount of salt water in a dish. Label the dish "salt water."
3. Cut two thin strips of potato about the thickness of thin French fries and at least 5 cm long. You should be able to completely submerge them in the water of the dishes. The two potato strips should be as nearly identical as you can make them.

Procedures and observations

Potatoes must be fresh. Frozen or old, rubbery potatoes will not work. Small glasses or paper cups can be used instead of dishes.

1. Place one strip of potato in the fresh water and the other in the salt water.
2. Leave the strips undisturbed for 30 minutes.
3. After 30 minutes take the potato strips out of the fresh water and the salt water and record your observations.
   - Describe the potato strip in fresh water. ***crisp***
   - Describe the potato strip in salt water. ***soft and flexible***

When making the salt-water solution, be sure that you use enough salt. We suggest that you use more salt than can be dissolved in the water, thus leaving a layer of salt on the bottom of your container.

Summing up

1. What is turgor pressure? ***Turgor pressure is the stiffness of plant cells caused by water pressure inside the cells.***
2. What conditions are necessary for plant cells to have turgor pressure? ***An abundant amount of water is necessary.***
3. At the end of your experiment, which of the two potato strips had turgor pressure? ***The one in the fresh water had turgor pressure.***

   How can you tell? ***It was crisp. The cells were full of water.***
4. Explain why the cells of the other potato strip lost their turgor pressure. ***The salt concentration caused water from the cells to go into the salt water. The loss of water caused the potato cells to lose turgor pressure and become limp.***

An alternative or additional activity would be to demonstrate the force of turgor pressure produced by germinating seeds. Fill a cup, pan, or similar container about half full with dry beans. (Tall, narrow containers give more dramatic results than short, wide containers.) Cover the seeds with water and place a plate or other flat object directly on top of the beans. You may wish to place a weight on top of the plate. Measure or mark the level of the plate. Allow the beans to soak overnight or longer, if necessary. As the beans imbibe the water they will swell and produce enough force to lift the plate and weight. Compare the final height of the plate to the initial height. Explain that the cells of the beans have absorbed water and become turgid. Be cautious if using glass containers since it is possible that the pressure generated will break the glass. An ambitious student could repeat the demonstration to determine the maximum weight a certain volume of seeds could lift.

Going Beyond

Determine a salt concentration that equals the solute concentration in the potato's cells. Place potato strips in a range of salt water concentrations. The highest concentration that does not change the crispness of the potato from its original crispness would have the same solute concentration as the cytoplasm of the potato's cells. Be sure to cut all strips from the same potato.

Name ______________________
Date __________ Hour __________

Class Investigation 5b

Anaerobic Cellular Respiration

Goal

- Observe the products of anaerobic cellular respiration.

Materials

apple juice, balloons, glass tubing, string, sugar, tape, thermometers, Thermos vacuum flasks, two-hole rubber stopper (to fit in the vacuum flasks), yeast

Setting up

1. Label the vacuum flasks *A* and *B*.
2. Prepare two rubber stoppers.
   - Place a thermometer through one hole in each stopper.
   - Place a short section of glass tubing through the other hole in each stopper.
   - Tie a balloon to the top end of each glass tube. Carefully tape each balloon so that no air escapes from it. The balloons should be stretched before attaching them to the glass tube. Fully inflate them a few times.

Procedures and observations

1. Pour 300 ml (9 fl. oz.) of apple juice into each vacuum flask.
2. Add 60 ml (4 tbsp.) of sugar into each apple juice vacuum flask.
3. In flask *A*, place one package (0.25 oz.) of yeast. Do not put yeast into flask *B*. Place the covers on the flasks and shake them well. Remove the covers and place the stoppers in each vacuum flask. Be sure that each balloon is deflated.
4. Wait for three minutes and then record your observations on the chart below. Observe the vacuum flasks for the next three days and record your observations on the chart below.

Flask *A*			Flask *B*		
Time	Temp.	Condition of balloon	Time	Temp.	Condition of balloon

Consider doing this investigation as a demonstration.

Home School Tip
If you have only one vacuum flask (Thermos bottle) then use your flask as "flask A" on one day and as "flask B" a few days later.

Any sugary fruit juice should work well in this investigation.

Lubricate the thermometer and the glass tubing before inserting them into the rubber stoppers. Be sure that the students hold the thermometers and the glass tubing in a towel. (If a thermometer or glass tube breaks, the towel will help prevent injuries.)

The thermometers you use should be long enough to extend into the apple juice and still be read above the stopper. You may want to assemble the stoppers before class begins and make sure that the suggested quantity of apple juice is sufficient.

Your vacuum flasks should be identical.

You will observe the primary results within the first couple of days (most likely within the first few hours).

It is essential that the stoppers make a good seal with the flasks.

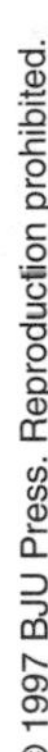

Summing up

1. After what period of time was the temperature in flask *A* the highest?

   ☐ 24 hr. ☐ 48 hr. ☐ 72 hr. ☐ The temperature did not change.

2. After what period of time was the temperature in flask *B* the highest?

   ☐ 24 hr. ☐ 48 hr. ☐ 72 hr. ☐ The temperature did not change.

3. After what period of time did the balloon on flask *A* expand the most?

   ☐ 24 hr. ☐ 48 hr. ☐ 72 hr. ☐ The balloon did not expand.

4. After what period of time did the balloon on flask *B* expand the most?

   ☐ 24 hr. ☐ 48 hr. ☐ 72 hr. ☐ The balloon did not expand.

5. Define anaerobic cellular respiration. ***Anaerobic cellular respiration is the process by which cells break down sugar and release energy without using oxygen.***

6. What are the products of anaerobic cellular respiration? ***Energy, carbon dioxide, and alcohol or lactic acid are the products of anaerobic cellular respiration.***

7. In which of the two vacuum flasks did anaerobic cellular respiration occur? ☒ A ☐ B Explain why you chose that answer. ***Answers will vary. The temperature in flask A increased, indicating that energy was released. The balloon on flask A expanded, indicating that a gas was given off.***

Name ______________________
Date ____________ Hour ______________

Class Investigation 5c

Starch from Photosynthesis

Goals

- To observe that the presence of starch can indicate that photosynthesis has occurred.
- To demonstrate that light is necessary for photosynthesis.

Materials     

alcohol (70% ethanol or 70% isopropyl), aluminum foil, 250 ml beaker, dark cabinet, geranium or coleus, hot plate or other heat source (not an open flame), iodine solution, sunny window, paper clips, petri dish, water

Your teacher will prepare the iodine solution as follows: Dissolve 10 g of potassium iodine in 100 ml of water. Add 5 g of iodine. This solution is used to test for starch. It causes materials that contain starch to become dark blue or black. The solution may be diluted if necessary and should be stored in darkness. Prepared iodine solutions may also be purchased. Tincture of iodine which is available in drugstores can be used as the iodine solution.

Setting up

1. Place a healthy geranium in a dark area for two days (a cabinet or cupboard works well). During this time, energy reserves in the leaf (starch) will become depleted since it will be unable to obtain energy from light.
2. Cut pieces of aluminum foil into various shapes or letters. Individual pieces should be large enough to cover one-third to one-half of one of the geranium or coleus leaves.
3. Use paper clips to attach the aluminum foil pieces to the upper surface of leaves that are still attached to the plant. (See diagram to right.)
4. Place the plant in a sunny window or other well lighted area for one or two days.
5. Heat the alcohol in a beaker until it is hot but not boiling. You should use enough alcohol to cover the leaves which will be placed in the beaker.
6. Remove the leaves with aluminum foil from the plant. Remove the aluminum foil.
7. Immerse the leaves in the hot alcohol for about five minutes. During this time the chlorophyll will be removed from the leaves.
8. Rinse the leaves with water and place each leaf flat in a petri dish.
9. To test for the presence of starch, cover each leaf with iodine solution in the petri dish for five minutes.
10. Rinse off the iodine solution and examine the leaves.

11. Make a drawing of your leaf in the space provided.

Summing up

1. Why at first did you have to put the plant in a dark area for two days? *so that respiration would use up any starch already stored in the leaves*

2. Did starch form in the covered or uncovered part of the leaf? *Starch formed in the uncovered part of the leaf.*

3. What does the presence of starch indicate? *Photosynthesis has occurred.*

4. What does the absence of starch indicate? *Photosynthesis did not occur.*

5. What would have been discovered during the test for starch if, after covering the leaves, you set the plant in a *dark* area for one or two days before testing for starch? *No starch would have been found and no pattern from the foil would have been seen.*

Going beyond

Explain an experiment that you could do (similar to this investigation) which would use different colors of plastic wrap or cellophane to determine the color(s) of transmitted light most useful in photosynthesis. *Students should describe an experiment that compares starch formation in leaves illuminated with different colors of light.*

Name ____________________
Date ____________ Hour ____________

6–Mitosis and Genes

Ideas 6a

Mitosis and Cell Division

Directions: Below is a series of diagrams illustrating cell division. Beside the diagrams is a column for the name of the phase being illustrated and another column describing what is happening in that phase. Fill in the missing names or descriptions. In your descriptions be sure to use the following words: *chromosomes, sister chromatids,* and *spindle.*

	Cell Division Phase	Description
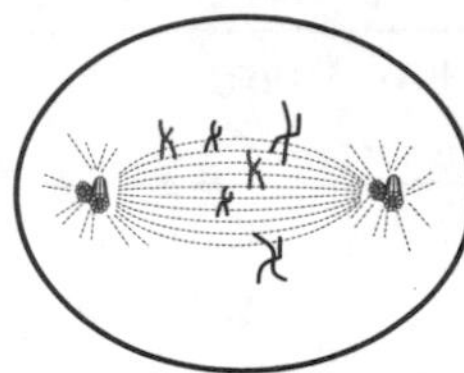	Mother cell (Interphase)	The cell is ready to divide.
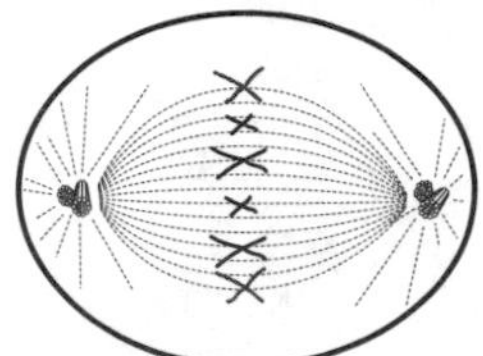	*Prophase*	The nuclear membrane disappears and the chromosomes coil up. The spindle begins to form.
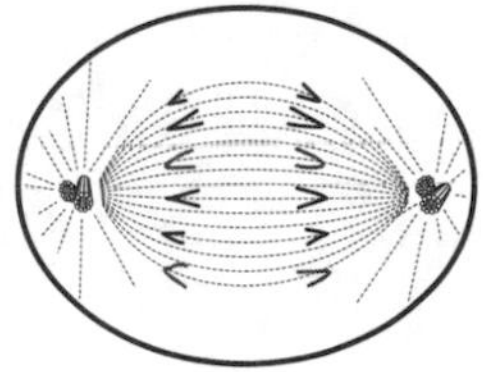	Metaphase	*Chromosomes (sister chromatids) line up at the center of the spindle.*
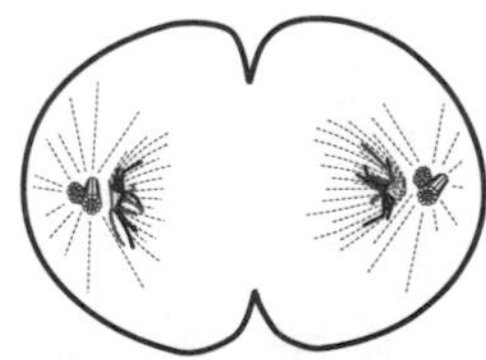	*Anaphase*	*Each pair of sister chromatids separates into two chromosomes and begins to migrate.*
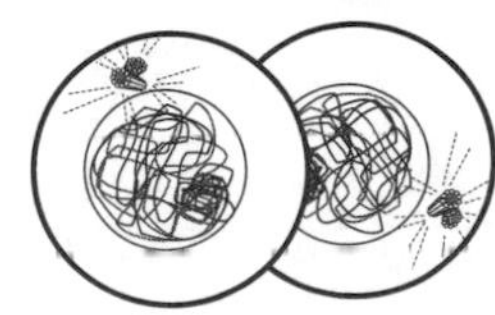	Telophase	*The new chromosomes reach the end of the spindle and begin to uncoil.*
	Cytokinesis	*The cytoplasm divides.*

Ideas 6b

Asexual Reproduction

Directions: Complete the table below by answering the question and filling in the missing words from the list provided.

amoeba
budding
planarian
regeneration
spores
yeast

Type	Must mitosis occur?	Must meiosis occur?	Example
mitosis of unicellular organism	***yes***	***no***	***amoeba***
budding	yes	***no***	***yeast***
regeneration	***yes***	no	***planarian***
spores	***yes***	***no***	bread mold

Name ______________________________

Date ____________ Hour ______________

Ideas 6c

Genes and Mitosis

Directions: Use the definitions below to choose the right words to fill in the blanks.

1. R E G E N E R A T I O N
2. S P O R E
3. A N A P H A S E
4. M E T A P H A S E
5. P R O P H A S E
6. T E L O P H A S E
7. G E N E S
8. S P I N D L E
9. M E I O S I S
10. F I S S I O N
11. C H R O M A T I D S
12. C Y T O K I N E S I S
13. N U C L E U S
14. B U D D I N G
15. A S E X U A L

1. The regrowing of missing body parts
2. A cell with a hard protective coat around it
3. The phase of mitosis that follows metaphase
4. The phase of mitosis in which the chromosomes are lined up in the middle of the spindle
5. The first phase of mitosis
6. The phase of mitosis during which cytokinesis takes place
7. Contain the information needed for cell functions
8. The structure on which chromosomes move during mitosis
9. Must precede sexual reproduction
10. Another name for cell division
11. The duplicate chromosomes that appear during mitosis
12. The dividing of the cytoplasm during cell division
13. The area where chromosomes are normally found in a cell
14. A form of asexual reproduction in yeast
15. The form of reproduction based on mitotic cell division

How Genes Function

Directions: Below are several groups of words. In each group three of the four words (or phrases) are related to one another. Draw a line through the unrelated word, and then write a sentence using the remaining words. Your sentence should show how the words are related. You may slightly change the form of the word in your sentence (for example, chromosome to chromosomes, replicate to replication).

The answers given here are the most logical. Students, however, may devise other good sentences that involve three of the four words in each group. The day after assigning this exercise, you may wish to work half of it in class and then grade the rest when you collect the assignment.

1. sugar / phosphate / ~~amino acid~~ / base ***A sugar, a phosphate, and a base make up a nucleotide.***

2. ~~uracil~~ / DNA / adenine / thymine ***Adenine and thymine are bases found in DNA.***

3. DNA / ~~RNA~~ / replication / nucleotides ***DNA replicates by lining up nucleotides.***

4. DNA / transcription / RNA / ~~amino acids~~ ***Transcription is the formation of an RNA molecule from DNA.***

5. ~~Mendel~~ / Watson / Crick / DNA ***Watson and Crick developed a model for DNA.***

6. proteins / ~~replication~~ / amino acids / ribosomes ***Amino acids combine on the ribosomes to form proteins.***

7. sequence / ~~factors~~ / amino acids / nucleotide ***The nucleotide sequence of m-RNA determines which amino acids to use to make the protein.***

8. ~~phosphate~~ / chromosomes / DNA / genes ***Chromosomes are made of genes, which are sections of DNA.***

9. ~~protein~~ / thymine / RNA / uracil ***In RNA, the base uracil replaces thymine.***

10. protein synthesis / ~~chromosome~~ / t-RNA / amino acids ***In protein synthesis, t-RNA transfers amino acids.***

Name ______________________

Date ____________ Hour ______________

Class Investigation 6a

The Phases of Mitosis

Goals

- Identify the phases of mitosis.
- Describe the sequence of the phases of mitosis.

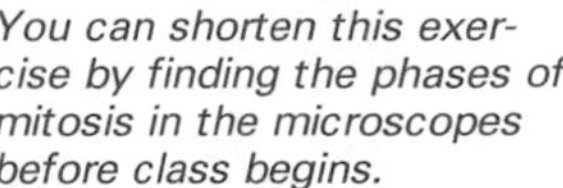

You can shorten this exercise by finding the phases of mitosis in the microscopes before class begins.

Arrange the phases in order. Then have the students view them and write the answers to the questions. This method is also good if you do not have enough microscopes for all of the students. To do this exercise as written, you will need to have about one microscope for every two to four students in your class.

Explain to your students that slide manufacturers slice the root tips when they prepare the slides. Sometimes the slice is made close to the edge of the cell. Thus occasionally the cell will appear empty. Actually, the chromosomes that belong in that empty cell are on another slide.

Establish the number of prophases, metaphases, anaphases, and telophases that you want your class to find; base that amount on the number of microscopes you have. Try to have an equal number of each phase so there will be opportunity for each student to conveniently view each phase. List the phases on the chalkboard with a certain number of lines under them. Tell students to write their names on the proper line when they have had their phase approved. This will then permit those who have not yet found a phase to know which ones not to look for.

Materials  

prepared slides of onion, lily, or hyacinth root tips showing the phases of mitosis; microscope

Setting up

1. Focus your microscope on one of the root tips on the preserved slide.
2. Locate the area just above the root cap. (See page 194 of your text.) In this area, mitosis happens rapidly to form new root cells so that the root can grow. When this root tip was killed and prepared for microscope viewing, many of the cells in this area were in various phases of mitosis. The root tip was then treated with special stains to permit you to see the chromosomes.
3. In order to see the chromosomes in the various phases of mitosis, you will need to focus your microscope on high power.

Procedures and observations

1. Scan your slide by slowly moving the slide back and forth. Look for cells in the various phases of mitosis.
2. Find what you think is a good example of one of the phases of mitosis. Position that cell in your microscope's viewing field.
   - What phase of mitosis do you believe this is? ***Answers will vary.***
   - Why do you think that you are viewing a good example of this phase of mitosis? ***Answers will vary.*** ______________________________
   - Ask your teacher to check your cell to be sure it shows a good example of the phase you think you are viewing.
3. After your teacher has agreed with your findings, you may enter your name on the list under the proper phase of mitosis. Once a list is filled up, no more of that phase should be found.
4. After you have found a phase of mitosis, observe other phases of mitosis through the microscopes of other students. Observe their slides only after they have had them approved by the teacher.
5. Once all the phases of mitosis have been found in your class, you should move from one microscope to another, viewing the various phases of mitosis **in order.** Carefully note the sequence of the movements of the chromosomes in mitosis.

Summing up

1. Write a brief description of the movements of chromosomes during mitosis as you saw them in the various microscopes.

   Prophase: ***In prophase the chromosomes began to coil up.***

   Metaphase: ***In metaphase the chromosomes lined up along the middle of the spindle.***

   Anaphase: ***During anaphase the chromosomes (sister chromatids) divided and moved away from each other on the spindle.***

   Telophase: ***During telophase the chromosomes uncoiled at the ends of the spindle.***

2. What other observations about mitosis did you make while observing these cells? ***Answers will vary. Students may notice that daughter cells are about half the size of regular cells. They may notice the division plate forming between the daughter cells. They may notice that interphase cells have fuzzy-looking nuclei.***

Name ______________________________

Date ______________ Hour ______________

Class Investigation 6b

A Model of DNA, RNA, and Protein Synthesis

Tell the students to color and cut out the nucleotides the day before you plan to use them in class.

You should use this investigation after you have used other visuals to present DNA, RNA, and protein synthesis. Use this exercise as a review rather than as an introduction.

Goal

- Model the processes of DNA replication, RNA transcription, and protein synthesis.

Materials

construction paper, colored pencils or crayons, scissors, tape

Setting up

1. Color the various nucleotides on pages 75-83 as indicated.
2. Cut out the nucleotides and bring them to class.

You may want to prepare the amino acids and the ribosomes rather than have the students do it.

Procedures and observations

1. As a class, build a DNA molecule on a large table or on the floor.
   - Form one side of a DNA molecule; then tape the nucleotides together.
   - Match your half-DNA molecule with the proper nucleotides to form a complete DNA molecule. Tape the two sides of the DNA molecule together.
2. Replicate your DNA molecule.
   - Unzip your DNA molecule.
   - Add the proper nucleotides to form two identical DNA molecules.
3. Transcribe a messenger RNA (m-RNA) molecule.
   - Unzip your DNA molecule.
   - Add the proper nucleotides to one side to form an m-RNA molecule. Remember that nucleotides in RNA are different from those in DNA.
   - Remove the m-RNA from the side of the DNA and zip the DNA molecule back together.
4. Manufacture a protein.
   - Make several differently colored and differently shaped amino acids from construction paper. Each amino acid should be about 8 inches in diameter.
   - Make a ribosome from construction paper.
   - Make transfer RNA (t-RNA) molecules. Each t-RNA molecule should be three nucleotides long and should be able to line up on your m-RNA molecule. Tape the nucleotides of the t-RNA together.
   - Attach an amino acid to each of the t-RNA molecules.
   - Slide the end of the m-RNA molecule over the ribosome.
   - Line up the proper t-RNA molecule with the m-RNA on the ribosome.
   - Tape together the amino acids that are lined up and detach them from the t-RNA.
   - Remove the t-RNA once it has released its amino acids.
   - Slide the ribosome along the m-RNA until the next three nucleotides are in it. Line up the proper t-RNA and attach its amino acid to the chain.
   - Continue the process for the length of the m-RNA.

The DNA molecule you manufacture should be at least twelve nucleotides long. (Fifteen or eighteen nucleotides are sufficient.) The number of nucleotides in your molecules should, however, be divisible by three.

It is profitable to have this exercise done over a period of several days. Manufacture your DNA molecule and replicate it on one day. If your class is large, you may be able to review the structure of DNA and replicate your DNA molecule again on the next day. If your class is small, you may only be able to review the structure and process on the next day. Then manufacture your messenger RNA. That night carefully decide how your transfer RNA molecules need to be made. The next day in class manufacture the protein.

To determine the sequence of nucleotide bases in your DNA molecule, you may want to randomly pull pieces of paper with the names of DNA's four bases on them from a container.

A ribosome pattern for this investigation appears on the last page of this teacher's edition of the activities manual.

Plan carefully for doing this if you have a large class constructing this together. (It could get out of hand easily.)

Cytosine
(light blue)

Cytosine
(light blue)

Cytosine
(light blue)

Guanine
(dark blue)

Guanine
(dark blue)

Guanine
(dark blue)

Thymine
(dark green)

Thymine
(dark green)

Thymine
(dark green)

Adenine
(light green)

Adenine
(light green)

Adenine
(light green)

Cytosine
(light blue)

Cytosine
(light blue)

Cytosine
(light blue)

Guanine
(dark blue)

Guanine
(dark blue)

Guanine
(dark blue)

Uracil
(gray)

Uracil
(gray)

Uracil
(gray)

Adenine
(light green)

Adenine
(light green)

Adenine
(light green)

Cytosine
(light blue)

Guanine
(dark blue)

Cytosine
(light blue)

Guanine
(dark blue)

Cytosine
(light blue)

Guanine
(dark blue)

Thymine
(dark green)

Adenine
(light green)

Thymine
(dark green)

Adenine
(light green)

Thymine
(dark green)

Adenine
(light green)

Cytosine
(light blue)

Cytosine
(light blue)

Cytosine
(light blue)

Guanine
(dark blue)

Guanine
(dark blue)

Guanine
(dark blue)

Uracil
(gray)

Uracil
(gray)

Uracil
(gray)

Adenine
(light green)

Adenine
(light green)

Adenine
(light green)

Cytosine
(light blue)

Guanine
(dark blue)

Cytosine
(light blue)

Guanine
(dark blue)

Cytosine
(light blue)

Guanine
(dark blue)

Thymine
(dark green)

Adenine
(light green)

Thymine
(dark green)

Adenine
(light green)

Uracil
(gray)

Adenine
(light green)

Name ______________________
Date ____________ Hour ____________

7–Genetics of Organisms

Ideas 7a

The Origin of Modern Genetics

Part 1

Directions: Gooney birds can have red beaks or white beaks. Beak color in gooney birds is controlled by two factors. Uppercase *R* represents the dominant factor, and it causes red beaks. Lowercase *r* represents the recessive factor and, when expressed, causes white beaks. Using this information, complete the chart below.

Letter representation	Dominant or recessive trait expressed?	Purebred or hybrid?	Color of beak
RR	*dominant*	*purebred*	*red*
rr	*recessive*	*purebred*	*white*
Rr	*dominant*	*hybrid*	*red*

Part 2

Directions: Write the proper terms next to the following definitions. Then find and circle the terms in the word puzzle on the next page. In the word puzzle the terms may appear horizontally, vertically, or diagonally, and may be forward or backward.

Mendel 1. The monk who studied genetics during the 1800s

purebred 2. An organism that has had the same characteristics for many generations

factors 3. The particles that, according to Mendel, caused inherited characteristics

cross 4. A test mating

genetics 5. The study of inherited characteristics

gene 6. Modern term for Mendel's term *factor*

pea 7. Organism Mendel observed in his study of genetics

dominant 8. The type of trait that masks the presence of another trait

fifty 9. About how many years Mendel's work went unnoticed *recessive* 10. The type of trait that can be masked

hybrid 11. Formed when two different purebreds are crossed

pollen 12. What Mendel transferred from one flower to another

two 13. How many factors each trait typically has

inheritance 14. The passing of characteristics from parents to offspring

characteristic 15. Trait that an organism expresses

Note: This puzzle contains distractors.

G G E C H R O M O S O M E S P
P E A B E V I S S E C E R A O
U N N H E S I T E C N N F E Y
M E P E S Z H Y B R I D I X E
E T I O T R O H S N D E R N N
B I R R A W T A R P O L L E N
E C N A T I R E H N I A F N A
R S A S R O T C A F C R I O N
E G G F L I L A D N E A Y I E
L D O M I N A N T V E S R R W
E L C O N F O M S T I E R A J
C H A R A C T E R I S T I C A
E R T T E G E Y E I T C F S F
P O D S P U R E B R E D G E N

Name ____________________

Date __________ Hour __________

Ideas 7b

Genes, Chromosomes, and Heredity

Directions: Write your answers to the following questions in the space provided.

1. How many chromosomes do normal human cells contain? ***46***
2. If an organism's normal chromosome number is 12, how many chromosomes would be in each of its egg or sperm cells? ***6***
3. Suppose someone reported that an animal's normal chromosome number was 17. Why would you say he is probably wrong? ***Chromosomes normally occur in pairs; thus there would normally be an even number of chromosomes.***
4. What does each small box of a Punnett square represent? ***possible gamete combinations or genetic possibilities of the offspring***
5. Do human males have *Y* chromosomes? ***yes***
6. How does incomplete dominance differ from simple dominant/recessive traits? ***Neither trait is dominant over the other; two traits blend to produce a different trait.***
7. Why should you not ridicule someone with an inherited disorder? ***Mockery is cruel; it ridicules something a person cannot control and mocks God's creation.***

Ideas 7c

Review

Directions: Read the following statements. In the space provided, write *True* if the statement is true and *False* if the statement is false and draw a line through the word or words that make the statement false. In the space in the margin, write the word or words necessary to make the statement true.

True 1. Organisms that are purebred for a trait will express the same characteristics for many generations.

True 2. Punnett squares show possible combinations of offspring.

True 3. Mendel used peas in his experiments to discover how organisms inherit traits.

twenty-three — *False* 4. Humans normally have ~~forty-eight~~ pairs of chromosomes in every cell.

True 5. If two purebred organisms that are different for a trait mate, they will produce hybrid offspring.

recessive; dominant — *False* 6. In hybrid tall pea plants, the gene for the ~~dominant~~ characteristic is hidden by the gene for the ~~recessive~~ characteristic.

True 7. Hybrids are organisms that have ancestors that are not alike.

True 8. A carrier has a gene for a certain trait but does not express that trait itself.

X — *False* 9. A sex-linked trait is caused by a gene located on the ~~*Y*~~ chromosome.

True 10. In incomplete dominance, two different genes for the same characteristic may each influence the expression of the characteristic.

True 11. A spotted calf produced by a brown bull and a white cow illustrates incomplete dominance.

True 12. Multiple gene inheritance deals with characteristics that are each controlled by several different sets of genes.

is not — *False* 13. It ~~is~~ possible for parents to pass to their children a gene that they do not have.

True 14. It is possible for parents to pass to their children a characteristic that they do not express.

one X *and one* Y *chromosome* — *False* 15. In humans, a female has two *X* chromosomes, and a male has ~~two *Y* chromosomes~~.

Name ______________________

Date ____________ Hour ______________

Personal Investigation 7a

Genetics Problems

If there is a Punnett square in the margin, be sure to work the problem using the Punnett square. Even if you feel you know the answer, work the problem in the Punnett square. The experience will help you to figure out the more difficult problems that come later.

1. One of the characteristics Mendel studied in his pea plants was the color of the pods. Usually the pea pods were green (the dominant characteristic), but sometimes they were yellow (the recessive characteristic). If Mendel crossed a plant that had purebred green pods (*GG*) with a plant that had purebred yellow pods (*gg*), what would the offspring be like? Place an *X* in the box(es) of the true statement(s).
   A. ☒ The offspring would have green pods.
   B. ☐ The offspring would have yellow pods.

	g	*g*
G	*Gg*	*Gg*
G	*Gg*	*Gg*

2. If Mendel crossed a plant that was purebred for green pods (*GG*) with a plant that was hybrid for green pods (*Gg*), what would the offspring be like? Place an *X* in the box(es) of the true statement(s).
   A. ☒ The offspring would have only green pods.
   B. ☐ The offspring would have only yellow pods.
   C. ☐ The offspring would have some green pods and some yellow pods.

	G	*g*
G	*GG*	*Gg*
G	*GG*	*Gg*

3. In the cross made above (#2), which of the following would be true of the offspring? Place an *X* in the box(es) of the true statement(s).
   A. ☐ They would all be purebred yellow-podded plants.
   B. ☐ They would all be purebred green-podded plants.
   C. ☐ Some would be purebred yellow-podded plants, and some would be purebred green-podded plants.
   D. ☒ Some would be purebred green-podded plants, and some would be hybrid green-podded plants.
   E. ☐ Some would be purebred yellow-podded plants, and some would be hybrid green-podded plants.

4. Mrs. Mitchell has curly hair (*HH*), which is the dominant characteristic, and Mr. Mitchell has straight hair (*hh*). If they have children, what kind of hair will the children have? Place an *X* in the box(es) of the true statement(s).
   A. ☐ All the children will have straight hair.
   B. ☒ All the children will have curly hair.
   C. ☐ Some of the children will have curly hair, and others will have straight hair.
   D. ☐ The girls will have curly hair; the boys will have straight hair.

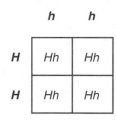

	h	*h*
H	*Hh*	*Hh*
H	*Hh*	*Hh*

	G	g
G	GG	Gg
g	Gg	gg

5. Starchy corn is dominant over sweet corn. If a farmer crosses two hybrid starchy corn plants (*Gg*), what will the offspring be like? Place an *X* in the box(es) of the true statements(s).

   A. ☐ All of the crop will be starchy.

   B. ☐ All of the crop will be sweet.

   C. ☒ Most of the crop will be starchy, but some of it will be sweet.

   D. ☐ Most of the crop will be sweet, but some of it will be starchy.

	r	r
R	Rr	Rr
R	Rr	Rr

6. In guinea pigs, a rough coat is a dominant characteristic, and a smooth coat is a recessive characteristic. If a guinea pig with a smooth coat (*rr*) mated with a guinea pig with a rough coat (*RR*), what would the offspring be like? Place an *X* in the box(es) of the true statement(s).

   A. ☒ All the offspring would have rough coats.

   B. ☐ All the offspring would have smooth coats.

   C. ☐ Some of the offspring would have rough coats, and some would have smooth coats.

   D. ☐ The dark-colored guinea pigs would have rough coats, and the light-colored guinea pigs would have smooth coats.

	f	f
f	ff	ff
f	ff	ff

7. In ducks, silky feathers are recessive to normal feathers. If two silky-feathered ducks mated, what kind of feathers would the ducklings have? Place an *X* in the box(es) of the true statement(s).

   A. ☒ All would have silky feathers.

   B. ☐ All would have normal feathers.

   C. ☐ Most would have silky feathers, but some would have normal feathers.

   D. ☐ Most would have normal feathers, but some would have silky feathers.

   E. ☐ Not enough information is given.

	H	h
H	HH	Hh
h	Hh	hh

8. Short hair is a dominant characteristic in most dogs. If a person crossed two hybrid short-haired dogs, what would the puppies look like? Place an *X* in the box(es) of the true statement(s).

   A. ☐ All the puppies would have short hair.

   B. ☐ All the puppies would have long hair.

   C. ☒ Most of the puppies would have short hair, but some would have long hair.

   D. ☐ Most of the puppies would have long hair, but some would have short hair.

   E. ☐ Not enough information is given.

Name ______________________

Date ____________ Hour ____________

9. In the Cross family, Kim, her father, and Grandmother Cross have blue eyes. Kim's mother and Grandfather Cross have green eyes. Green is the dominant characteristic. Which of the following statements is/are true?
   A. ☒ Kim's mother is hybrid for green eyes.
   B. ☐ Kim's mother could be either hybrid or purebred for green eyes.
   C. ☐ Grandfather Cross is purebred for green eyes.
   D. ☒ Grandfather Cross is hybrid for green eyes.
   E. ☐ Grandfather Cross could be either hybrid or purebred for green eyes.

Grandmother (B) Grandfather (G)

Mother (G) Father (B)

Kim (B)

B = blue eyes

G = green eyes

Problems Dealing with Incomplete Dominance

10. In snapdragons white and red are purebred characteristics, and pink is the hybrid characteristic. If a gardener crossed a red snapdragon (R^rR^r) with a white snapdragon (R^wR^w), what flower colors would be produced? Place an *X* in the box(es) of the flower color(s) that could be produced.
    A. ☐ red
    B. ☐ white
    C. ☒ pink

	R^r	R^r
R^w	R^rR^w	R^rR^w
R^w	R^rR^w	R^rR^w

11. What flower color(s) would be produced if two pink snapdragons were crossed? Place an *X* in the box(es) of the flower color(s) that could be produced.
    A. ☒ red
    B. ☒ white
    C. ☒ pink

	R^r	R^w
R^r	R^rR^r	R^rR^w
R^w	R^rR^w	R^wR^w

12. In shorthorn cattle, red (C^rC^r) and white (C^wC^w) are purebred colors and roan is the hybrid condition. If a white shorthorn bull mated with a roan shorthorn cow, what would the calves look like? Place an *X* in the box(es) of the true statement(s).
    A. ☒ The calves could be white.
    B. ☒ The calves could be roan.
    C. ☐ The calves could be red.

	C^w	C^w
C^r	C^rC^w	C^rC^w
C^w	C^wC^w	C^wC^w

13. A farmer had two prize animals in his stock. One was a shorthorn bull, and the other was a shorthorn cow. Every year he bred these two animals and sold the calf. Among the calves that these two shorthorn animals produced were four roan calves, two red calves, and one white calf. What did the two parents look like? Place an *X* in the box(es) of the true statement(s).
    A. ☐ One was red, and the other was white.
    B. ☐ One was red, and the other was roan.
    C. ☐ One was white, and the other was roan.
    D. ☐ Both were red.
    E. ☐ Both were white.
    F. ☒ Both were roan.

Problems Dealing with Sex-linked Traits

	X^H	X^H
X^h	X^HX^h	X^HX^h
Y	X^HY	X^HY

14. If a hemophiliac male (X^hY) married a normal woman (X^HX^H), what type of children could they have? (Hemophilia is a recessive characteristic.) Place an *X* in the box(es) of the true statement(s).
    A. ☒ They could have a normal son (X^HY).
    B. ☐ They could have a hemophiliac son (X^hY).
    C. ☐ They could have a normal daughter (X^HX^H).
    D. ☒ They could have a daughter who is a carrier (X^HX^h).
    E. ☐ They could have a hemophiliac daughter (X^hX^h).

	X^D	X^d
X^d	X^DX^d	X^dX^d
Y	X^DY	X^dY

15. If a woman who is a carrier for the Duchenne type of muscular dystrophy (X^DX^d) married a man who has the disease (X^dY), what type of children could they have? Place an *X* in the box(es) of the true statement(s).
    A. ☒ They could have a normal son (X^DY).
    B. ☒ They could have a son who has the disease (X^dY).
    C. ☒ They could have a daughter who is a carrier (X^DX^d).
    D. ☐ They could have a daughter who does not have a gene for the disease (X^DX^D).
    E. ☒ They could have a daughter who has the disease (X^dX^d).

Name ______________________

Date ____________ Hour ______________

Class Investigation 7b

Inheritance of Traits

Goals

- Illustrate the relationship between the inheritance of traits and the inheritance of chromosomes.
- Model the expression of dominant, recessive, and incompletely dominant traits.

Materials

coins (penny, nickel, and quarter), bags with parent chromosomes, miniature marshmallows (several colors), pipe cleaner, popped popcorn, potato, puffed wheat, pushpins or thumbtacks (several colors), toothpicks

Many substitutions are possible in this investigation. If different colors of miniature marshmallows are unavailable, then use highlighters to color some. Students may work in pairs.

Procedures and observations

In this investigation you will build an imaginary creature called a spudoodle. The traits of your organism will be determined by the genes on the chromosomes your spudoodle inherits from its parents. The spudoodle chromosome number is 16. Thus, the spudoodle you build will have 8 chromosome pairs. One chromosome in each pair will come from its mother and one from its father.

Assemble these bags before class; you will need two bags for each spudoodle to be assembled. The chromosomes are strips of paper approximately ½-inch wide and variable in length. There should be eight pairs of chromosomes in each bag. A chromosome pair consists of the two which are the same length. On each member of a pair, write a single letter representing a gene (allele) for a particular trait. Each chromosome of a pair should have the same letter, but may differ in case (uppercase/lowercase). A complete set of parent chromosomes should consist of eight pairs of chromosomes with each pair having a unique length and letter. Appendix B may be photocopied and cut into such chromosomes to save time. It may also be helpful to use red and blue paper to designate "mother" and "father" chromosomes.

1. Obtain two bags from your teacher, each containing the chromosomes of a potential spudoodle parent.
2. Remove the chromosomes of one potential parent from one bag and turn the chromosomes upside down so you cannot see the letters on them. Organize the chromosomes by length. Put the two longest ones together, then put the two second-longest ones together, and so on. Sort the chromosomes for the other potential parent in the same manner, but be careful not to mix the chromosomes of the two parents together.
3. Pick one chromosome from each parent's longest pair of chromosomes. Put the two chromosomes you selected in a separate "baby spudoodle" pile. Do the same for the second-longest chromosome pairs, and so on for all the chromosome pairs.
4. Return the remaining parent chromosomes to their bags, and move them out of your way.
5. Arrange the baby spudoodle's chromosomes in pairs by length. The baby spudoodle should have eight pairs of chromosomes. Turn the chromosomes so the letters on them are facing up.
6. The traits coded for by the letters on the baby spudoodle chromosome pairs can be found in the table on the next page. The letter from each chromosome in a pair must be used to form the two-letter code in the table. Record your baby spudoodle's two-letter codes in the table.
7. Assemble your baby spudoodle according to the traits coded for in its chromosomes. To show where the various body parts belong, one spudoodle is drawn on the next page.

Two-letter code	Trait	My spudoodle's code
HH or Hh hh	has hair no hair	
AA Aa aa	large mouth (quarter) medium mouth (nickel) small mouth (penny)	
EE or Ee ee	popcorn ears puffed wheat ears	
BB or Bb bb	blue eyes white eyes	
DD Dd dd	blue dorsal spines pink dorsal spines white dorsal spines	
RR or Rr rr	curly tail straight tail	
GG Gg gg	green legs red legs white legs	
NN or Nn nn	two-nostril nose one-nostril nose	

Dorsal spines = back spines

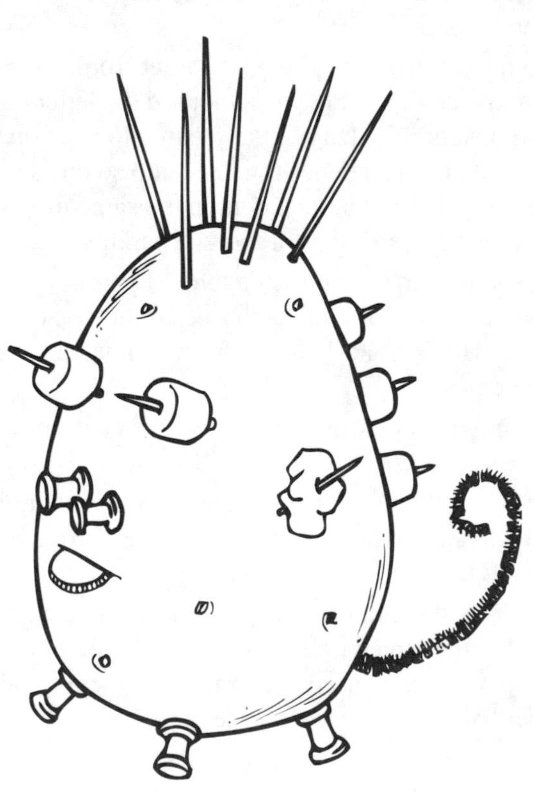

Students should observe the other spudoodles and pay particular attention to how their traits are similar or dissimilar.

8. When you are finished, name your spudoodle and place it in the spudoodle-holding area designated by your teacher.

Name ______________________

Date ____________ Hour ____________

Summing up

1. What is your spudoodle's name? ______________________

2. List the spudoodle body parts whose traits are controlled by simple dominant/recessive genes. *hair, ears, eyes, tail, and nose*

3. List the spudoodle body parts whose traits are controlled by incompletely dominant genes. *mouth, dorsal spines, and legs*

4. Does the inheritance of the longest pair of chromosomes have any effect on spudoodle eye color? Why? *No, eye color traits are inherited with a different chromosome pair.*

This answer assumes that you have not coded eye color on the longest chromosomes.

5. What letters would a baby spudoodle need to inherit from its parents for it to have red legs? *G and g (or Gg)* Does it make any difference which letter came from the mother spudoodle? *no*

6. Is it possible for a spudoodle having blue dorsal spines to have a baby spudoodle with white dorsal spines? Why or why not? *No, if the parent had blue dorsal spines it would have the genes or letters DD for that trait and would thus be unable to pass the gene or letter d on to its offspring. The offspring must get a "d" from each of its parents.*

Compare each spudoodle with its corresponding code provided by the students in the table. The student's decoding should be evaluated and included in the grading of this investigation. This is why the name of the spudoodle is asked for in question #1.

Name ______________________

Date ____________ Hour ______________

Personal Investigation 7c

Constructing Family Pedigrees

Have you ever wondered if a baby soon to be born into a family will have blue eyes, red hair, or a long nose like that of other family members? In order to predict the inheritance of any genetic trait, scientists construct pedigrees. Pedigrees are diagrams that show the presence or absence of a particular trait in several generations of a family. On page 113 of your text is a pedigree of a trait in a family. A pedigree for dimples is shown below.

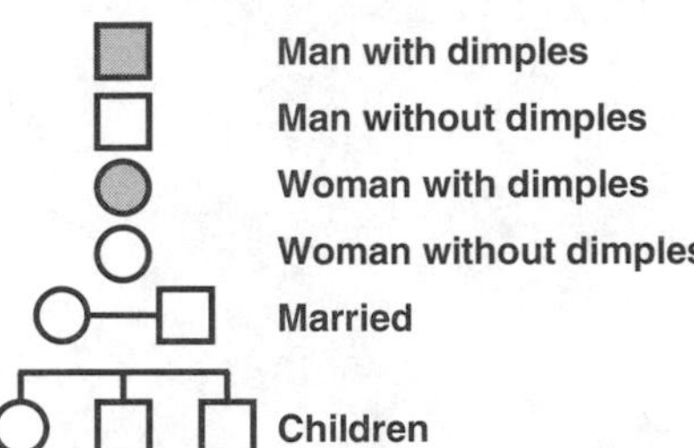

Have the students determine the genes for each member in this pedigree.

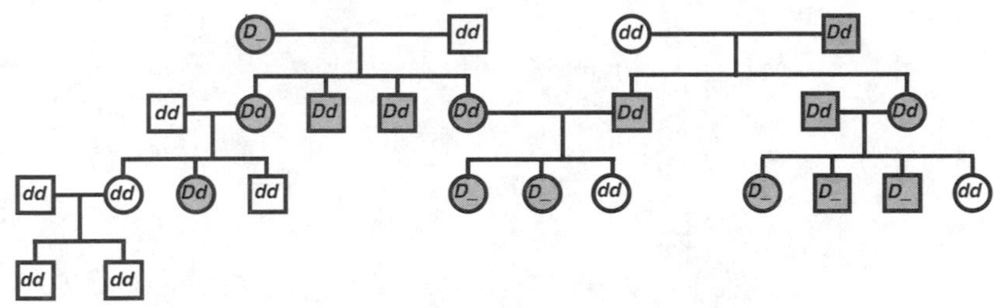

As an alternative or in addition to this investigation you could have students construct the "taste pedigree" of their family. Human genetics taste paper sets can be purchased for about $5. These include papers impregnated with substances that only some people can taste. The tasting abilities are inherited.

Choose a family that has many of its members in your area. Then choose one of the simple inherited characteristics listed on page 105 of your text. Construct a pedigree for this trait in that family. (Use the pedigree above as an example.) To gather your information you will need to visit or interview various members of the family to determine whether they have the characteristic. Ask certain members of the family for information about the characteristic in the family members who are not available for an interview. Photographs of grandparents and great-grandparents will occasionally be helpful. In your pedigree, include as many members of the family as possible.

After you have gathered the information, try to construct Punnett squares of the crosses illustrated in your pedigree. By determining which genes the current generation of people have, you should be able to predict what the future generations of people will look like.

Scientists use pedigrees to learn about other inherited characteristics. The inheritance of various disorders, such as sickle cell anemia, red-green colorblindness, hemophilia, the Duchenne type of muscular dystrophy, cystic fibrosis, or Tay-Sachs disease, can affect a person's life far more than his hair color or nose length can. (See pages 94-95, 112, and 118-20 of your text for discussion of these diseases.)

Name ____________________
Date __________ Hour __________

8–Genetic Changes

Ideas 8a

Mutations

Directions: Complete the words missing in the following statements by filling in the necessary letters. The circled letters form a brief definition of mutation.

1. A mutation that changes the sequence of bases in DNA is called a (G) E N E mutation.
2. A G (E) R M mutation can influence offspring.
3. Mutations usually occur R A (N) D O M L Y.
4. When God C U R S (E) D the ground (Gen. 3:17), a major change occurred in living things.
5. A mutation that results in the death of the organism is a L E (T) H A L mutation.
6. A seedless watermelon that has three sets of chromosomes is a type of P L O (I) D Y mutation.
7. A N (C) O N is a breed of short-legged sheep.
8. A S O M A T I (C) mutation will not affect the offspring.
9. A C (H) R O M O S O M A L mutation may involve entire chromosomes.
10. A M U T (A) T I O N is a change in genetic material.
11. Some mutations have so little effect that they are U (N) N O T I C E A B L E.
12. A mutation in the P I (G) M E N T - P R O D U C I N G gene causes albinism.
13. Down's S Y N D R O M (E) usually involves the human twenty-first chromosome.

A brief definition of mutation is G E N E T I C C H A N G E.

G	E	N	E	T	I	C	C	H	A	N	G	E
1	2	3	4	5	6	7	8	9	10	11	12	13

Ideas 8b

Man's Use of Genetics

Directions: Below are examples of the use of genetic information. Choose the proper term from the list below to describe what is being done in the examples. You may use each term more than once.

a. cloning
b. crossbreeding
c. genetic engineering
d. selection

*b*______ 1. A farmer decides to mate his neighbor's exceptionally large Angus bull with his own Hereford cow that gives the most milk.

*a*______ 2. After years of breeding roses, a man finally grows a beautiful, strong, fragrant rose that resists certain diseases and insects. The man then grafts stems of this rose onto roots of other rose plants to produce many rose plants that are genetically alike.

*b*______ 3. A grape vine that cannot withstand cold winter temperatures but can produce sweet grapes is used to pollinate flowers of a grapevine that can withstand severe winter temperatures but cannot produce sweet grapes.

*d*______ 4. A golden retriever (hunting dog) that has won several prizes is mated with a golden retriever that has also won in many dog shows.

*a*______ 5. A beautiful black tulip was found growing in a man's yard. A company purchased the bulb of this tulip and carefully grew the bulb so that it would produce many smaller bulbs, each of which grow into black tulip plants.

*c*______ 6. Using a virus, scientists add a lethal gene to a protozoan's genes.

*a*______ 7. You cut a potato into several sections, each of which contains an eye (bud), and plant the sections.

*b*______ 8. In an attempt to produce a peach without fuzz, a scientist pollinates a peach flower with pollen from a plum.

*c*______ 9. A gene that produces a human hormone is isolated and put into a bacterium cell. The bacterium then grows and uses the gene to produce the hormone. Later the hormone can be purified and used to treat people who need the hormone.

*d*______10. You save seeds from your largest pumpkin to plant next year.

Name ______________________

Date __________ Hour __________

Ideas 8c

Review

Part 1

Directions: In the spaces provided tell the difference between the terms given.

Answers will vary.

1. gene mutation / chromosomal mutation ***In a gene mutation the sequence of nucleotides is changed and new proteins are produced. Chromosomal mutations involve the number of chromosomes or the number or location of genes on a chromosome.***

2. somatic mutation / germ mutation ***Somatic mutations are in body cells and are not inherited by offspring. Germ mutations occur in gamete-producing cells; thus they may not affect the organism that has them, but they may affect the offspring.***

3. ploidy mutation / diploid ***A ploidy mutation is a change in the number of chromosomes. Diploid describes the normal number of chromosomes in an organism.***

4. selection / genetic engineering ***Selection involves choosing desirable traits in organisms and reproducing organisms with those traits. Genetic engineering involves manipulating an organism's genes to obtain desirable traits in offspring.***

5. inbreeding / crossbreeding ***Inbreeding is breeding an organism with a close relative or with itself. Crossbreeding is breeding different varieties of organisms.***

6. genetic engineering / Human Genome Project ***Genetic engineering is the use of special techniques, such as transferring individual genes, to control the genetic makeup of an organism. The Human Genome Project is a scientific effort to map (find and identify) all the genes on human chromosomes.***

Part 2

Answers will vary.

Directions: Record your responses in the spaces provided.

1. At what two times did God directly alter His physical creation? ***God altered His creation when He cursed the earth (Gen. 3) and when He sent the Flood (Gen. 7-9).***

2. There are several ways in which a cell in an organism can have a gene mutation that will not significantly affect the organism. List three ways and explain why they would be insignificant. ***(1) A gene mutation occurring in a gene that a cell does not use will probably not affect the organism. (2) A single mutation in a large multicellular organism will affect only a small number of cells and will probably result in a minor deformity. (3) A lethal gene mutation in a large multicellular organism will kill only the cell with the mutation and will probably be unnoticed.***

3. Discuss the following statement: "Harmful mutations are sometimes helpful." Give one example from the chapter. ***A mutation that may hinder an organism's ability to survive in the wild may produce a characteristic that man finds desirable. Ancon sheep, silver minks, and seedless bananas are examples of organisms whose mutations have produced desirable characteristics.***

4. What is the difference between identical and fraternal twins? ***Identical twins have the same genetic makeup since they come from a single zygote. Fraternal twins are not genetically identical since they develop from separate zygotes that are in the womb at the same time.***

Name ______________________
Date __________ Hour __________

Class Investigation 8a

Observing Radiation Effects on Seedlings

The seeds used in this investigation require 3-10 days to germinate. Consider starting the investigation during your coverage of Chapter 7.

Goals

- Observe examples of radiation-induced mutations.
- Compare the rate of mutation with the amount of radiation.

Materials

flowerpots, irradiated seeds, potting soil, warm and well-lighted area

Home School Tip

You may find a dentist or x-ray technician who is willing to x-ray some seeds for you. However, it is usually a great inconvenience for them to do this. Irradiated seed sets are well worth their cost (approximately $13).

Procedures and observations

Irradiated seeds are usually sold in kits that contain an unirradiated control group and four treatment groups that have been exposed to different amounts of radiation. Sow each group of seeds in a different flowerpot. Record the number of seeds sown in each group. Label each pot with the type of seed and amount of irradiation. Place the pots in the same or identical warm, well-lighted area(s). After one week observe the pots and the plants.

These kits are available from Carolina Biological Supply Company and can also be used in Class Investigation 14b.

Plant name ______________________

Treatment	Number of seeds planted	Number of live seedlings after one week	Average seedling height	Number of unusual seedlings
control				

Describe any unusual seedlings. *Descriptions will vary.*

Your teacher may want you to transplant the plants and grow them to maturity at home.

Summing up

1. Did exposure to radiation increase or decrease how tall the seedlings grew? *Radiation usually results in decreased seedling height.*

2. Did exposure to radiation increase, decrease, or have no effect on the number of unusual seedlings? *increase or possibly no effect (other than height or less germination)*

3. Did more or fewer seeds germinate with increased radiation? *fewer*

4. Why was it important to include an unirradiated seedling group in your observations? *They were the control group. Radiation effects on the treated seed is determined by comparison with this group.*

5. Why was it necessary to place all the flowerpots in the same conditions (temperature and light)? *to be certain that observed differences in the plants were not due to differences in growth conditions such as temperature and lighting*

6. How do you think radiation caused the differences that you have observed? *probably by causing mutations in the seed's genes*

7. Your answer to question 6 may not be the only correct explanation. What might be another possible explanation? *The radiation could have caused these effects without causing mutations.*

Go a step further

Explain an experiment that you could do to determine which of the two explanations (6 and 7) is the correct one. *Answers will vary but should suggest that observations of subsequent offspring generations of the irradiated seeds would help differentiate between true mutations and other effects. The mutations could persist in subsequent generations.*

Name ______________________________
Date ____________ Hour ______________

Personal Investigation 8b

Chromosomal Mutations

Goals

- Identify examples of chromosomal mutations.
- Make a karyotype.

Materials

ruler, scissors, tape or glue

Procedures and observations

The three drawings below show how chromosomes appear through a microscope after they have been prepared for counting in a genetics laboratory. One drawing is the chromosomes of a normal watermelon cell. One drawing is the chromosomes of a watermelon cell that had a chromosomal mutation resulting in one extra chromosome. One drawing is of a watermelon cell with a triploid mutation. Label each drawing as either "normal diploid," "extra chromosome," or "triploid."

1. *extra chromosome*

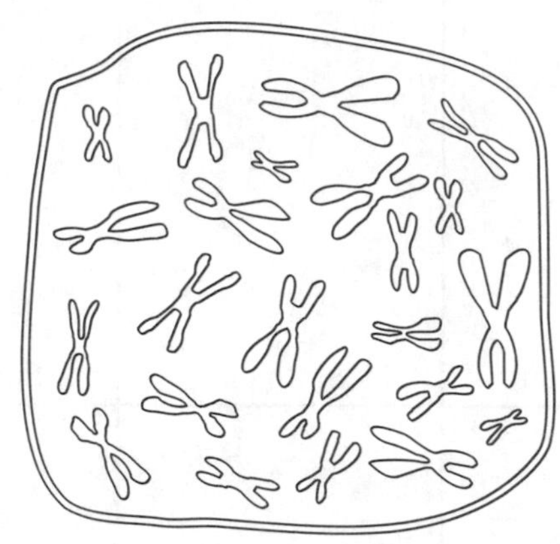

2. *triploid*

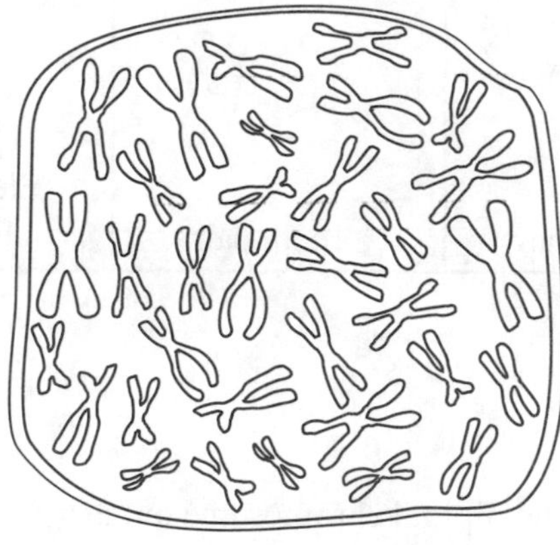

3. *normal diploid*

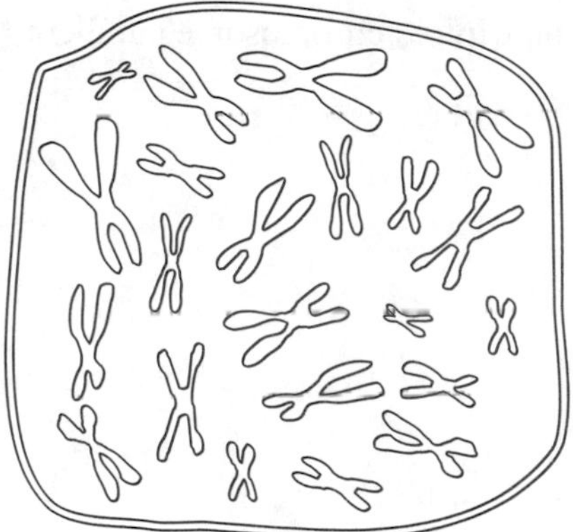

The drawing on page 107 shows how the chromosomes of a diploid watermelon appear through a microscope after they have been prepared for counting in a genetics laboratory.

Using your scissors, cut out each chromosome and then glue or tape pairs of identical chromosomes side by side in the spaces provided below. Start with the longest chromosomes first, then the second longest, and so on. End with the shortest chromosomes. When finished, you will have constructed a *karyotype* for watermelon.

First pair (longest)	Second pair	Third pair	Fourth pair
Fifth pair	Sixth pair	Seventh pair	Eighth pair
Ninth pair	Tenth pair	Eleventh pair (shortest)	

Summing up

1. What is the diploid chromosome number of watermelon? *twenty-four*

2. What is the triploid chromosome number of watermelon? *thirty-three*

Name ______________________
Date ____________ Hour ______________

Name ______________________
Date __________ Hour __________

9–Biblical Creationism

Ideas 9a

What the Bible Teaches About Creation

Directions: Complete the words missing in the following statements by filling in the necessary letters. The circled letters will spell a word representing something that must be accepted by faith.

1. "In the beginning God (C) R E A T E D" (Gen. 1:1).
2. Man is (R) E S P O N S I B L E to God.
3. God created by D I R (E) C T acts.
4. God specially C R E (A) T E D man.
5. God S U S (T) A I N S His creation.
6. "All things were made by H (I) M" (John 1:3).
7. God reveals His P (O) W E R in creation.
8. God created M A (N) in His own image.
9. E V O L U T (I) O N contradicts God's Word.
10. God has revealed the (S) E Q U E N C E of creation.
11. The F I R (M) A M E N T shows God's handiwork (Ps. 19:1).

C	R	E	A	T	I	O	N	I	S	M
1	2	3	4	5	6	7	8	9	10	11

Ideas 9b

Creationist Views

Directions: Write the proper terms next to the following definitions or descriptions. Then find and circle the terms in the word puzzle below the definitions. The terms may appear horizontally, vertically, or diagonally and may be forward or backward.

antediluvian 1. The period of time before the Genesis Flood

long-day 2. The theory that ties Genesis 1 with "one day is with the Lord as a thousand years, and a thousand years as one day" (II Pet. 3:8).

leviathan 3. The biblical creature whose description in Job includes smoke, coals, and fire

local 4. A flood that happens only in a small area

genealogy 5. A list of a family tree

greenhouse 6. The effect that a thick canopy of water would have on the earth

old-earth 7. The theory that the earth is millions or even billions of years old

universal 8. A flood that covers the entire earth

Apatosaurus 9. A huge dinosaur that probably ate plant matter

canopy 10. A layer of water above the earth

gap 11. The theory that there was a creation that was destroyed when Satan fell

behemoth 12. A large animal called "the chief of the ways of God" in the book of Job (Job 40:19)

begat 13. A word often used in biblical genealogies to describe the relationship of parent to child

short-day 14. The theory that the days described in Genesis 1 are each twenty-four hours long

Stegosaurus 15. A 10-ton dinosaur that had a 2.5-ounce brain

fossil 16. The preserved remains of an organism

young-earth 17. The theory that the earth is only a few thousand years old

sedimentation 18. The process in which material settles out as a moving substance slows down

Name ______________________

Date ____________ Hour ____________

nongap ______ 19. The theory that states there was no first creation that was destroyed at the time of Satan's fall

cubit ______ 20. Unit of length used in the Bible in the description of Noah's ark

P	S	U	R	U	A	S	O	G	E	T	S	A	N
O	S	U	R	U	A	S	O	T	A	P	A	B	O
A	N	T	E	D	I	L	U	V	I	A	N	D	I
T	H	A	R	T	A	Y	N	E	B	E	G	A	T
Y	P	O	N	A	C	A	I	C	A	N	T	Y	A
O	D	L	O	N	D	D	V	G	U	T	S	A	T
C	E	T	A	B	A	G	E	S	A	B	T	G	N
D	R	V	D	C	Y	N	R	E	H	T	I	E	E
L	E	E	R	E	O	O	S	Y	S	L	G	T	M
N	M	E	Y	G	O	L	A	E	N	E	G	R	I
D	A	S	M	L	I	D	L	H	P	V	A	O	D
B	F	L	O	O	T	D	R	A	E	I	S	I	E
A	E	P	B	R	I	N	T	O	A	A	Y	R	S
U	F	H	O	P	E	P	L	A	R	T	A	G	P
R	O	H	E	O	E	D	E	M	G	H	U	A	E
A	S	T	A	M	E	L	O	E	N	A	G	E	R
D	S	E	R	A	O	R	G	E	V	N	P	N	L
E	I	O	R	B	E	T	T	E	O	S	A	U	R
M	L	T	E	S	U	O	H	N	E	E	R	G	O
S	H	T	R	A	E	G	N	U	O	Y	N	O	D

Ideas 9c

In Defense of Creation

Consider assigning one question to each student and then discussing the answers in class.

Directions: Record your responses in the spaces provided.

1. List at least five creationist theories and briefly explain each one. *(1) long-day theory: Each day of creation represents a long period of time. (2) short-day theory: Each day of creation was twenty-four hours long. (3) gap theory: A "first creation" (Gen. 1:1) was destroyed at Satan's fall, and the earth was re-created (Gen. 1:2-31). (4) canopy theory: A layer of water vapor above the earth fell at the time of the Flood. (5) nongap theory: There was only one creation; there was no gap between Genesis 1:1 and 1:2.*

2. List at least two reasons to believe that the earth is not millions or billions of years old. *(1) The genealogies and ages recorded in the Bible indicate that the earth's age is only six thousand years. (2) Dates of events recorded in sources other than the Bible indicate that the earth is not millions of years old.*

3. List at least five reasons to believe that the Genesis Flood was a universal flood. *(1) The Bible says that the Flood covered the whole earth. (2) The purpose of the Flood was to destroy mankind. (Man could escape a local flood.) (3) The ark would not have been necessary for a local flood. (4) God's promise not to send another similar flood would be broken by the occurrence of local floods. (5) Random arrangement of fossils supports the idea of a universal flood. (6) The water covered the highest mountain. This would have been possible only if the entire earth had been flooded.*

Name ______________________

Date ____________ Hour ____________

Ideas 9d

Review

Directions: In each of the following statements draw a circle around the correct choice in the parentheses. On the lines below each statement, tell why the incorrect choice is not acceptable.

Students should easily choose the correct answers, but they may have difficulty giving reasons for their choices. Emphasize that reasons are important and that the students should not give up because the exercise seems difficult.

If you feel that your students will have extreme difficulty giving explanations, you may omit that part of the assignment.

1. Biblical creationism and evolution are both accepted by (faith / scientific evidence.) ***There is no scientific evidence to prove either creationism or evolution.***

2. God (did / did not) reveal enough about creation to contradict evolutionary theory. ***The Bible clearly contradicts evolution, and scientific observations of the physical and natural world do not support evolution.***

3. God created (but does not sustain / and sustains) what He created. ***The Bible says that God designed, created, and sustains His creation (Ps. 104).***

4. God (created / did not create) plants, animals, and man in the same way. ***Man was not spoken into existence; he was specially formed.***

5. The creation has (degenerated / stayed the same) since God created it. ***God created the world in a perfect form, but He later cursed the ground because of man's sin (Gen. 1:31; 3:6-19).***

6. The canopy theory deals with the conditions on the earth before the (Flood / gap). ***The canopy theory deals with the conditions on the earth before the Flood; not the conditions in a "first creation."***

7. The fact that many fossils are found in mixed heaps supports (the evolutionary theories of fossil formation / the Flood theory of fossil formation). ***Many believe that the Flood was the only catastrophe that could have deposited the organisms that formed sedimentary fossils in the arrangements found today.***

8. Using genealogies, men can determine the age of the earth to be about (six thousand / six million / six billion) years old. ***Genealogical records in the Scriptures account for approximately four thousand years before Christ's birth. Four thousand years plus two thousand years (the time since Christ's birth) equals six thousand years.***

Name ______________________

Date ____________ Hour ______________

Personal Investigation 9a

The Animals in Noah's Ark

Materials

encyclopedia or other reference book, ruler

Procedures and observations

Genesis 6:15 states that Noah's ark was 300 cubits long, 50 cubits wide, and 30 cubits high. A cubit is the distance between the end of the longest finger and the elbow. Although some Bible scholars disagree as to the exact size of a cubit used by Noah, most agree that a cubit of about 0.46 m (18 in.) long is probably accurate.

Using a 0.46 meter cubit, Noah would have made the ark about 138 m (450 ft.) long by 23 m (75 ft.) wide, and 14 m (45 ft.) high. According to Genesis 6:16 the ark had three internal decks. If the ark were a boxlike structure, it would have had over 9,500 sq. m (100,000 sq. ft.) of deck space. In other words, the deck space of the ark was about the size of twenty basketball courts.

It is difficult for most people to visualize the size of such a structure. To help visualize the size of the ark, draw a cross section of the ark to scale. Consider using a scale in which 1 cubit equals about 3 mm (0.13 in.). Your ark would then be 90 cm (37.5 in.) long, 15 cm (6.3 in.) wide, and 9 cm (3.8 in.) high.

If a man were 1.8 m (6 ft.) tall, he would be 4 cubits tall. Based on the scale you used to draw the ark, he would be 1.2 cm (0.5 in.) tall. Draw a figure of a man 1.2 cm tall, cut it out, and place it on the ark drawing.

Look up the average sizes of various land animals that were probably taken on the ark. Make drawings of these animals using the same scale that you used to draw Noah's ark. Cut out these animals and place them on your drawing of the ark.

Remember that the drawing you have made of Noah's ark is only two-dimensional. The ark was actually 23 m (75 ft.) wide. Thus the ark could have had many more animals in it than you can put on your diagram. Bring your diagrams to class and discuss them.

Rather than assigning this investigation as individual projects, you can profitably do this as a class exercise. Use a bulletin board for the ark drawing. If possible, you can use a whole wall and a roll of paper to draw your ark. A scale of 2.5 cm (1 in.) per cubit is possible if your room is large enough.

Consider also drawing a football field (300 ft. x 160 ft., not including the end zones) for comparison.

Have the students suggest a list of animals; then assign different students to look up the sizes of the various animals and make drawings of them. Small animals, such as rabbits, mice, snakes, and insects, will be almost impossible to draw to scale if the scale you use is not very large. Remind students that small animals like these were possibly put in cages or other containers and thus would have required very little deck space.

Occasionally a student will become very interested in the topic of dinosaurs while they are being discussed in class. This investigation would be a good extra-credit project for him.

Some books dealing with dinosaurs are: (1) The Answer s Book *(second edition): Ham et al., 1991; (2)* Dinosaurs: Those Terrible Lizards: *Gish, 1977; (3)* Dinosaurs by Design: *Gish, 1992.*

Depending on your students' backgrounds, strengths, and maturity, you might consider using a secular dinosaur reference book as well. Be very careful to separate evolutionary bias from observations.

Consider dividing the class into groups and having each group research a different dinosaur. If you do this, form small groups of only two or three students. You may want to have each group report orally about its dinosaur. If reports are given orally, you can have other students in the class evaluate the acceptability (from a nonevolutionary viewpoint) of the material presented.

Make sure that students understand that one of the major purposes of this exercise is to evaluate the material they read. You may want them to review the material in Chapter 1 regarding true statements.

Home School Tip
An individual student should research 3-4 dinosaurs.

Research Investigation 9b

Dinosaurs

Materials

encyclopedia or other reference book

Procedures and observations

The term *dinosaur* was first used by Sir Richard Owen in 1842. At this time men were discovering large animal bones for the first time. The word *dinosaur* means fearful or monstrous lizard. Most dinosaurs were not monstrous or fearful. Some scientists believe that the average size of the reptiles called dinosaurs was probably about the size of a chicken.

Much has been written about dinosaurs. Some of the material that has been written is probably true. By carefully observing an animal's bones, scientists can tell about its size, its method of moving, the type of food it ate, and a few other things. By observing a skeleton, however, scientists cannot easily tell when the animal lived, where it lived, or what other kinds of organisms lived around it. Often, however, evolutionists will guess at this kind of information.

Read about dinosaurs in an encyclopedia and choose several different dinosaurs. Find encyclopedias and other books that discuss dinosaurs and read about the ones you chose. Try to determine the difference between information that scientists gather through observation and that which is probably someone's guess. Write a brief report about the dinosaurs you chose. Include in your report the material that you believe to be true. Exclude any material that is evolutionary. If possible, include drawings of the dinosaurs you discuss in your report.

Name ____________________
Date __________ Hour __________

10–Biological Evolution

Ideas 10a

Defining Concepts of Evolution

Directions: In the spaces provided tell the difference between the terms given.

1. evolution / theory of evolution ***Answers will vary. Evolution is a change that makes something more complex. The theory of evolution is the belief that the physical world was not created but that it evolved into its present form.***

2. theory of evolution / biological evolution ***Biological evolution is a part of the theory of evolution. Biological evolution is the belief that organisms have evolved from other organisms by gradual changes.***

3. theory of inheritance of acquired characteristics / evolution-mutation theory ***The theory of inheritance of acquired characteristics is the belief that offspring will have the same traits that the parents acquired. The mutation theory is the belief that only mutations produce the necessary changes for biological evolution.***

4. theory of natural selection / mutation-selection theory (Neo-Darwinism) ***The theory of natural selection is the belief that certain organisms will survive because they are superior. The mutation-selection theory is the belief that mutations will provide superior organisms that will then be acted upon by natural selection.***

Ideas 10b

How Biological Evolution Supposedly Took Place

Directions: Four evolutionary theories are listed below. Imaginary examples of evolution are also given. Tell which of the evolutionary theories is being illustrated in the example by writing the letter of the proper theory in the space provided. You may use each theory once or twice.

a. Theory of inheritance of acquired characteristics
b. Mutation theory
c. Theory of natural selection
d. Mutation-selection theory

a ______ 1. A duck is in an accident and receives a hole in its lower bill. Because of this hole, the material the duck scoops up from the bottom of the pond drains more rapidly, and the duck is able to eat more quickly than other ducks of the same species. When its ducklings hatch, they too have holes in their lower bills and thus have an advantage over other ducks.

b ______ 2. An orange tree that normally produces orange oranges grows a branch that produces red oranges. The local newspaper prints a headline: "Evolution Happening in Local Orchard."

c ______ 3. A long drought caused the smaller plants in an area to die. An exobbie, a small leaf-eating animal that normally lives and eats on the ground, started climbing trees to find leaves to eat. Exobbies with longer claws were able to climb trees easily, and they began spending long periods of time on tree branches. When the drought ended, short-clawed exobbies returned to the land and ate small plants, but long-clawed exobbies stayed in the trees and ate tree leaves. There are now two types of exobbies: tree exobbies and land exobbies.

a ______ 4. A fox caught its tail in a trap. After much pain the fox escaped, leaving half of its tail in the trap. The pups of this fox had tails that were shorter than normal.

c ______ 5. A factory began dumping a chemical into a stream. This chemical caused the stream to become murky. Most of the animals and plants in the stream died off. Some animals left the area. An unusual variety of plant began to live in the area. One fish found this new plant to be a suitable diet. The tiny feelers that grew around this fish's mouth helped it to find the plant in the murky water. Those fish with the longer and more sensitive feelers found the most plants and were able to breed, passing on the long, sensitive feelers to their offspring.

Name ______________________________

Date ____________ Hour ______________

b ________ 6. One of the problems with Dochie pigeons is that they have small wings and cannot fly very far without tiring. They appear to be very intelligent and can be trained to do many useful things. These pigeons can carry messages from one place to another even though they must cover miles of unfamiliar territory where other pigeons would get lost. But Dochies are much slower than other pigeons because they must stop and rest. One purebred Dochie pair, however, produces a bird that looks and behaves like a Dochie but has large wings. The owner hopes to begin a breeding program to produce more large-winged Dochies.

d ________ 7. The red-bottomed sea turtle has short flippers. Because of its lack of speed, it is often caught by predators. Once a red-bottomed sea turtle with long flippers hatched. It swam better and was able to escape its predators. When it mated, some of its offspring also had long flippers. The red-bottomed sea turtles with long flippers were able to swim quickly enough to escape predators, while the short-flippered sea turtles were caught and eaten. As the short-flippered red-bottomed sea turtles died off, the long-flippered red-bottomed sea turtles began to thrive.

A Record of Evolution

Directions: Use the clues below to choose the right word to fit in the blanks. Most of the words deal with evolution. The letters in the shaded rectangle will spell out one of the supposed proofs of evolution. Answer the question at the bottom of the clues once you have determined what the supposed proof is.

1. R E C A **P** I T U L A T I O N
2. **H** E R R I N G
3. L A **Y** E R S
4. M I S S I N G **L** I N K
5. F L **O** O D
6. **G** I L L S L I T S
7. R **E** L A T E D
8. S A T A **N**
9. **E** M B R Y O S
10. M A S **T** O D O N
11. F O S S **I** L
12. C O M M O N A N **C** E S T O R
13. **T** R I L O B I T E S
14. **R** E P T I L E S
15. Z Y G O T **E**
16. A R C H A **E** O P T E R Y X
17. C L A S **S** I F I C A T I O N

1. The theory that the embryos of many different organisms look very similar at some time in their development
2. Four square miles of rock layers in California contain only this type of fish fossil.
3. Fossils are found in rock __________.
4. An organism that evolutionists believe existed but for which they have found no physical evidence
5. Many Christians believe in the __________ theory of fossil formation.
6. People who believe the theory of recapitulation often believe that when humans are embryos, they have ________ ________.
7. Christians should avoid saying that two different groups of organisms are __________.
8. The one who wants men to believe in the theory of evolution
9. The theory of recapitulation deals with the study of __________.
10. A large elephant with thick hair
11. The preserved remains of an organism
12. An organism that supposedly gave rise to two different kinds of organisms
13. Extinct organisms that would probably be classified as arthropods
14. Most evolutionists believe that birds evolved from __________.
15. Cell resulting from the union of a sperm and an ovum
16. An extinct organism that was probably a bird
17. The grouping of organisms

If someone spoke to you using the supposed proof of evolution that appears in the rectangle above, what would you tell him? *The arrangement of organisms on a tree (classification) does not support or prove anything. People can construct many different phylogenetic trees using the same organisms.*

Name ____________________
Date __________ Hour ______________

Ideas 10d

Review

Directions: Complete the crossword puzzle on the back of this page.

Across

5. The ______ tribesmen consider long necks to be a sign of feminine beauty.
7. A ______ mutation usually causes a reshuffling or doubling of genes already in existence.
9. ______ mutations occur in cells that form gametes.
10. The Creator of the world
13. A division of time on the earth; part of an era
14. One of the sense organs
16. The ______ Islands are found off the coast of Ecuador.
20. Small
21. Evolution by mutation is a theory of ______.
22. According to evolutionists, reliving the past before being born is ______.
25. Evolution is ______ true.
28. Trait resulting from an organism's environment (two words)
30. Darwin proposed the theory of ______ (two words).
34. A large elephant with thick hair
37. An idea that appears to be supported by observations
39. The number of people who are righteous (Rom. 3:10)
40. A group of organisms that are now extinct
41. The missing organisms that would fit between existing organisms on a phylogenetic tree

Down

1. ______ trees attempt to show the path of biological evolution.
2. The ______ record is a record of past living things.
3. A universal ______ probably produced the random order of fossils.
4. Allowing only those with the best traits to survive is ______.
5. Evening
6. Paleontologists often ______ to find fossils.
8. Psalm 104:16 says that the trees of the land are filled with ______.
11. ______ studied to become a preacher but instead became an evolutionist.
12. Human embryos were said to have ______s (two words) resembling those of fish.
15. Having no specific pattern
17. Student
18. A physician who performs operations in the mouth is an ______ surgeon.
19. The process in which something improves or becomes more complex
20. Changes in the peppered ______ population illustrate natural selection.
23. Lamarck ______ the giraffe's long neck to support his theory.
24. The spinning of the earth
25. On the *Beagle* Darwin was a ______.
26. A genetic change in an organism
27. Beth hopes that Matthew will ask her to go on a ______ sometime soon.
28. Evolutionists believe that different groups of organisms have descended from common ______.
29. The kind of bird that catches the worm
31. ______ started the belief that offspring will possess the acquired characteristics of their parents.
32. Opposite of west
33. Divisions of a period
35. A French word for Christmas
36. In Genesis 1:29, God told Adam and Eve that they could eat fruit and ______.
38. Shout

	1 P		2 F							3 F			4 S		5 P	A	6 D	A	U	N	G
7 C	H	R	O	M	O	8 S	O	M	A	L		9 G	E	R	M		I				
	Y		S			A				O			L				10 G	O	11 D		12 G
	L		S			13 P	E	R	I	O	D		14 E	A	15 R				A		I
	O		I							D			C		A				R		L
	16 G	A	L	A	17 P	A	G	18 O	S				T		N		19 E		W		L
	E				U			R		20 M	I	N	I		21 D	E	V	R	I	E	S
	N				P			A		O			O		O		O		N		L
22 R	E	C	A	P	I	T	23 U	L	A	T	I	O	N		M		L				I
	T				L		S			H				24 R			U		25 N	O	T
	I		26 M				E					27 D		O			T		A		
28 A	C	Q	U	I	R	29 E	D	C	H	A	R	A	C	T	E	R	I	S	T	I	C
N			T			A						T		A			O		U		
C		30 N	A	T	U	R	A	31 L	S	32 E	L	E	C	T	I	O	N		R		33 E
E			T			L		A		A				I					A		P
S			I			Y		34 M	A	S	T	O	D	O	35 N		36 H		L		O
37 T	H	E	O	R	38 Y			A		T				39 N	O	N	E		I		C
O			N		E			R							E		R		S		H
R					L			C				40 T	R	I	L	O	B	I	T	E	S
S					41 L	I	N	K	S								S				

Name ______________________

Date ____________ Hour ____________

Class Investigation 10a

Making a New Gene

This investigation is best done with the whole class cooperating as a single group.

Goals

- Model the improbability that gene mutations might produce a new gene.
- Illustrate the harmful nature of mutations.

If you did not cover Section 6B in the textbook, you should briefly explain the relationship between DNA, genes, codons, and nucleotides.

Materials

number spinner, paper

Setting up

Make a number spinner from the plastic lid of a coffee can or margarine container, a split-tack fastener or cotter pin, and a pointer cut from another plastic lid. The spinner should have twelve numbered sectors (see diagram). Letter twenty-six small pieces of paper each with a different letter of the alphabet. Keep these in a container from which you will randomly select letters.

Number spinners made from plastic spin much more freely and are more durable than those made from paper.

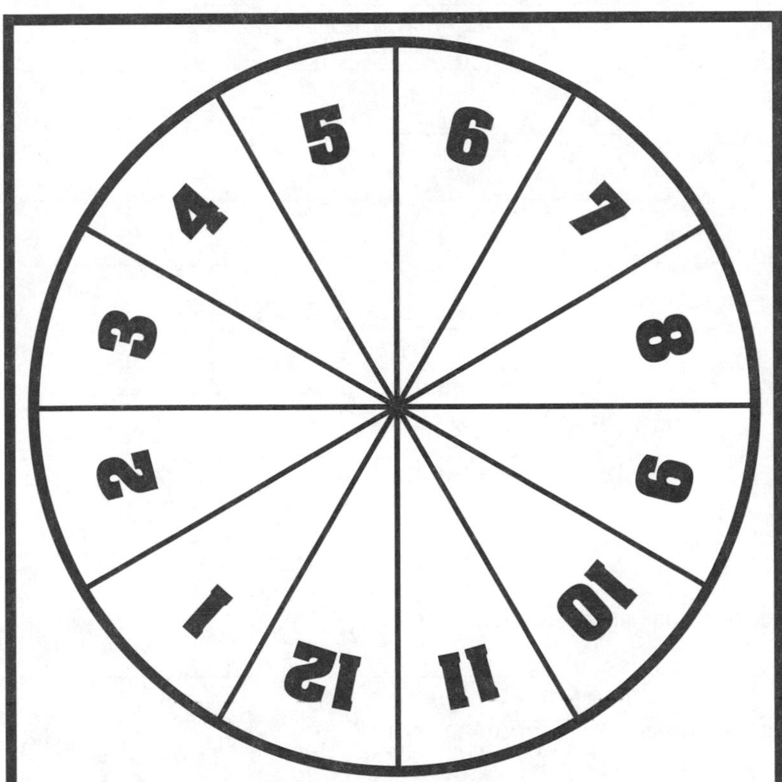

One limitation of this model is that the four nucleotides found in DNA are represented by twenty-six letters in the model. This means that there are many more alphabetic codons possible in the model than the sixty-four possible with four nucleotides. You could limit the substitution to vowels for vowels. Also, different codons sometimes code for the same amino acid. Even so, the model is valid for illustrating that the mutation of one gene into a completely different, beneficial gene is highly unlikely. Also, these limits on making a correct sentence are balanced by using a short, four-codon-long sentence. (Genes are hundreds of codons long.)

Procedures and observations

A way to demonstrate new genes produced by mutations is to compare a gene to a sentence. The sentence used in this investigation consists only of three-letter words which represent codons. The letters in the words represent nucleotides. (Recall from Chapter 6 of your text that genes are made of nucleotides that are read in groups of three called codons.)

1. Use your number spinner to randomly select which letter position (numbered 1-12) to mutate. Record this number in the "position to change" column.
2. Randomly pick a lettered piece of paper from your supply of letters. Record this letter in the "new letter" column. Return the lettered paper to the container.
3. Rewrite the sentence in the space provided, substituting the letter selected from the container for the letter you selected with the number spinner.

There are some initial substitutions that will work to make correct sentences. The likelihood of these random substitutions is 1 or 2 per every hundred students.

4. Repeat steps 1-3 beginning with the newly formed sentence from the previous turn until all the spaces for new sentences have been filled.

Position to change	New letter	1	2	3	4	5	6	7	8	9	10	11	12
		H	I	S	M	O	P	W	A	S	W	E	T

Summing up

1. Did some letter positions never mutate? *Answers will vary, but usually some do not mutate.*

2. Did some letter positions mutate more than once? *yes*

3. How many mutations (letter substitutions) did it take for you to make a new, grammatically correct sentence? *Answers will vary. For most it will never happen randomly.*

4. If the sentence used in this investigation were twice as long, would it be more likely or less likely that a new, correct sentence could be produced by this type of mutation? *less likely*

5. Genes consist of thousands of nucleotides (letters). How do you think this would affect the likelihood of a mutation's making a new, beneficial gene? *It would be very unlikely, even impossible.*

Name ______________________________
Date ____________ Hour ______________

Research Investigation 10b

Darwin's Finches

Materials

encyclopedia or other reference book

Procedures and observations

Finches are small seed-eating songbirds in the family Ploceidae. In this group are the goldfinch, bunting, grosbeak, cardinal, towhee, canary, and many others. In fact, approximately one out of every seven birds is a member of the Ploceidae family.

Some of the most famous finches are those living on the Galápagos Islands. Charles Darwin studied the Galápagos finches during his travels on the HMS *Beagle.* Although close together, many of these islands have vastly different environments. On the various islands, Darwin observed different kinds of finches. Darwin believed that these different finches illustrated his theory of natural selection.

In various biology books and in other library resources, look up the Galápagos finches. How do these birds differ from one another and from other finches? According to Darwin, how did the Galápagos finches develop into the different varieties that he found? Explain why this is an evolutionary belief. What explanation would you offer to explain why the Galápagos finches have the various characteristics that they have? Write a report telling of your findings and your answers to these questions.

You may want to preview sources and recommend certain books for the students who work on this exercise. You can find discussions of these birds in many sources, but you may need to give your students some direction in finding them.

Some students will have difficulty sorting out the evolutionary information and applying the anti-evolutionary ideas they have read in their text and heard in class. The primary purpose of this assignment is to show the students the problems and to give them guidance in such applications.

Rather than having your students write a report, you may want to have them do the research and then discuss these finches and their evolutionary significance orally.

This could be a good extra-credit assignment for an eager, good student. If his paper is good, have him read it to the class; then you can comment on it.

This investigation is a good class activity. When the students bring in photocopies of phylogenetic trees, post the photocopies on a bulletin board. Have all the students compile the list of differences. You can mark the differences they find on the photocopies. You may want to find the phylogenetic trees yourself, photocopy them, and post them for the students to view. You may also find different phylogenetic trees and then make your own drawings of them. Duplicate your drawings and have the students find the differences.

Research Investigation 10c

Phylogenetic Trees

Materials

encyclopedia or other reference books

Procedures and observations

Scientists who support evolution do not agree on the way in which biological evolution took place. Since these scientists use phylogenetic trees to illustrate the path of evolution, there are almost as many different phylogenetic trees as there are opinions of how evolution took place.

In various books, read about evolution and find different phylogenetic trees. You should look for phylogenetic trees that cover all of the evolution of life (from "amoeba to man") and not just a section of evolution (such as the evolution of fishes or plants). Make photocopies of these different phylogenetic trees and study them carefully. Look for significant differences in evolutionary paths and in common ancestors on these phylogenetic trees. (Differences in the methods of drawing the phylogenetic trees are not significant.) Mark the significant differences on the photocopies and compile a list of these differences.

Name ____________________

Date __________ Hour __________

11–Little-seen Kingdoms

Ideas 11a

Kingdom Monera

Directions: In the space provided, write a sentence that indicates the relation between each pair of words or phrases below.

1. bacteria / cyanobacteria *Bacteria and cyanobacteria are grouped together in Kingdom Monera.*

Answers will vary.

2. nucleus / prokaryote *Prokaryotes do not have a nucleus.*

3. antibiotics / yogurt *Antibiotics and yogurt are two products bacteria help to produce.*

4. rapid growth rate / crowded conditions *Bacteria are capable of rapid growth rates, but problems related to crowded conditions limit their growth.*

5. flagella / movement *Those bacteria capable of movement have flagella.*

Kingdom Protista

Directions: Write clues that relate to Kingdom Protista for each of the crossword answers below.

Answers will vary, but accept only those that correctly relate the word to Protista. "______ is a disease" would be an unacceptable clue for malaria.

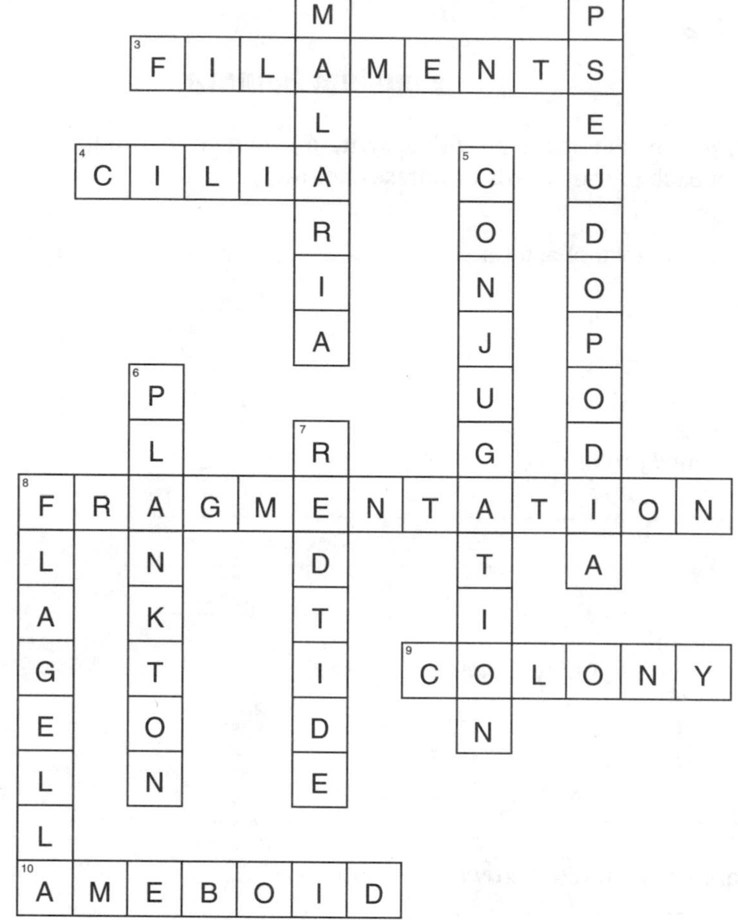

Across

3. *Long, threadlike types of colonies*
4. *Many short, hairlike projections used for movement*
8. *A form of asexual reproduction*
9. *Capable of living alone but usually forms a group*
10. *Type of movement that involves flowing cytoplasm*

Down

1. *A protistan-caused disease*
2. *Bulges of cytoplasm*
5. *A form of sexual reproduction*
6. *Oceanic food*
7. *Makes shellfish toxic*
8. *Long, whiplike propulsion system*

Name ______________________
Date __________ Hour __________

Ideas 11c

Structural Characteristics of Fungi

Directions: Below is a diagram of a mushroom. Around the diagram are various labels or definitions. For each definition write the term in the blank provided; then draw a line from the term to the structure on the diagram.

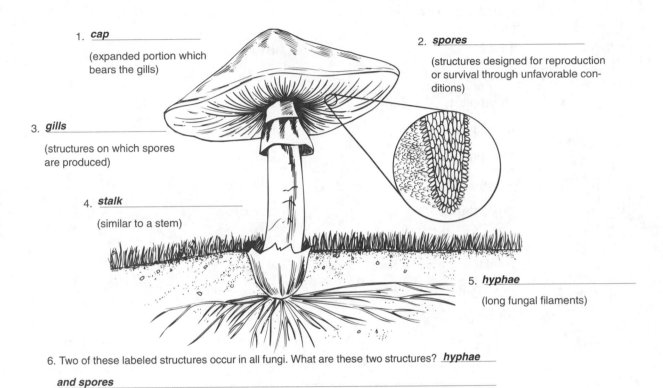

1. *cap* ______
(expanded portion which bears the gills)

2. *spores* ______
(structures designed for reproduction or survival through unfavorable conditions)

3. *gills* ______
(structures on which spores are produced)

4. *stalk* ______
(similar to a stem)

5. *hyphae* ______
(long fungal filaments)

6. Two of these labeled structures occur in all fungi. What are these two structures? *hyphae and spores*

Ideas 11d

Kingdom Fungi

Directions: Write the answer to each question in the space provided.

1. A long filament of fungal cells is a *hypha*.
2. A *saprophyte* absorbs food from dead material.
3. A fungus and an alga that live as a single organism are called a *lichen*.
4. *Mycorrhizae* aid plant roots in absorption of minerals.
5. Reproductive cells formed on mushroom gills are called *spores*.
6. Fungi and bacteria perform the important function of *decomposition*.
7. Mold is classified in kingdom *Fungi*.
8. *Mushrooms* are a commonly eaten, fungal pizza topping.
9. List five products that fungi were involved in producing and which can be purchased at a store near you. *Answers will vary: mushrooms, cheese, chocolate, bread, antibiotics, alcohol, acetone.*

Ideas 11e

Review

Grading: *Give credit for each word in the first column correctly matched with its kingdom. Then, give additional credit if the second column words are correctly paired with the kingdom / first column combination. Only one solution will correctly match all the words once.*

Directions: Match each word or phrase from List 1 with the correct kingdom by writing the word or phrase in the blank provided. Similarly match each word or phrase from List 2 with the *best* kingdom / word List 1 combination. Each word is used once. Use a pencil since you may need more than one try.

List 1	List 2
cilia	*Amoeba*
chloroplasts	bacteria
dinoflagellates	*Euglena*
food poisoning	mold
~~mushrooms~~	no nucleus
mycorrhizae	oceanic food
Penicillin	*Paramecium*
plankton	red tide
prokaryote	root association
pseudopodia	~~spores~~
stem rust	wheat

Kingdom	Words from List 1	Words from List 2
Monera	*food poisoning*	*bacteria*
	prokaryote	*no nucleus (or bacteria)*
Protista	*cilia*	*Paramecium*
	chloroplasts	*Euglena*
	dinoflagellates	*red tide*
	plankton	*oceanic food (or red tide)*
	pseudopodia	*Amoeba*
Fungi	mushrooms	spores
	mycorrhizae	*root association*
	Penicillin	*mold (or spores)*
	stem rust	*wheat (or spores)*

Name ______________________

Date ____________ Hour ____________

Class Investigation 11a

Composting

Since this investigation requires so much time, consider starting it early in the school year. It can also be used as a science fair project.

Goals

- Identify which materials in household trash and garbage will decompose.
- Evaluate composting as a method of trash and garbage disposal.

This investigation works best if it can be done during a warm season of the year.

Materials

area of land where you have permission to compost trash and garbage, gloves, household trash and garbage (include plastic, paper, vegetable, and glass wastes), scales or balance, shovel, wood and nails or other materials to build a compost bin (optional)

If land is a problem, you may be able to layer soil and wastes in a 20 gallon or larger trash can.

Setting up

1. (optional) Build a compost bin. A 1 m square wooden box 90 cm tall with a lid, possibly hinged, and no bottom will serve adequately. Construct the sides of the bin with half-inch gaps between the boards. Many other designs are possible. The purpose of this box is to keep the waste materials in a confined space and to keep out animals.
2. Prepare the composting area by using the shovel to turn or loosen the soil in a 1 m square area. If you are using a composting bin, this is the area enclosed by the bin.

Discarded wood pallets are an inexpensive source of wood for building a compost bin. You can also confine the materials in a cage made of chicken wire and stakes driven into the ground.

Some cities regulate composting to guard against pests and odors. Check your local laws.

Procedures and observations

1. Save your family's trash and garbage for one week. Trash includes materials such as glass, paper, plastic, cardboard, and so forth. Garbage is mostly food wastes such as vegetable peelings, apple cores, and the vegetables you did not eat for supper.
2. Wearing gloves, sort and categorize the trash and garbage. Several categories likely are listed in the table on the next page.
3. Weigh and record the material in each category.
4. Mix all the wastes together again and prepare to put it in the compost bin. You should have enough waste to fill the bin. If necessary, collect trash for more than one week or combine the trash of several families.
5. Fill the compost bin with alternating layers of waste and soil. The waste layers should be six inches thick, and the soil layers should be two inches thick. The top layer should be a soil layer.
6. If only a small amount of rain falls during the next two to six months, water the compost occasionally during that time.
7. After one month turn (mix) the soil and wastes using a shovel.
8. After about two to six months, return to the compost bin and retrieve the remains of the wastes (wear gloves). Record how well each type decomposed. Collect ***only*** those wastes that decomposed partially or not at all and record their weights. If an item decomposed completely, simply record 0 as its final weight.

There may be some items in the trash that you may not want the students to see (confidential letters, financial statements, certain personal hygiene products). Alert the parents to remove any such items before the students collect the trash.

The wastes will probably not decompose as rapidly as compost piles normally do since nondecomposable materials are included. Contents and weather conditions will affect the rate of decomposition. In actual practice, nondecomposable items are not included in the pile and neither are some decomposable items such as meat and fat scraps. The composition of an avid composter's pile probably consists mostly of yard wastes, leaves, and animal manures.

Type of waste	Initial weight	How well did it decompose? (completely, partially, not at all)	Final weight
Paper			
Cardboard			
Glass			
Plastic			
Vegetable matter			
Bones			
Meat, skin, fat			
Metal cans			
Total		Weight that was not decomposed =	
		Weight that was decomposed =	

Summing up

1. Which materials decomposed best? ***Answers will vary. However, the vegetable material usually decomposes rapidly.***

2. Which materials did not decompose at all? ***Answers will vary but may include glass, plastic, and metal items.***

3. How would the results be different if you let the compost set for six more months? ***The partially decomposed items such as bones and some types of paper may be more decomposed.***

4. Why do you think soil was important in this investigation? ***Soil was a source of the microorganisms that decomposed the trash and garbage. It also helped to retain water.***

Name ______________________________
Date ______________ Hour ______________

5. How do you think weather and climate conditions affected your results? *Answers will vary, but decomposition should be more rapid during warm, wet periods than at other times.*

6. What uses can you think of for the compost produced in this investigation? *Answers will vary but may include being used as soil products (mulch, fertilizer, potting soil).*

7. What living organisms were important in this investigation (consult your textbook if necessary)? *fungi and bacteria (and people)*

8. What is the initial weight of your family's weekly trash and garbage that will decompose rapidly? ______ How much would a year's worth of this type of trash and garbage weigh? ______

9. Suppose your family composted that portion of its trash and garbage that will rapidly decompose. What problems might arise? *Answers will vary. Consider smell and pest problems and how to use the finished product.*

10. Is composting a good method for *your family personally* to dispose of its trash? Why or why not? *Answers will vary.*

11. Define *compost*. *decomposed organic matter (leaves, paper, etc.) or the process of decomposing such organic matter*

Go a Step Further

Directions: Use the compost you made to enrich the soil in one part of a flower bed or garden. Compare the growth of plants in this area with a control area.

T.E. only: *"Shrinking the Trash Heap."* BioScience, *42:90-93, Feb. 1992.*

Supplementary reading:

"Turn Your Fall Waste into Future Gold." *Organic Gardening,* 40:46-50, Sept./Oct. 1993.

"Cleaning up Compost." *Science News,* 40:56-58, Jan. 23, 1993.

"Don't Let Cold Weather Cool Your Compost." *Organic Gardening,* 35:50-53, Nov. 1992.

Name ______________________

Date __________ Hour __________

Class Investigation 11b

Raising Protists

The most important goal in this investigation is that students observe different types of living protists.

Goals

- Observe various kinds of protists.
- Culture protists found in pond water.

Materials

blank microscope slides (depression slides are best), rice, compound microscope, plant food, pond water, stereoscopic microscope, two culture bowls

You may substitute purchased cultures of various protists for the pond water. Amoeba, Euglena, Paramecium, *and algae such as* Spirogyra *and* Volvox *are good organisms to observe.* Hydra *would also be good to observe although it is not a protist.*

Procedures and observations

1. Collect pond water in culture bowls or other containers. Include a few dead leaves and a little mud from the pond bottom.
2. Examine the pond water with the stereoscopic microscope. Be sure to examine the surface of the dead leaves and bottom mud. In the space below draw five different organisms that you find.

Students may be excited about creatures other than protists. This is fine, but their drawings should be only of protists.

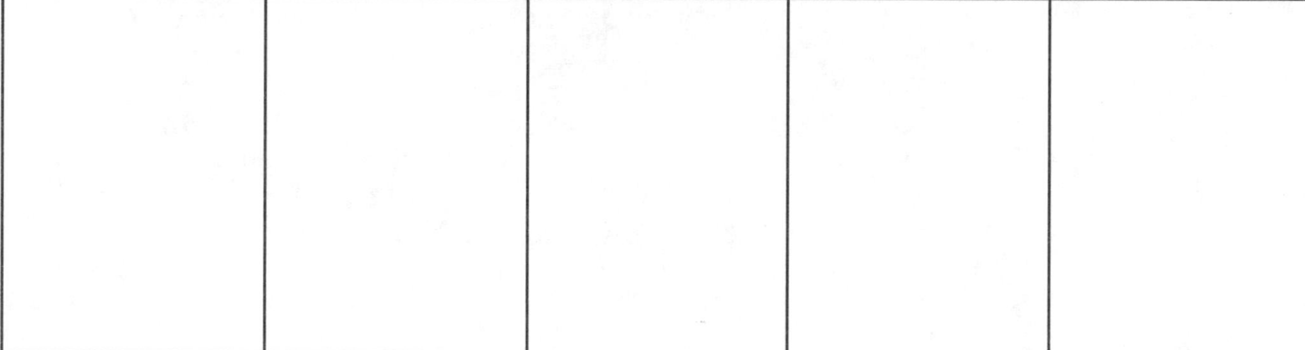

3. Add a few grains of rice to one culture bowl and set it aside for a week.
4. Add a small amount of soluble plant food to another bowl and set it in a brightly lit area for a week (full sunlight is fine).
5. After one week reexamine the entire cultures first with the stereoscopic microscope; then examine a drop on a slide with a compound microscope. In the space below, draw the two most numerous types of organisms found in each bowl.

Home School Tip

Examine a drop on a slide using the lowest power (4x) of your compound microscope in place of the stereoscopic microscope. A good hand lens may also work.

Although algae may not be apparent the first week, they will probably be visible the second week.

Summing up

1. What differences did you notice between the types of organisms growing in each bowl after one week? *Answers will vary. The culture receiving plant food and sunlight will probably be rich in filamentous algae. The other will likely have protozoans although not necessarily the same types as observed the previous week.*

2. Did you see types of organisms the second week that you did not see the first week? *Answers will vary.*

3. Were certain organisms visible when using the compound microscope that were not visible with the stereoscopic microscope? *yes*

Name ______________________

Date ____________ Hour ____________

Class Investigation 11c

Examining a Mushroom

Goals

- Observe the parts of a mushroom.
- Make a spore print.

Materials

black and white paper, knife, microscope, fresh mushrooms (wild or cultivated), prepared slide of a mushroom, spray shellac (optional)

Home School Tip
If you have young children in your home, take the same precautions with mushrooms collected from the wild as you would with poison.

Procedures and observations

Making a spore print

1. Choose a mushroom with a fully expanded cap and cut the stalk as close to the cap as possible.
2. Place the cap gill-side down, on a piece of white paper. If the mushroom has pores instead of gills, lay it pore-side down.
3. Cut another cap from another mushroom and likewise place it on a piece of black paper.
4. Allow the caps to lie undisturbed for at least a day. Spores will fall out of the cap and make a pattern on the paper similar to the gill or pore pattern. Sometimes mushroom caps decompose overnight, and sometimes they are filled with insects that emerge as the cap sits overnight.
5. Remove the caps from the papers and observe the spore prints. What colors are your mushroom spore prints? ***Answers will vary.***

   Are they the same color as the gills? ***Answers will vary. Gill color and spore print color are not necessarily the same.***
6. Using the point of a pencil or another sharp object, transfer a few spores to a microscope slide. Examine the spores with a microscope. Are they perfectly round? ***Answers will vary.***
7. Make a sketch of a single spore in the space below.

8. (optional) If you wish to preserve your spore print, lightly spray it with shellac. Several light sprayings are better than one thick coat.

Examining a mushroom

1. Collect a mushroom growing on the soil, including any parts that resemble roots. These are not roots but they do absorb nutrients from the soil.
2. Examine the stalk. Sometimes a ring of tissue surrounds the stalk. This is the remnant of where the cap was attached to the stalk before the cap expanded. Does your mushroom have such a ring? *Answers will vary.*
3. The stalk base in some mushrooms is expanded; in others it is the same diameter as the remainder of the stalk. Is the stalk base expanded on your mushroom? *Answers will vary.*
4. Mushroom caps may have gills or pores on the lower surface. Spores are produced on microscopic structures on the gills or in the pores. Which does your mushroom have, gills or pores? *Answers will vary.*
   If your mushroom has gills, are they connected to the stalk? *Answers will vary.*
5. The stalk base may sit in a cup-shaped structure. Does your mushroom have such a cup-shaped structure? *Answers will vary.*
6. Examine a prepared slide of a cross section through a mushroom. You should notice the structures on the gills that form the spores.
7. Make a drawing of your mushroom in the space below. Be sure to include all the details mentioned above and any others that you may notice.

Remind the students to wash their hands, especially if there is any possibility that the mushrooms could be poisonous.

The perfect conclusion to this investigation is a sampling of fungal foods, [e.g., grocery store mushrooms (ordinary type and a special variety such as shitake), morels, yeast (fresh yeast rolls), etc.].

Name ______________________
Date ____________ Hour ____________

12–Kingdom Plantae: Plant Structure

Ideas 12a

Form and Structure

Part 1

Directions: Label the drawing below using the terms below. Write each term near the structure it names; then draw a line from each term to the proper structure.

1. blade
2. node
3. petiole
4. root
5. stem

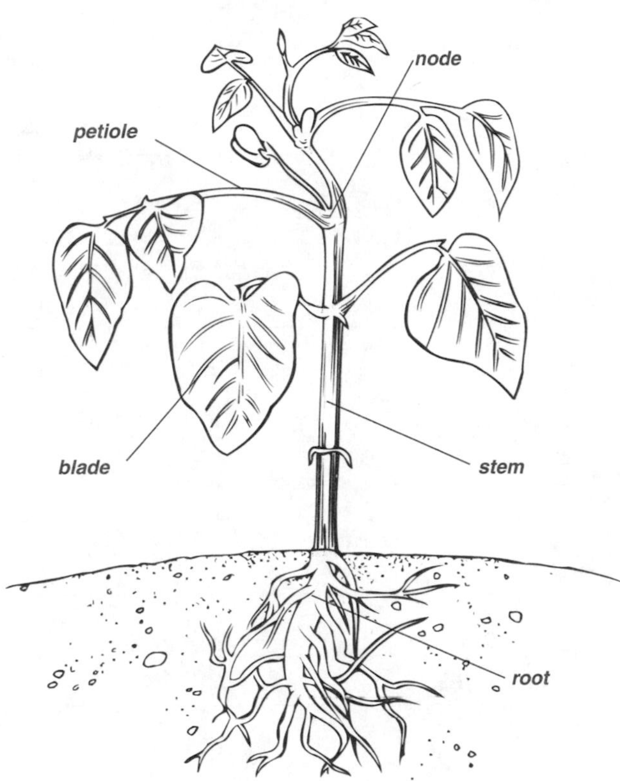

6. What type of root system does this plant have? *tap root system*

7. What type of leaf venation does this plant have? *pinnate*

8. What type of leaf arrangement does this plant have? *alternate*

Tell the students to not use the first two leaves when answering the alternate/ opposite question.

Part 2

Directions: Draw another plant next to the one above but with a different type of root system, a different type of leaf venation, and a different type of leaf arrangement.

1. What type of root system does your plant have? *fibrous root system*

2. What type of leaf venation does your plant have? *parallel or palmate*

3. What type of leaf arrangement does your plant have? *opposite or whorled*

Ideas 12b

Leaf Characteristics

Directions: Write a sentence for each pair of words below that includes both words and shows how the words are related. You may slightly change the words, such as *blade* to *blades*.

Answers will vary.

1. blade / compound *A leaf that has a blade that consists of many parts is a compound leaf.*
2. leaf / node *Leaves are attached to stems at nodes.*
3. alternate / stem *An alternate leaf arrangement has only one leaf attached at a node on a stem.*
4. leaf / veins *Veins conduct water and sugar in leaves.*
5. petiole / blade *A petiole connects a leaf blade to the stem.*
6. blade / leaflets *A leaf blade may be divided into leaflets.*
7. parallel / veins *A leaf's veins may be arranged parallel to each other.*
8. opposite / whorled *An opposite leaf arrangement has two leaves attached at a node; a whorled arrangement has three per node.*

Ideas 12c

Anatomy

Directions: Complete the words missing in the following statements by filling in the necessary letters. The circled letters form the answer to the final question.

1. The (C) U T I C L (E) is a waxy protective layer.
2. Two especially important characteristics of plant cells are C E L (L) W A L L S and P (L) A S T I D S.
3. T (U) R G O R pressure is water pressure in plant cells.
4. Wood is made of X Y (L) E M tissue.

Name ______________________

Date ____________ Hour ____________

5. Sugar is transported in P H L (O) E M tissue.
6. Long, tough, tapered plant cells are called F I B E R (S).
7. The outermost tissue of young plant organs is the E P I D (E) R M I S.
8. C E L L U L O S E is a major component of plant cell walls.

Ideas 12d

Major Plant Groups

Directions: Use the concept words from the list below to fill in the chart showing the relationships between the concepts. Words on the arrows show the relationships. Each concept word is used only once, and *there is only one correct way to use all the concept words* in this chart. Three words have already been placed in the chart to get you started.

Concept words

angiosperms	gymnosperms
club moss	~~naked seeds~~
cones	nonseed plants
covered seeds	rhizomes
~~ferns~~	~~seed plants~~
fronds	spores
fruits	vascular plants

Allow the students to use the textbook. Give credit for any correctly connected concepts and bonus points for correctly connecting all concepts.

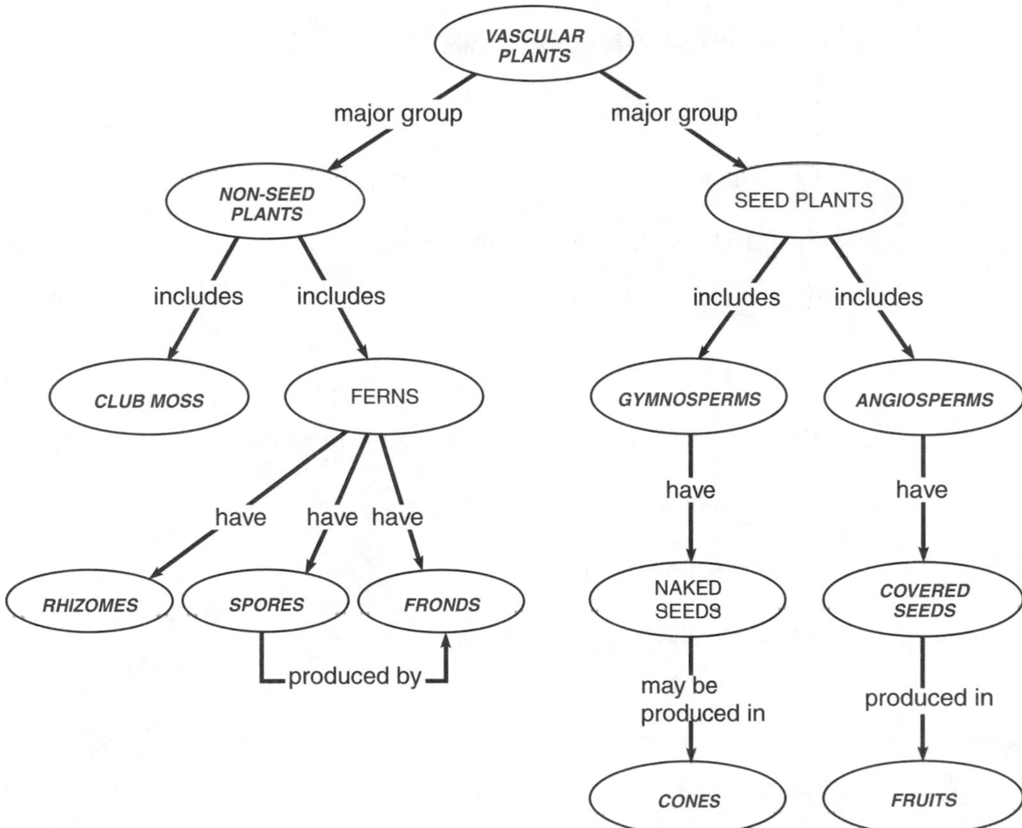

Ideas 12e

Review

Directions: Read the following statements. In the space provided, write *True* if the statement is true and *False* if the statement is false and draw a line through the word or words that make the statement false. In the space in the margin, write the words necessary to make the statement true.

multicellular	*False*	1. Plants are eukaryotic and ~~unicellular~~.
	True	2. Leaves are attached to stems at nodes.
	True	3. An alternate leaf arrangement has one leaf at a node.
blade	*False*	4. The flat, green part of a typical leaf is the ~~petiole~~.
	True	5. Vascular bundles contain xylem and phloem.
Anatomy	*False*	6. ~~Morphology~~ is the bodily construction of an organism.
Wood	*False*	7. ~~Bark~~ is layers of old xylem.
spores	*False*	8. Mosses reproduce by ~~seeds~~.
	True	9. A fibrous root system does not have one main root.
	True	10. Herbaceous stems are soft and flexible.
cellulose	*False*	11. Plant cell walls are mostly ~~protein~~.
	True	12. Ferns have vascular tissue.
Turgor	*False*	13. ~~Chlorophyll~~ pressure helps to support plants.
rhizoids	*False*	14. Moss ~~roots~~ anchor moss to the soil and absorb water.
	True	15. Fern leaves are called fronds.
fruits (or seeds)	*False*	16. Angiosperms produce flowers and ~~cones~~.
	True	17. Horsetails were once used as a cleaning abrasive.
	True	18. Rope can be made from plant fibers.
plastids	*False*	19. All plants have ~~chloroplasts~~.
Phloem	*False*	20. ~~Xylem~~ conducts sugar solution.

Name ______________________________

Date ______________ Hour ______________

It is possible to do this investigation during the winter if you direct the students to evergreen plants, indoor plants, and even fallen, brown leaves.

Avoid using ferns, grasses, pines, and spruces.

Field Investigation 12a

Leaf Characteristics

Goal

- Observe and identify leaf traits.

Materials

leaves collected locally, tape, paper, folder

Procedure

1. Collect one leaf (or stem with leaves) for each of the descriptions below. You should collect a separate specimen for each description. You may, however, use different leaves from the same plant to illustrate more than one of the descriptions.
2. Label each specimen by taping a leaf (or stem with leaves) to a sheet of paper with the leaf's description neatly printed on the paper. Keep these papers in a folder.

Descriptions

1. *Simple* leaves in an *alternate* arrangement
2. *Simple* leaves in an *opposite* arrangement
3. *Compound* leaves in an *alternate* arrangement
4. *Compound* leaves in an *opposite* arrangement
5. *Simple* leaves with *parallel* veins
6. *Simple* leaves with *palmate* veins
7. *Simple* leaves with *pinnate* veins
8. *Simple* or *compound* leaves with a *toothed* blade
9. A leaf with a *petiole* and a *deeply-lobed* blade
10. *Hair* or *fuzz* on the underside of a leaf

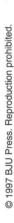

Personal Investigation 12b

Germinating Fern Spores

This investigation is best done as a teacher demonstration or by an interested student. It takes about 3-6 weeks for fern spores to germinate. The underlying goal is to demonstrate reproduction by nonseed plants.

Goal

- Germinate fern spores.

Materials

boiling water, clay flowerpot with saucer base, fern fronds with spores, newspaper, plastic wrap, potting soil, rubber band, sand, small stones or pieces of broken clay pottery

Once the spores germinate, show them to the students even though you may be teaching a different unit by then. If you sow spores once every few months during the year, you will eventually have all stages of the fern life cycle available at one time.

Clay pots work best for this investigation.

The potting soil, whether it is purchased or mixed on your own, should have much water-absorbent material such as sphagnum, peat moss, or leaf litter.

If possible, provide ferns or fern fronds of different ages or different stages of development to insure that at least some viable spores will be collected.

Alternatively, you could boil or bake the clay pot, rocks, and sand (boil for 10 minutes or bake at 170 degrees for 2-3 hours). You could try baking the soil, but that might destroy its organic matter. Rinsing the soil with boiling water should be sufficient.

The sand layer is not absolutely necessary, but it does make it easier to see the young fern plants.

Home School Tip

If you do not already have a good place to set up this investigation, consider starting a terrarium, leaving a space for the flowerpot with fern spores described in this investigation. A small aquarium with a glass plate cover should work fine.

Procedure

1. Collect three or four fern fronds that have spore-producing structures on the underside of the fronds. The spore-producing structures often appear as dots on the lower surface of the fronds.
2. Place your fronds spore-side-down on a piece of newspaper or a large piece of white paper, and allow them to lie undisturbed for a day or two. Spores, resembling fine dust, should be released from the fronds during this time.
3. Wash the clay pot and stones (or broken pottery pieces); then rinse them with boiling water. If the potting soil and sand are not labeled "sterilized," you should rinse them with boiling water.
4. Put an inch-thick layer of stones in the bottom of the clay pot. Cover this with a thick layer of potting soil, then add a thin layer of sand. The top of the sand layer should be about one-half inch below the top of the pot.
5. Water the pot thoroughly. Sprinkle the spores that you collected onto the surface of the sand. Cover the pot with plastic wrap and secure it with a rubber band. Set the pot in its saucer base. Place the pot in an area with normal room temperature and medium light (not direct sunlight nor in dim light). You should maintain a water level in the base for the next few weeks.
6. The spores should germinate in about 3-6 weeks. The fern plants that grow from the spores will be small (no larger than your fingernail). At first you will need a hand lens to see them. They will not be shaped like the fern plants you are used to seeing. It will take an additional month or more for "normal appearing" fern plants to appear.

The gametophyte fern plants (the stage that grows from spores) will grow into flattened, heart-shaped structures, each about the size of a fingernail. When they reach this size, water them from the top so that a film of water temporarily remains on the surface of the gametophyte fern plants. This will allow them to reproduce sexually (microscopic reproductive organs on gametophytes require water to facilitate fertilization) and eventually produce the typical sporophyte fern plant with which most people are familiar.

In our tests, spores germinated within a month produced heart-shaped structures about two weeks later and produced the first sporophyte about two weeks after that. Numerous sporophytes were present two and one-half months from the initial sowing.

Name ______________________

Date ____________ Hour ____________

13–Kingdom Plantae: Plant Activities

Ideas 13a

Photosynthesis and Leaves

Directions: Label the following drawing by supplying the missing terms or definitions and then drawing a line from each term to the proper structure in the cross section of the leaf.

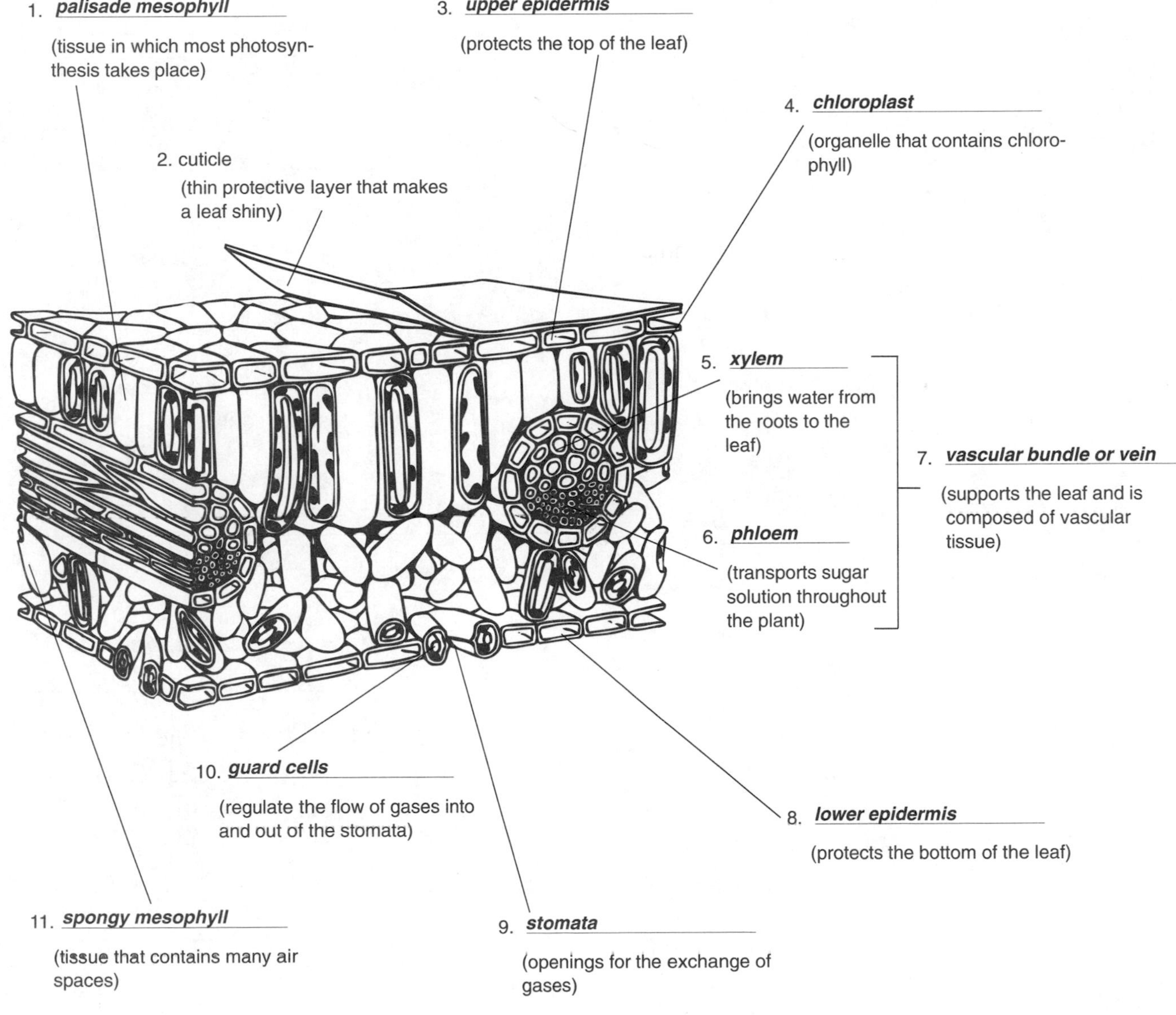

Ideas 13b

Functions of Plants

Directions: Unscramble the words and write them in the blanks. For some of the words a definition has been supplied. For those that lack a definition, you must write one in the space provided.

1. toro srhai — *root hairs* — Extension of root epidermal cells that help absorb water
2. mottasa — *stomata* — *Openings in leaves that allow gases to pass through*
3. spirittranano — *transpiration* — *Water exiting through stomata of leaves*
4. cellesitn — *lenticels* — *Openings in the bark of woody plants that allow gas exchange*
5. poygns yesmlhplo — *spongy mesophyll* — *Area in a leaf where the cells have many air spaces between them*
6. helpmo — *phloem* — Plant tissue that transports sugar solution
7. reimmtess — *meristems* — *Regions in a plant where growth occurs*
8. roomehn — *hormone* — *Chemical substance made by a plant that controls its growth*
9. gyexno — *oxygen* — A gas produced during photosynthesis
10. robcan dexdiio — *carbon dioxide* — *A gas required for photo-synthesis*

Name ______________________

Date __________ Hour ____________

Ideas 13c

The Environment and Plant Responses

Directions: Match the terms below with their definitions by writing the proper letter choices in the blanks provided. You may use each term only once. Some terms are not used.

a. auxin
b. day-neutral plants
c. germination
d. long-day plants
e. negative geotropism
f. negative phototropism
g. photoperiodism
h. positive geotropism
i. positive phototropism
j. short-day plants
k. tropisms

h 1. Roots growing toward pull of gravity

j 2. Plants that flower when exposed to short days and long nights

a 3. Hormone involved in phototropism

i 4. Stems and leaves growing toward light

b 5. Plants that flower regardless of the length of the day or night

k 6. The growth responses of plants to factors in their environment

e 7. Stems growing away from the pull of gravity

g 8. A plant response to the length of day and night

Ideas 13d

Review

Directions: In the spaces provided, tell how the pair of terms are similar; then tell how they are different.

If this seems too difficult for your students, then let them find only the similarities or only the differences. You may wish to specify which choice to answer for each number.

1. lateral meristem / apical meristem
   similar: ***Both are areas where growth occurs in plants.***
   different: ***Apical meristems are found at the tips of stems and roots. Lateral meristems are found at places other than at the tips.***

2. auxin / hormone
   similar: ***Both substances are made by plants and control growth.***
   different: ***Auxin is only one kind of hormone.***

3. guard cells / stomata
similar: ***Both help control gas exchange in leaves.***

different: ***Stomata are the openings in leaves; guard cells are the special cells that regulate the stomata.***

4. lenticels / stomata
similar: ***Both help control gas exchange in plants.***

different: ***Lenticels are found on stems. Stomata are usually found on leaves and are surrounded by guard cells.***

5. palisade mesophyll / spongy mesophyll
similar: ***Both are leaf layers where photosynthesis occurs.***

different: ***Palisade mesophyll is closely packed and has more chloroplasts. Spongy mesophyll is beneath the palisade mesophyll, has many air spaces and fewer chloroplasts.***

6. starch / cellulose
similar: ***Both are made from sugar.***

different: ***Starch is a storage material. Cellulose is a cell wall component.***

7. positive tropism / negative tropism
similar: ***Both are growth responses of plants to factors in the environment.***

different: ***Growth toward a factor is positive; growth away from a factor is negative.***

8. photosynthesis / phototropism
similar: ***Both are plant responses that require light.***

different: ***Photosynthesis stores energy in the form of sugar. Phototropism is a plant's growth toward or away from light.***

9. photoperiodism / phototropism
similar: ***Both are plant responses that require light.***

different: ***Photoperiodism is a response to the length of day. Phototropism is a plant's growth toward or away from light.***

10. transpiration / root hairs
similar: ***Both are involved in the movement of water in plants.***

different: ***Transpiration is the exiting of water vapor and other gases through stomata in leaves. Root hairs absorb water into the plant.***

Name ______________________
Date ____________ Hour ____________

Class Investigation 13a

How Much Water Is Lost During Transpiration?

Goals

- Observe the results of transpiration.
- Determine the weight of the water lost by a plant during transpiration.

Materials

plastic bag, balance, putty or modeling clay, a potted geranium (or other plant with a single stem), twist tie or tape

Setting up

1. Thoroughly water a geranium plant and allow the excess water to drain.
2. Place the pot in a plastic bag. Put a small amount of putty or modeling clay around the stem where you will close the bag. Close the bag around the stem and use tape or a twist tie to secure the bag to the stem.

Procedures and observations

1. Weigh the plant and record its weight on the chart below.
2. Place the pot in direct sunlight or in a well-lighted area of the room.
3. For the next four days weigh the plant and record its weight. Record any other observations in the column specified for notes.

Day	Weight	Weight lost	Notes
1			
2			
3			
4			
5			

Summing up

1. Calculate the amount of weight that the plant lost each day and record the amount on the chart above.
2. Define *transpiration.* ***Transpiration is the process by which plants release water into the atmosphere.***
3. On which day did the plant lose the most weight? ______________
   Why do you think the plant lost more weight on that day? ***Answers will vary. Exposure to sunlight, wind, or higher temperatures could have caused the plant to lose more water. On the first day it would have the most water available to lose.***

You will need an actively growing potted plant. A flowering plant is good to use. Water the plant several hours before class time so that its soil will be drained when you place it in the bag.

This investigation is best done as a demonstration. Begin this investigation on Monday, if possible. If you do not begin on Monday, you may wish to continue the observation for fewer days.

Home School Tip

Bathroom scales are usually not sensitive enough to use in this investigation unless the potted plant is exceptionally large (like a five-foot rubber tree with many leaves). Kitchen scales may work.

Initially watering the plant is important; there must be some water present for the plant to transpire.

Sealing the pot in the plastic bag will eliminate any weight change due to water evaporation from the soil.

In our test of this investigation, a store bought geranium in a 4 in. pot lost approximately 40 g per day over a three-day period.

4. On which day did the plant lose the least weight? ____________

Why do you think the plant lost less weight on that day? *Answers will vary.*
Exposure to little sunlight and exposure to cool temperatures could have caused the plant to lose a smaller amount of water. On each successive day there would be less water available to lose.

5. How much weight did the plant lose altogether? *Answers will vary. (grams or ounces)*

6. One gram of water has a volume of 1 ml; one ounce of water has a volume of 1/4 cup. What volume of water did the plant transpire? *Answers will vary. (milliliters or cups)*

Name ______________________

Date ____________ Hour ______________

Class Investigation 13b

Movement in Stems

This investigation is best done as a demonstration.

Goals

- Demonstrate and understand water movement in stems.
- Determine whether light and air currents affect the rate of transpiration.

Materials

cardboard box, electric fan, knife, two fresh stalks of celery with leaves, two wide-mouth jars, red or blue food coloring, ruler

The celery that you use should have as many leaves as possible. Celery that has several leaves will have many stomata and will be able to carry on a large amount of transpiration. Try to have about the same number of leaves on each of the stalks of celery that you use.

Setting up

1. Mix ten drops of food coloring in 100 ml (8 tsp.) of water and divide it equally between the two jars.
2. Holding the base of the celery stalks underwater, cut off about 2 cm (0.8 in.) of the base of each stalk. Remove the cut-off piece. Expose the cut end of the celery stalk to air as little as possible.
3. Quickly place a stalk of celery in each jar.
4. Label one jar *A* and the other jar *B* and put them in the following places.
   - Place jar *A* under a cardboard box.
   - Place jar *B* by a fan or air duct where it will receive drafts.

Try to make the celery stalks relatively equal. Do not use the heart of the celery or the tough outer stalks. Obtain the freshest celery that you can for this experiment.

Procedures and observations

1. Periodically during the day measure the height to which the food coloring has risen in the celery.
2. Measure from the bottom of the celery stalk to the highest point to which the food coloring has risen.
3. Do not remove the celery from the water. If the food coloring does not show above the level of the water, do not measure it but record *0* for its measurement.
4. Record your observations on the chart below.

To avoid staining your fingers, you may want to use plastic gloves when cutting the bases of the celery.

	Distance Food Coloring Has Risen	
Time	Stalk *A* (Jar *A*)	Stalk *B* (Jar *B*)

This investigation may take several hours. We suggest that you explain it to your class one day and indicate that you will set the experiment up the next day. If possible, make arrangements for various students to make the necessary observations periodically throughout the day. Record the observations on a sheet of paper. The next day write the data from this sheet of paper on the chalkboard for students to copy.

You may want to make your last observation the day after you start the experiment.

You need to make observations only every few hours. It is not crucial that the intervals of time between the observations be exactly the same, but you should keep the intervals somewhat similar.

Summing up

1. What part of the celery carried the colored water toward the leaves?

   ☒ xylem ☐ phloem

2. What is transpiration? ***Transpiration is the process by which a leaf loses water vapor.***

3. How does the process of transpiration cause water to move in the stem?
   When transpiration causes the loss of water at the top of a plant, water will move up the stem to replace the water that is lost.

4. In which stalk did the colored water rise the highest?

   ☐ A ☒ B

5. In which stalk did the colored water rise the least?

   ☒ A ☐ B

6. In which stalk did the colored water rise the fastest?

   ☐ A ☒ B

7. In which stalk did the colored water rise the slowest?

   ☒ A ☐ B

8. Why do you think these results occurred? ***Answers will vary. The draft increased transpiration, which increased water movement.***

Name ______________________
Date ____________ Hour ____________

Class Investigation 13c

Leaf Design and Function

The secret to a successful investigation of leaf structures is a good prepared slide. Avoid ordering monocots (corn, grass, lily, onion). Some good typical leaves include apple, geranium, holly, lilac (Syringa), privet (Ligustrum), rose, and tomato.

Goals

- Observe the structures and tissues within a leaf.
- Recognize how a leaf's design aids photosynthesis.
- Observe guard cells and stomata.

Materials

coverslip, eyedropper, glass slide, leaf (geranium, lettuce, or philodendron are good), microscope, prepared slide of a leaf cross section, scissors, toothpicks

Students may have difficulty with the last question in the Summing Up section. The material is covered in the text, but the students may become confused by the question. You may wish to discuss the question (not the answer) before they begin the activity. If they understand the question, they should be able to answer it.

Part 1: The Structure of a Leaf

Procedures and observations

1. Obtain and set up your microscope.
2. Place the prepared slide of a cross section of a leaf on the stage of your microscope and focus it.
3. Find a section of the leaf that is not damaged and that does not have a section of a vein in it.
4. Observe the structures and tissues of the leaf from the top to the bottom of the leaf.
   - Recall that what you see in the microscope is the reverse of what you have on the microscope stage.
   - As you do this exercise, you may want to change back and forth between low and high power.
5. Find the following structures and tissues. Describe their size, shape, thickness, and other characteristics as you see them.

Some prepared leaf slides do not have cuticles on them. Sometimes they are removed as the slide is being made. If your slides contain leaves that lack cuticles, make sure that the students are aware of that fact so that they do not attempt to write a description of the cuticle.

   - Cuticle ***Answers will vary. The cuticle is a thin, clear layer.***
   - Upper epidermis ***Answers will vary. The upper epidermis is a single layer of small, boxlike cells.***
   - Palisade mesophyll ***Answers will vary. The palisade mesophyll is a thick layer of thin cells packed closely together.***
   - Spongy mesophyll ***Answers will vary. The spongy mesophyll is a thick layer of irregular cells with many spaces between the cells.***
   - Lower epidermis ***Answers will vary. The lower epidermis is similar to the upper epidermis; it has guard cells and stomata.***
   - Cuticle ***Answers will vary. The cuticle is a thin, clear layer. Both the upper and lower leaf surfaces have a cuticle.***

Locate guard cells and stomata. Describe them. *Answers will vary. Guard cells usually look like opposing letter Cs. The spaces between them are the stomata.*

6. Find a cross section of a vein. Avoid the vein that runs down the middle of the leaf and avoid veins that are cut lengthwise.
   - What tissues do you see in the vein? How can you tell which is which? *Xylem, phloem, and strengthening tissues are visible. The xylem is above the phloem, and the strengthening tissues form a circle around the xylem and phloem.*
   - What is the function of a vein? *A vein carries water and dissolved minerals to the leaf cells and carries sugar dissolved in water away from the leaf.*

Summing up

1. Which of the tissues or cells of the leaf you observed contain chloroplasts and thus carry on photosynthesis? *The palisade mesophyll and the spongy mesophyll carry on photosynthesis. Some students may correctly include guard cells.*

2. God designed the leaf to carry on photosynthesis. In what ways does the placement of the leaf structures and tissues make the leaf ideal for carrying on photosynthesis? Tell how the requirements for photosynthesis are easily met and the products of photosynthesis easily removed because of the leaf's structure. *Answers will vary. The palisade mesophyll contains the most chlorophyll because its cells are closely packed. Since the palisade mesophyll is the upper mesophyll layer, a maximum amount of chlorophyll is exposed to the sun. The spaces in the spongy mesophyll permit oxygen and carbon dioxide to be exchanged easily. The stomata and guard cells permit these gases to be exchanged with the environment. The veins carry water to and sugar away from the cells that carry on photosynthesis.*

Name ______________________

Date ____________ Hour ____________

Part 2: Guard Cells and Stomata

Procedures and observations

1. Obtain and set up your microscope.
2. Wash and dry a glass slide and coverslip.
3. Place a drop of water on the slide.
4. Carefully tear the leaf, pulling away a section of the lower epidermis.
5. Being careful not to damage the epidermis, use scissors to remove the epidermis with a tiny portion of the leaf attached to it.
6. Place the epidermis and leaf portion on the water on the slide. Using toothpicks, make sure part of the epidermis is flat in the water. Do not damage the epidermis.
7. Place the coverslip on top of the water and epidermis.
8. Place the slide on the microscope stage and find the epidermis on low power.
9. Observe the epidermis using high power.
10. Locate guard cells and stomata.
11. Check the box that indicates what you observed:
    - ☐ All of the stomata are open.
    - ☐ All of the stomata are closed.
    - ☐ Some of the stomata are open, and some are closed.
12. Describe the stomata. ***Answers will vary. Some will say that they are tiny holes between the guard cells; others will say that they are spindle shaped.***
13. What do the guard cells look like? ***Answers will vary. Some students will compare them to half-moons or C-shaped balloons.***

To save time, you may want to prepare the slides and have them set up on microscopes before class begins. You can then prepare a mock slide as a demonstration for the class. The students can then observe the specimens and answer the questions.

You may need to demonstrate how to tear the leaf to obtain a section of epidermis.

You can use plants other than the ones listed in the materials section, but it is difficult to remove the epidermis from many of them. You may want to test your leaves before you have students try them.

If you take your leaf from a plant that has been well watered and is in a well-lighted area, it will be actively carrying on photosynthesis, and its stomata should be open. If you prepare your slide quickly and place the epidermis in the drop of water before the guard cells have a chance to lose their turgidity, the stomata should remain open. For closed stomata use a slightly wilted leaf. Most students will handle the leaf epidermis long enough for some of the stomata to close.

Curling epidermis is always a problem. Tell students that they do not need to have the entire epidermis flat on the slide; they need only enough to look at through their microscopes.

Summing up

1. What is the function of the stomata? ***Answers will vary. Stomata permit gases to be exchanged between the leaf and the atmosphere.***
2. What is the function of the guard cells? ***Answers will vary. Guard cells open and close the stomata (openings), regulating the exchange of gases.***
3. How do you suppose the guard cells open and close the stomata? ***Answers will vary. When the guard cells have turgor pressure (are filled with water), they are crescent shaped, which causes the stomata to be open. When they lack turgor pressure, they collapse, and the stomata close.***

The final Summing Up question will be difficult for many students. Have your students do the Summing Up for homework, omitting the last question. Discuss the answer to the last question in class the next day.

Name ______________________
Date ____________ Hour ____________

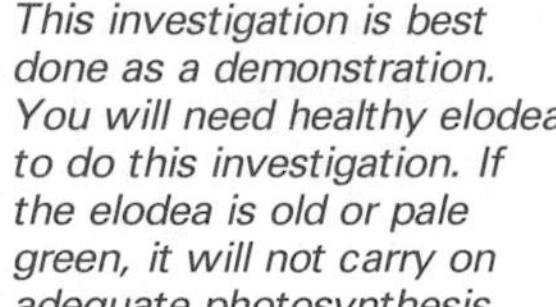

This investigation is best done as a demonstration. You will need healthy elodea to do this investigation. If the elodea is old or pale green, it will not carry on adequate photosynthesis.

Anacharis *is another name for elodea.*

Class Investigation 13d

Is Light Necessary for Photosynthesis?

Goals

- Determine whether light is necessary for photosynthesis.
- Determine whether the amount of light affects the rate of photosynthesis.

Materials

cardboard box; elodea; lamp; three large, clear, flat dishes; three nails; three ring stands; three test tubes; burette clamps; thread

Setting up

1. Fill three dishes and three test tubes with water. Carefully mount the test tubes above the dishes as illustrated in the diagram. The test tubes must be filled with water (no air in the top of the tube), and their openings must be below the surface of the water but still about 2.5 cm (1 in.) from the bottom of the dish.
2. Using a sharp knife, cut three equal lengths of elodea. Each of the elodea pieces should have the same number of leaves. Be careful not to damage the elodea's leaves as you cut the stem.
3. Tie a piece of thread to a nail. Tie the other end of the thread to the bottom end of the elodea.
4. Measure the length of your thread and elodea. With the nail on the bottom of the dish and the elodea in the test tube, there should be about 5 cm (2 in.) of water-filled test tube remaining above the top end of the elodea. If necessary, adjust the length of the thread by twisting the thread around the nail.
5. Place the elodea inside the test tube as shown in the diagram. Do the same for the other two test tubes.

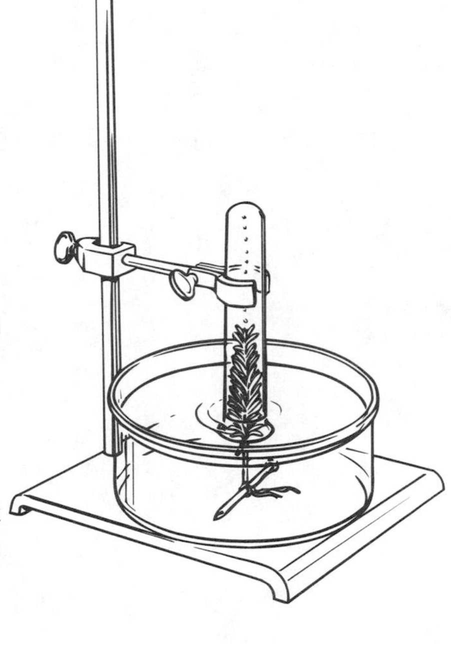

Procedures

1. Place one test tube-elodea-dish apparatus in an area where it will receive normal room light.
2. Place a box over another apparatus.
3. Place the third apparatus in an area where you can leave a lamp shining on it overnight. The lamp should be near enough to give the elodea bright light but not close enough to heat the water.

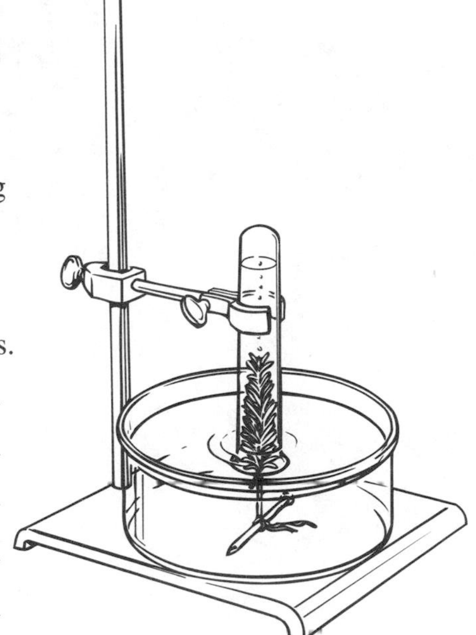

Observations

1. One half-hour after you begin the experiment, record your observations.
   - In normal room light: ***There should be little change. There may be some air at the top of the tube but not a steady stream of bubbles.***
   - In the dark: ***There should be no change.***
   - Under the lamp: ***There should be a small amount of oxygen collected at the top of the test tube. There may be a stream of small bubbles coming from the elodea.***

For best results, boil and then cool the water used in this investigation to remove dissolved gases. Then add 2 ml of sodium bicarbonate (baking soda) solution to provide abundant carbon dioxide. The bicarbonate solution is made by dissolving 0.84 g (2½ tbsp.) of sodium bicarbonate in 100 ml of water. Higher concentrations of sodium bicarbonate will hinder photosynthesis.

Instead of using ring stands, you may devise any other method that will hold the test tubes in place.

If the thread tends to slip off the nail, you can use a large hexagonal nut in place of the nail.

Students may have difficulty with some of the Summing Up questions. You may want to discuss some of them in class.

2. Twenty-four hours after you begin the experiment, repeat your observations.
   - In normal room light: ***There should be a small amount of oxygen collected in the top of the test tube.***
   - In the dark: ***There should be no change. Occasionally some cellular respiration will have released some carbon dioxide if the room is very warm.***
   - Under the lamp: ***There should be a large collection of oxygen at the top of the test tube.***

Summing up

1. What process was the elodea carrying on in order to produce the results you observed in the test tubes? ***It was carrying on photosynthesis.***

2. What observations led you to this conclusion? ***Light is necessary for photosynthesis. Since the elodea in the light produced the gas, and the elodea in the dark did not, we can assume that photosynthesis was responsible for the gas produced.***

3. What was the gas that was being produced and that was collecting at the tops of the test tubes? ***The gas was oxygen.***

   Why do you believe that this was the substance being produced? ***Photosynthesis produces oxygen.***

Go a step further

You can add carbon dioxide to the water by adding baking soda to the water. Find the amount of baking soda to add that will result in the fastest rate of oxygen production. Be sure to keep all other conditions equal.

Name ______________________________
Date ______________ Hour ______________

Class Investigation 13e

The Effect of a Hormone on Plant Cuttings

Goals

- Demonstrate the effect of a hormone in plants.
- Propagate a plant using a stem or leaf cutting.

Materials

flowerpots or similar containers; plant(s) (African violet, begonia, tomato, willow, and holly work well); potting soil, sand, or vermiculite; rooting hormone; warm and well-lighted area

Be careful not to use dormant plants.

Rootone is a common brand name of rooting hormone and is available in the garden section of department stores as well as from nurseries.

Setting up

Obtain one or more of the plants listed above. The plants should be healthy and growing. You will eventually have to remove the cuttings from the soil to observe your results. Thus, the soil that you use should not be heavy or have a high clay content since this may break the roots when you remove the cuttings. Have at least two flowerpots for each kind of plant tested—one for the control group and one for the treatment group.

Procedures and observations

1. Fill the flowerpots with potting soil.
2. Cut entire leaves, including the petioles, from African violet and begonia plants or make stem cuttings 3-4 inches long from the other plants listed. Stem cuttings from the tip of a stem are best; otherwise, use sections from young stems. Do not use old, thick stems.
3. Divide your cuttings from each plant into two groups.
4. With the first group, moisten the bottom inch of each cutting; then dip the moistened end in the rooting hormone.
5. Plant these cuttings in a pot and water them lightly. You may plant one or more cuttings per pot, depending on the sizes of the cuttings and pots. Label this pot "treatment."
6. Similarly, plant the second group of cuttings without applying rooting hormone. Label this pot "control."
7. Place all pots in a warm, well-lighted area.
8. After approximately 3 weeks carefully remove each cutting from its pot and wash off most of the soil from the end of the cutting. Be careful not to mix the treatment and control groups.
9. Count how many roots have formed on each cutting and observe how long they are. Also observe where the roots formed (on the tip of the cut end or on the sides). Record your observations in the table on the next page.
10. If you wish, repot your plants and continue to let them grow.

Home School Tip
A single student would only need to test one or two kinds of plants with three to four cuttings per treatment.

Plant name		Average number of roots	Typical length of roots	Location of roots on the cutting
	Treatment			
	Control			
	Treatment			
	Control			
	Treatment			
	Control			

Summing up

1. Did the treatment groups have more roots? *yes*
2. Did any roots form on the control cuttings? *Answers will vary.*
3. Did some kinds of plants form more roots than others? If so, which ones? *Answers will vary.*
4. Did rooting hormone stimulate roots to form in the plants you used? How do you know for certain? *Yes, we know for certain by comparison with the control group in which all other conditions were the same except for the absence of rooting hormone.*
5. What kind of businesses might use rooting hormones? *Answers will vary but may include garden centers and nurseries.*

Name ______________________________
Date ____________ Hour ______________

Class Investigation 13f

Tropisms in Seedlings

Goals

- Demonstrate and observe geotropism in seedlings.
- Demonstrate and observe phototropism in seedlings.

Materials

bean seeds, cotton, eyedropper, two glass plates (panes), lamp, paper towels, plastic or Styrofoam egg cartons, rubber bands, scissors, shoe boxes

Experiment 1

Setting up

1. Place several folded paper towels on a glass plate. Place rubber bands around the glass plate and paper towels to hold the towels in place.
2. Place eight small cotton balls on the paper towels; then place bean seeds in the center of each cotton ball. Be sure that the bean seeds "face" up, right, left, and down, as indicated in the diagram.
3. Slowly wet the cotton and the paper towels.
4. Place another glass plate over the top of the bean seeds and secure it in place with more rubber bands.
5. Using a marking pencil, draw an arrow on the top glass plate.
6. Set this assembly, with the arrow pointing upward, in a dark, warm area.

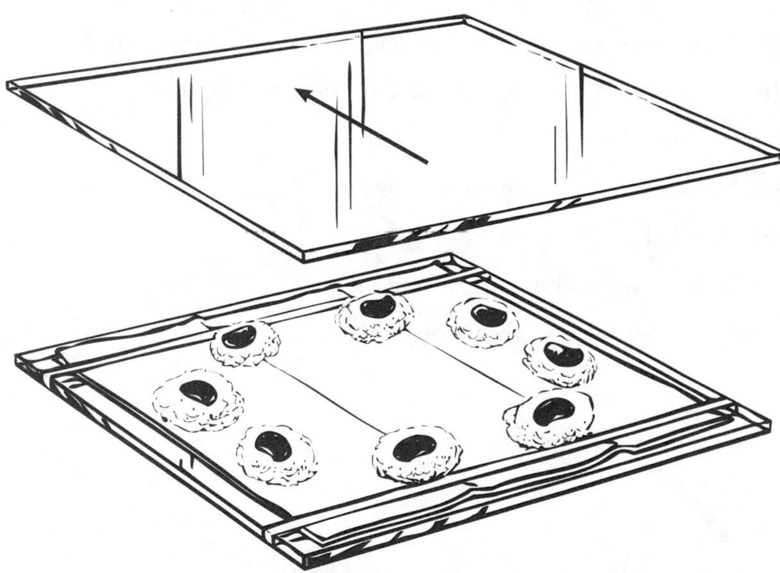

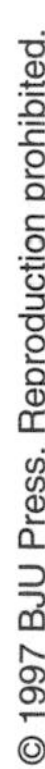

Procedures and observations

1. Using an eyedropper, daily add water to the assembly.
2. Observe the bean seeds daily.
3. Once the seeds begin to grow, record their growth patterns on the chart on the next page. Record the growth of the root and the stem shoots.

Use windowpane glass available from a hardware store and cut to approximately 6" x 6". You may want to tape the sharp edges.

Dry beans (lima, pinto, kidney, navy, etc.) from a grocery store usually work well, but be sure to test them for germination before beginning this investigation.

You can substitute other seeds for the bean seeds. If you use small seeds (such as radish seeds), you may not need the cotton. You may have problems "facing" the smaller seeds in a proper direction. Corn seeds can also be used.

To speed sprouting, soak the seeds in water overnight before planting them. Plant the bean seeds about three days before you start the second experiment.

Home School Tip
You can substitute a clear drinking glass or the bottom of a clear glass baking dish if you do not have plate glass. You will need to improvise with ways to hold the seeds in place.

Date	Facing upwards	Facing right	Facing left	Facing down

Summing up

1. What is geotropism? *Geotropism is a plant's response to gravity.*
2. Did the roots of the bean seedlings exhibit ☒ positive geotropism or ☐ negative geotropism? (Place an *x* in the proper box.)
3. Did the stems of the bean seedlings exhibit ☐ positive geotropism or ☒ negative geotropism? (Place an *x* in the proper box.)
4. Did the way in which the seeds were positioned affect their response to geotropism? If so, what were the differences? *There should be no differences.*

Experiment 2

Setting up

1. Several days before you begin this experiment, cut five sections with four cups each from plastic egg cartons. Fill the cups with potting soil and plant a bean seed in each cup.
2. Prepare four shoe boxes by cutting an 8-by-8-cm hole in the end of each. Number the boxes 1-4.
3. Water the seeds. Keep the soil moist, but not too wet.
4. When the first seedlings break through the soil, begin the experiment.

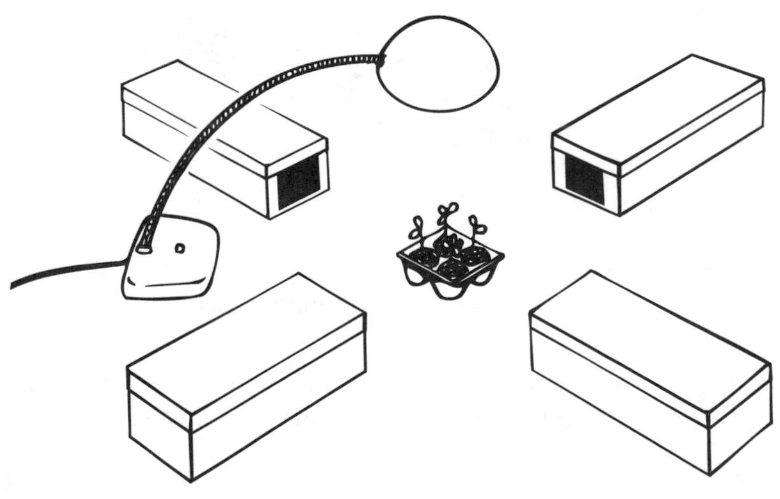

Name ______________________

Date ____________ Hour ____________

Procedures and observations

1. Place a section of egg carton containing sprouting bean seeds in each of the shoe boxes. The egg carton should be on the side farthest from the hole. Arrange the shoe boxes around a lamp as indicated in the diagram.
2. Place the fifth set of sprouting bean seeds below the lamp.
3. Continue keeping the soil moist but not wet.
4. Observe the seedlings daily for several days. Record your observations in the chart below.

Date	Box 1	Box 2	Box 3	Box 4	Center

Summing up

1. What is phototropism? *Phototropism is a plant's growth in response to light.*

2. Did the plants in the boxes exhibit positive or negative phototropism?

Plants in box 1: ☒ positive phototropism ☐ negative phototropism

Plants in box 2: ☒ positive phototropism ☐ negative phototropism

Plants in box 3: ☒ positive phototropism ☐ negative phototropism

Plants in box 4: ☒ positive phototropism ☐ negative phototropism

Plants in the center section: ☐ positive phototropism ☐ negative phototropism

It will be difficult to separate negative geotropism from positive geotropism in the center section.

3. Was there any significant difference in appearance between the five different sets of plants? If so, what was the difference? *The plants in the boxes should have long, thin stems that grew toward the holes. The plants in the fifth section should be shorter, sturdier, and greener.*

4. Can you account for any difference in the appearance between the plants that were in the boxes and the ones that were in the fifth section? ***The intensity of the light accounts for the difference in the growth of the plants. The sturdier plants in the fifth section received a higher intensity of light.***

Name ______________________
Date __________ Hour __________

14–Kingdom Plantae: Plant Reproduction

Ideas 14a

Flowers

Directions: Below is a diagram of a flower. Around the diagram are various definitions. For each definition write the term in the blank provided; then draw a line from the term to the structure on the diagram.

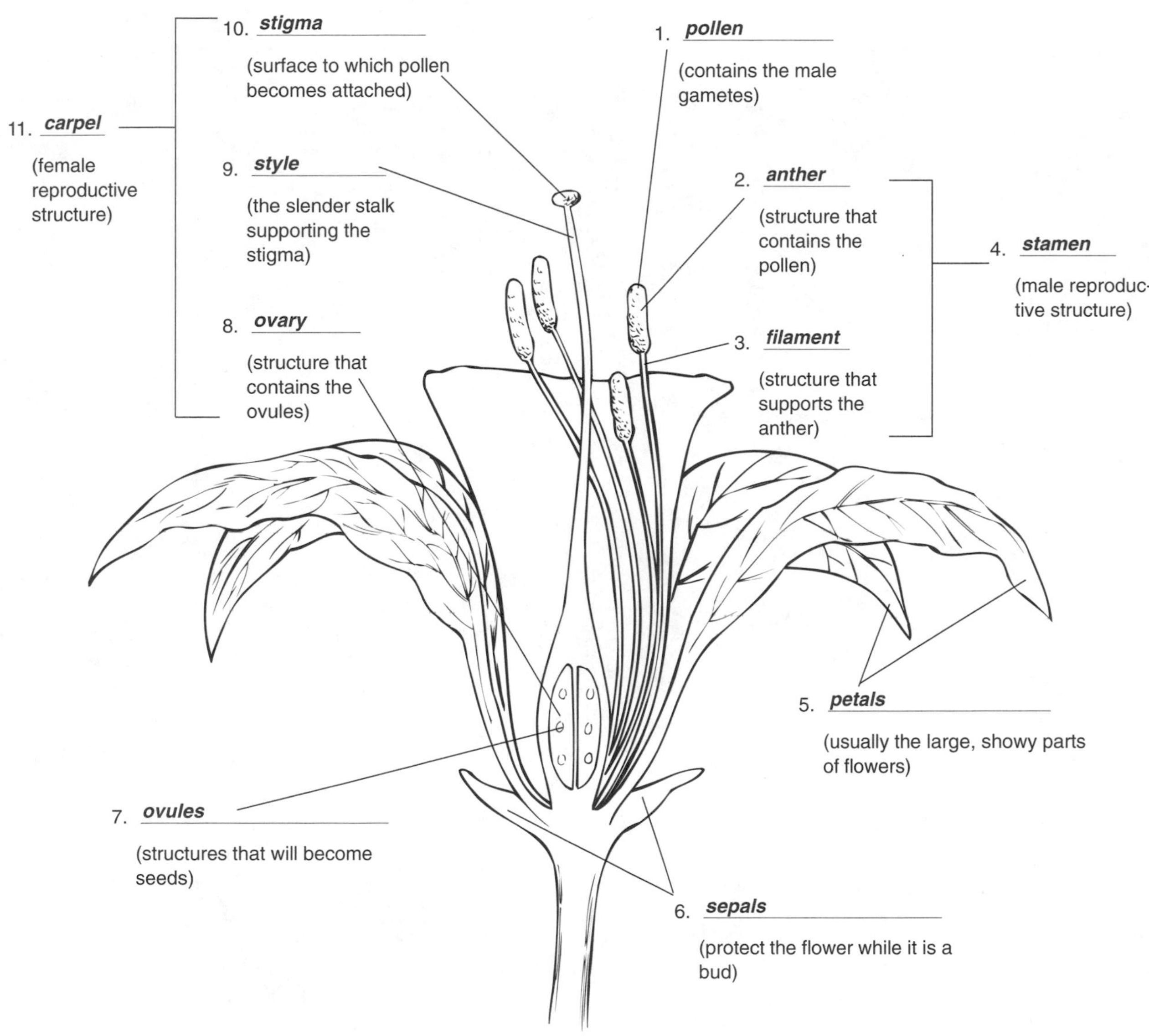

Name ______________________
Date __________ Hour __________

Ideas 14b

Pollination

Directions: Arrange the following sentences so that they describe the normal sequence of pollination and fertilization. Arrange the sentences in order by writing *1* by the event that occurs first, *2* by the event that occurs second, and so forth.

3 ______ The pollen tube grows.

2 ______ Something (insect, wind) transfers pollen to a stigma. ***pollination***

1 ______ The flower produces pollen in its anthers.

5 ______ An ovule develops into a seed containing an embryo.

4 ______ Male gametes enter an ovule. ***fertilization***

Write *pollination* beside the sentence above that defines pollination.

Write *fertilization* beside the sentence above that defines fertilization.

Ideas 14c

Scattering Seeds

Directions: Record your responses in the spaces provided.

1. How can decaying fruit help seeds to sprout and grow? ***It can enrich the soil by providing nutrients.***

2. How can a bird unknowingly spread the seeds of its favorite fruit tree by eating the seeds? ***They may pass unharmed through its digestive tract to be deposited elsewhere.***

3. Give an example of a plant whose seeds are dispersed by wind. ***dandelion, tumbleweed (Students may give other correct answers.)***

4. Give an example of a plant whose seeds are dispersed by water. ***water lily, coconut (Students may give other correct answers.)***

5. Why is it important for a plant not to have its seeds accumulate all in one place? ***There would not be enough nutrients, water, and light for them all to survive.***

Review

Directions: Write the proper terms next to the following clues. Then find and circle the terms in the word puzzle below the clues. In the word puzzle the terms may appear horizontally, vertically, or diagonally and may be forward or backward.

sepals 1. The outermost flower parts that often resembles leaves

fruit 2. A ripened ovary

stigma 3. The top, outermost part of a carpel

anther 4. The flower part where pollen develops

stamen 5. A male reproductive part of a flower

carpels 6. The female reproductive parts of a flower

petals 7. Usually the most colorful parts of a flower

diploid 8. Describes an organism that has two copies of each chromosome in each of its cells

gametes 9. Special sex cells designed to transfer or receive chromosomes

flowers 10. The reproductive organs of many plants

seeds 11. Contain embryos, stored food, and a protective coat

pollination 12. Transferring pollen to a stigma

runners 13. Structures involved in asexual reproduction of strawberries

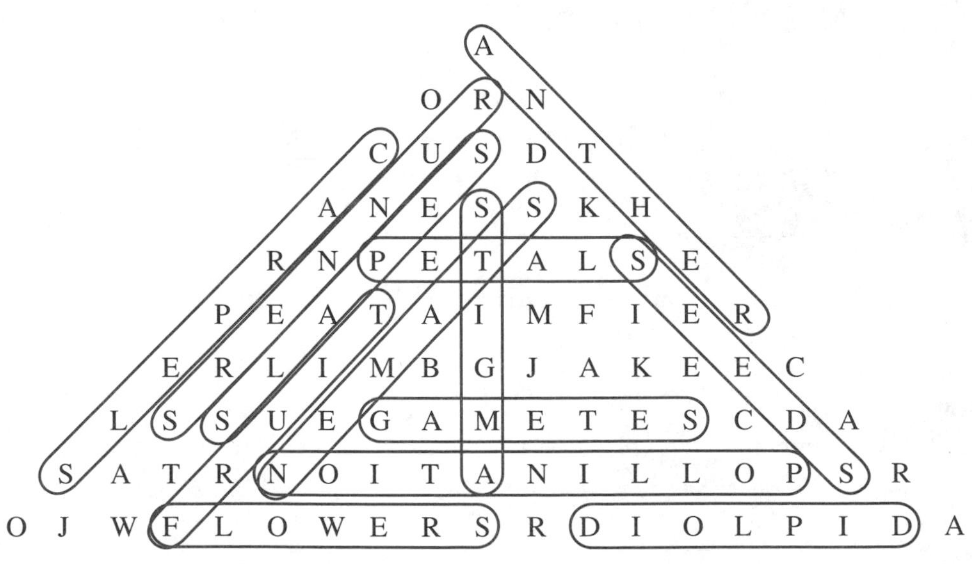

Name ______________________

Date ____________ Hour ______________

Class Investigation 14a

Dissection of a Flower

You can obtain flowers from local gardens or a florist, or you can grow them for this exercise.

Avoid the composite flowers, such as carnations, daisies, dandelions, and mums. You can use these flowers, but they will require some research on the part of the students and will also require magnification in order to be studied.
Roses, gladioluses, hibiscuses, petunias, geraniums, African violets, tulips, daffodils, orchids, hollyhocks, most fruit or vegetable blooms, apple or other fruit tree blossoms, and many others will make good dissection materials.

Goals

- Identify the parts of a flower.
- Observe some of the variations in flower parts.

Materials

fresh flowers, probes, scalpel or single-edged razor blade

Procedures and observations

1. Each group in your class will be assigned a number and given a different kind of flower. As you read the following questions, record your answers in the chart on the line for the number of your flower.
2. Without cutting, find as many flower parts as you can. Are any missing? Fill in your answer on the chart below.
3. Count the number of flower parts asked for in the chart below and record your findings. (If there are more than twenty-five of any one flower part, just record the word *many*.)

No.	Flower Name	Missing flower parts	Number of							Ovary placement*
			Sepals	Petals	Stamen	Stigmas	Ovaries	Ovary chambers	Ovules	
1.										
2.										
3.										
4.										
5.										
6.										
7.										
8.										
9.										
10.										
11.										
12.										
13.										
14.										
15.										

*__ABOVE__ or __IN__ the receptacle

Since students are making only one cut and the rest of the exercise consists of observations, you may be able to give instructions and then allow the students to work on their own while you carefully check their progress.

Home School Tip

A single student need dissect no more than five different flowers.

4. Locate and examine the carpel(s) and ovary(ies).
   - Is the ovary above the receptacle or in the receptacle? Record your answer in the "Ovary placement" space on the chart.
   - Using a very sharp scalpel or razor blade, cut the pistil and ovary from the top to the bottom. Examine the ovary.
   - Does the ovary have a single chamber or many chambers? Record your answer on the chart.
   - Locate and examine the ovules.
   - How many ovules are there? Record your answer on the chart. (If there are more than a dozen, write the word *many* on the chart.)
   - What do ovules become? ***They become seeds.***

Summing up

Go to the other groups in your class and observe the flowers they dissected. On your chart, fill in information for these flowers.

Name ____________________

Date __________ Hour __________

Class Investigation 14b

Factors that Affect Germination

You should start this exercise several days before starting Chapter 14 in class. This will give you time to hand out the beans, have students expose them to various factors, and have the seeds ready to plant on the first day that you discuss Chapter 14. You may not need to observe the seeds for a full two weeks to obtain enough data to complete the investigation.

Goals

- Determine whether seeds are alive.
- Identify the effects of various factors on the ability of seeds to sprout and grow.
- Gain experience in recording observations accurately.

Materials

bean seeds, potting soil, potting tray(s), labels, factors to be used in the experiment (See box below.)

When students are choosing factors that their bean seeds will be exposed to, make sure that all of the groups do not choose the factors that will be the most extreme and the most harmful to the seeds. Some of the groups should expose their seeds to the minor factors in order to give good answers and draw proper conclusions in the Summing Up section.

Setting up

Your teacher will divide the class into several groups and will give each group twenty seeds. Each group will choose one of the factors from the list of suggestions below and will apply its factor to all twenty of its seeds.

Procedures and observations

1. All the groups should plant their seeds at the same time. Your teacher will plant twenty seeds that were not exposed to any factor to serve as the control group.
2. Plant the seeds in large potting trays. All seeds should be planted oriented in the same direction and about 1.3 cm (0.5 in.) deep in the soil. If possible, plant all the seeds for the entire class in different rows of the same large planting tray.
3. Label the rows of seeds according to the factor they experienced.
4. Water the seeds enough to keep the soil moist but not too wet.
5. Place the plant tray(s) in a sunny, warm spot.

A large planting tray can be constructed of wood. It needs to be only 8 to10 cm (3 or 4 in.) deep. The size of the tray depends on the number of groups you have in your class. Plan to allow about 8 cm (3 in.) between rows of seeds. Twenty seeds will require a row that is about 40 to 50 cm (16 to 20 in.) long. You can line the planting tray with plastic; be sure to have some drainage holes in the plastic. Overwatering is a common problem. If you choose to plant your seeds in different containers, make sure the conditions are as nearly identical as possible in the various containers.

Factors

Below is a list of factors that you can use in this experiment. Perhaps you can think of additional factors. Each group in your class should choose one factor to test.

Hydrogen peroxide Soak the seeds in hydrogen peroxide for one, five, ten, or twenty-four hours. (Choose one.)

Radiation Irradiated seed sets available from science supply companies provide seeds that have been exposed to various amounts of radiation.

Microwaves Expose the seeds to microwaves in a microwave oven at low setting for five, ten, fifteen, or thirty seconds. (Choose one.)

High temperature Expose the seeds to temperatures of 300°, 350°, or 400°F in a conventional oven for five, ten, or fifteen minutes. (Choose one combination.)

Refrigeration Place the seeds in a refrigerator for five minutes, one hour, five hours, or twenty-four hours. (Choose one.)

Freezing Place the seeds in a freezer for five minutes, one hour, five hours, or twenty-four hours. (Choose one.)

Water Soak the seeds in water for one, five, ten, or twenty-four hours. (Choose one.)

Alcohol Soak the seeds in rubbing alcohol for one, five, ten, or twenty-four hours. (Choose one.)

Petroleum jelly Coat the outside of the seeds with petroleum jelly.

Liquid fertilizer Soak the seeds in water containing liquid fertilizer (at the strength recommended for lawn use) for one, five, ten, or twenty-four hours. (Choose one.)

Weed killer Soak the seeds in water containing weed killer for one, five, ten, or twenty-four hours. (Choose one.)

Bleach Soak the seeds in water containing bleach for one, five, ten, or twenty-four hours. (Choose one.)

Sunlight Expose the seeds to direct sunlight for one day, five days, or ten days. (Choose one.)

As an alternative you could germinate the seeds in seed rolls. Roll the seeds up in several layers of paper towels and moisten the towels. The disadvantage to this method is that observations of leaves after two weeks will not be reliable because they tend to be malformed or die when grown for extended lengths of time in seed rolls. But, if you are recording only germination, the method is fine.

Each group should record the data for their treatment on one row of the summary chart. On the last day of observations you should oversee the sharing of this data. Remember to plant and observe the control group.

6. Observe the seeds daily. Record your daily observations in your notebook. On the chart below, summarize your observations of your experimental group on one line.

Summing up

On the last day of observations, the teacher will lead the class in compiling the data on the following chart. Make sure you copy the information onto this chart as your class discusses it.

Summary Chart

Factor	Total number of sprouts after two weeks	Number of days for first sprout to appear	Average height of leaves at the end of two weeks	Average number of leaves at the end of two weeks	Other observations
Control					

If you use dry beans from a grocery store, be sure to verify that they will germinate before beginning this investigation. There are other experiments that will use bean seeds. Buying in quantity is less expensive, but you will not want to buy more than one year's supply of seeds at a time.

Consider appointing two students from every group to observe the bean seedlings daily and report to the class. This will alleviate crowded conditions that could arise at the planting tray with the whole class trying to observe the seedlings at the same time.

Home School Tip

With your help, a single student could test approximately five of the factors plus a control group.

1. Which factor(s) in this experiment caused the seeds to sprout *more quickly* than the seeds in the control group? ***Answers will vary. Soaking the seeds in water and hydrogen peroxide may speed sprouting.***

2. Which factor(s) in this experiment caused the seeds to sprout *more slowly* than the seeds in the control group? ***Answers will vary. Radiation, high temperatures, microwaves, petroleum jelly, and other factors may delay sprouting.***

3. Which factor(s) caused significantly *more* seeds to sprout in the experimental groups than in the control group? ***Answer will vary. Few, if any, of these factors will increase the number of sprouts.***

Name ____________________
Date __________ Hour __________

4. Which factor(s) caused significantly *fewer* seeds to sprout in the experimental groups than in the control group? ***Answers will vary. Radiation, heat, microwaves, and weed killer are some factors that may cause fewer seeds to sprout.***

5. Which factor(s) in this experiment had *little or no effect* on the number of seeds that sprouted? ***Answers will vary. Water and short exposures to heat and cold are some factors that will not affect sprouting.***

6. Based on your observations, do you think that the bean seeds were alive when the factors were applied to them? ☒ Yes ☐ No Explain your answer. ***The seeds must have been alive because they began to grow. They demonstrated that they were alive by having the attribute of life.***

7. What did you notice about the seeds before they were planted that indicated they were alive? ***Answers will vary. By observation, nothing indicated that they were alive.***

8. Why do you think the seeds in some groups did not sprout or sprouted more slowly than those in the control group? ***Certain factors damaged or killed the seeds.***

9. What other significant or unusual conclusions can you make based on observations of the bean seeds that your class planted? ***Answers will vary.***

10. Do you think that your conclusions about bean seeds are true of seeds in general? ☐ Yes ☐ No Why or why not? ***Answers will vary. Some students may feel that the other seeds need to be tested.***

If you use an irradiated seed set, then be sure to purchase nonirradiated seeds for the other factors from the same supplier. It would be invalid to compare the results of the different factors if the seeds used for each factor came from different sources. Irradiated seeds can also be used in Class Investigation 8a.

Another factor would be to use a heating cable to provide bottom heat to the potting tray. Such cables are available from garden supply stores and through seed catalogs.

Home School Tip

You may find a dentist or x-ray technician who is willing to x-ray some seeds for you. However, it is usually a great inconvenience for them to do this. Irradiated seed sets currently cost about $13.

Name ______________________
Date ____________ Hour ____________

15–Invertebrates I: Sponges, Jellyfish, and Worms

Ideas 15a

Sponges and Jellyfish

Directions: Read the following descriptions and decide whether a sponge or jellyfish is being described. In the space by each statement, write *S* if it describes a sponge, *J* if it describes a jellyfish, and *SJ* if it describes both.

SJ 1. Has no backbone

S 2. Body filled with pores

J 3. Has a water skeleton

J 4. Possesses tentacles

S 5. Is a filter feeder

SJ 6. Most live in oceans

S 7. Classified in phylum Porifera

J 8. Digests food in a gastrovascular cavity

J 9. Can sting you with nematocysts

S 10. Skeleton made of spongin or spicules

SJ 11. Classified in Kingdom Animalia

S 12. Has collar cells with flagella

Ideas 15b

The Planarian: A Type of Flatworm

Directions: In the spaces below, write the words that are described by the following statements.

1. F R E E - L I V I N G
2. B I L A T E R A L
3. G A N G L I O N
4. G A S T R O D E R M
5. W A S T E S
6. N E U R O N S
7. N E R V E
8. S T I M U L U S

1. Not permanently attached to an object
2. Body symmetry in which one side is like a mirrored copy of the other side
3. A simple brain
4. Secretes digestive enzymes in the intestine
5. Removed by flame cells and excretory pores
6. Long, thin cells that run through the body and carry impulses from place to place
7. A collection of neurons wrapped in protective coverings
8. Something an organism can sense

Ideas 15c

The Planarian's Digestive System

Directions: Arrange the following sentences so that they describe the normal process of planarian digestion. Put the sentences in order by writing the correct numbers in the blanks provided.

2 ______ The gastroderm secretes enzymes.

4 ______ The cells of the gastroderm absorb the small pieces of food, and cellular digestion begins.

1 ______ The planarian attacks food and pulls it through the mouth into its intestine.

5 ______ Nutrients are absorbed into the tissues of the planarian from the cells of the gastroderm.

6 ______ Indigestible material is pushed out through the mouth.

3 ______ Enzymes break food down into small pieces.

Name ______________________
Date __________ Hour __________

Ideas 15d

The Earthworm's Digestive System

Directions: Label the following drawing by supplying the missing terms or definitions and then drawing a line from each term to the proper structure in the drawing.

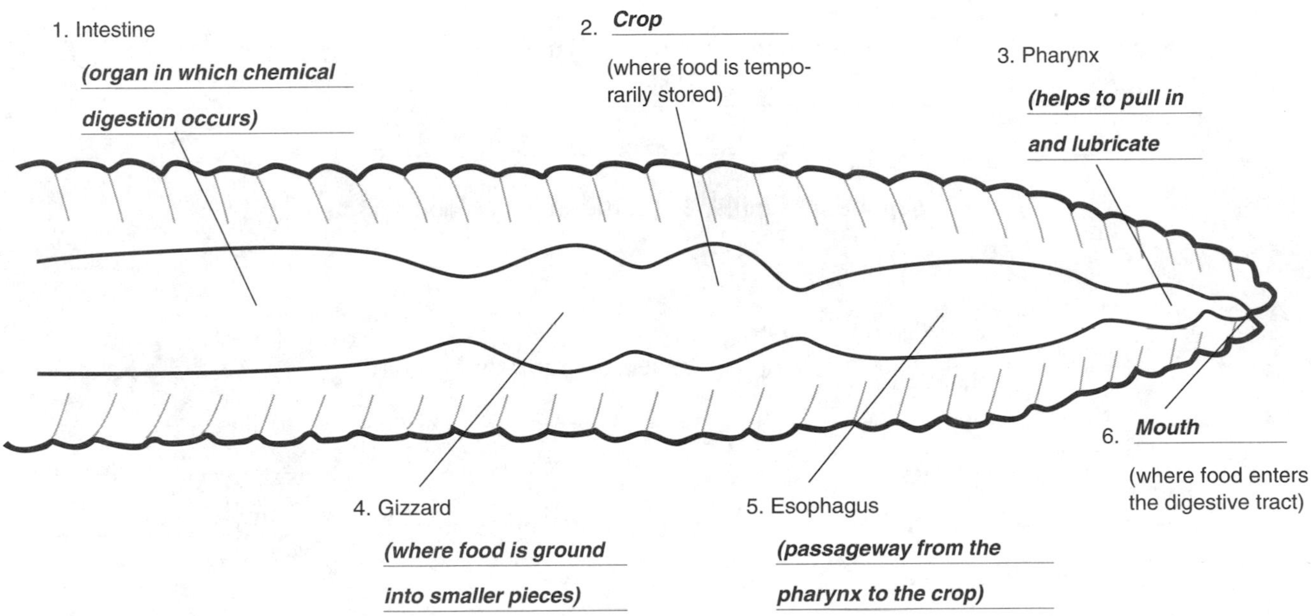

Ideas 15e

The Earthworm and Other Segmented Worms

Directions: Below are several groups of words. In each group three of the four words (or phrases) are related to one another. Draw a line through the unrelated word and then write a sentence using the remaining words. Your sentence should show how the words are related. (You may slightly change the form of the word in your sentence.)

1. bristles / ~~flagella~~ / muscles / earthworm *An earthworm moves by using its muscles and bristles.*

2. neurons / ganglia / impulses / ~~cuticle~~ *Neurons carry impulses between ganglia and sensory receptors.*

3. ~~nephridia~~ / capillaries / aortic arches / blood vessels *An earthworm's circulatory system consists of blood vessels, capillaries, and aortic arches.*

4. pharynx / esophagus / ~~sensory receptor~~ / gizzard *An earthworm's food passes from its mouth to the pharynx, to the esophagus, then to the gizzard.*

5. earthworm / leeches / segments / ~~planaria~~ *The body plan of earthworms and leeches is segmented.*

Name ______________________
Date __________ Hour __________

Class Investigation 15a

Earthworm Dissection

Students should carefully read the material in the box on page 180 before beginning this investigation. Instruct them not to play with the equipment.

Goals

- Learn how to dissect.
- Learn about the structures of an earthworm.

Materials

dissection pan, dissection pins, preserved earthworm, probes, scissors, scalpel or single-edged razor blade

BJUP carries a dissection kit that includes the specimens as well as the tools and instructions needed to dissect a frog, an earthworm, a crayfish, and a perch. A videocassette is also available from BJUP that shows the dissection of these four animals. Actual dissection by the student is preferable.

Procedures and observations

Examine the earthworm's exterior

1. Find the clitellum, which is the smooth enlarged area on the body of the worm. This structure is closest to the "head" end of your earthworm.
2. Notice that the earthworm has many segments. Count the number of segments from the tip of the "head" to the clitellum. How many are there? *There are thirty-two segments.*
3. Carefully feel for the earthworm's bristles. The bristles are located on the lower side of the earthworm. Determine which surface of the earthworm is the upper surface and which is the lower surface.
4. Place the earthworm in the dissection pan; place its lower surface down.
5. Often you can see a dark line extending down the middle of the earthworm's upper surface. This is the dorsal blood vessel. (See page 237 of your text.)

Aristotle wrote that earthworms grew spontaneously (spontaneous generation) from mud and humid ground, that eels emerged out of earthworms, and that if you cut an earthworm open you may occasionally find eels. This seems humorous to us, but before observation and scientific inquiry were used, such speculations were considered facts. Challenge your students to disprove Aristotle.

Open the earthworm's body

1. With your scissors cut a small opening (1 mm long) in front of the clitellum.
2. Insert the point of your scissors into the slit and cut an opening along the middle of the earthworm's back. Cut just to the side of the dorsal blood vessel. You can see the dorsal blood vessel if you lift the cut edge of the body wall with your probes. Be sure you are cutting only the body wall!
3. Carefully pull apart the sections of the body wall. Note the partitions inside the body. These partitions separate the inside of the earthworm's body. Use a probe to break apart these partitions.
4. Pull the body walls back; insert pins through the body walls and into the wax of the dissection pan. Place the pins into segments 5, 10, 15, 20, and 25. The earthworm's reproductive structures are light-colored masses in segments 9-12.* The reproductive structures lie over the aortic arches. (See pages 236-37 of your text.) Carefully remove the reproductive structures but do not destroy the aortic arches, the dorsal blood vessel, or the digestive system structures beneath.

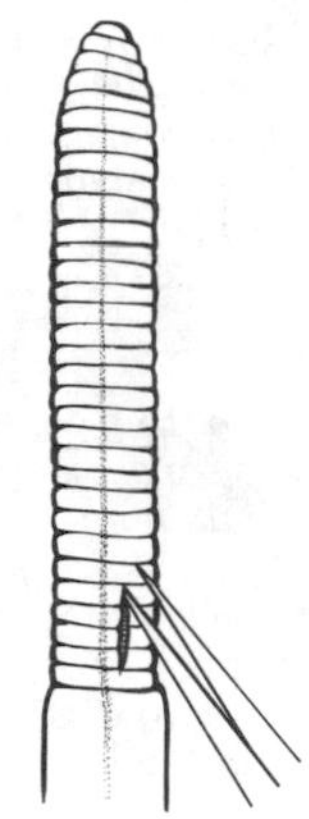

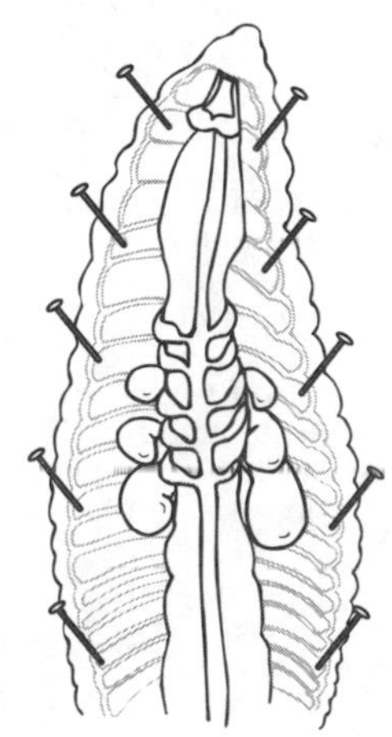

*Locations for the particular structures may vary somewhat. The segment numbers given tell the approximate locations.

5. Find all the aortic arches. They are located near segment 10. The aortic arches come in pairs, one on each side of the earthworm. How many pairs of aortic arches are there? ***There are five pairs of aortic arches.***

6. Locate the dorsal blood vessel in segments 20-25. Move the intestine carefully to one side and locate the ventral blood vessel.
   The dorsal blood vessel pumps blood in which direction? ***It pumps blood forward.***

   The ventral blood vessel pumps blood in which direction? ***It pumps blood backward.***

7. What type of circulatory system does the earthworm have?
   ☐ open ☒ closed Describe this type of circulatory system. ***In this type of circulatory system, the blood never leaves the blood vessels.***

Home School Tip

Although you can use fresh earthworms (killed with alcohol), the preserved ones that you can purchase are far superior. You can purchase as few as ten for less than $4 from BJUP. A preserved earthworm is included in the BJUP dissection kit.

Take the students step by step through this exercise. Have one of them read the instruction aloud. You can comment on it and answer any questions. Let the students then pick up the tools and follow the instruction. Most students would not be able to do this exercise by themselves with the limited instructions given here. The students who race ahead usually have poor dissections.

You may want to give two grades on this exercise: one on the dissection and another on the answers to the questions. Giving these two grades may encourage a serious approach to dissection. This, however, will require you to examine each student's dissection before the organisms are thrown away.

Supply one earthworm for every two students. One earthworm per student is advisable if you are grading the dissections as well as the answers to the questions. Allowing more than two students to work on a single earthworm is not advisable.

Procedures and Tools for Dissection

Never use the dissection equipment for anything other than dissection. Since this equipment can be very dangerous, **do not** play with it.
Do not carve in the wax or foam pad of the dissection pan.
Before you begin a dissection, read the entire investigation thoroughly. In your textbook, look up pictures of the organism that you will be dissecting.
Reread the directions before you begin to cut.
Be sure that you have identified the proper structure before you cut.
When you are told to cut something but you are not told which tool to use, you must decide whether to use the scissors or the scalpel (razor blade).
When you are finished with your specimen, wrap it in a paper towel and place it in the trash can.
If you must keep your specimen overnight, wrap it in a wet paper towel and place it in a plastic bag. Gently remove most of the air from the bag and tightly close it.

Locate the following organs of the digestive system

Tell which segments the following organs are located in and describe their functions.

1. Pharynx ***located in segments 4-5; sucks in food***
2. Esophagus ***located in segments 6-14; passageway from the pharynx to the crop***
3. Crop ***located in segments 15-16; temporary storage chamber for food***
4. Gizzard ***located in segments 17-18; grinds food (mechanical digestion)***
5. Intestine ***located in segments 19-anus; chemical digestion and absorption***

Name ______________________________

Date ______________ Hour ______________

Research Investigation 15b

Other Sponges, Jellyfish, and Worms

You may want to have the students responsible for finding the information for only ten of the animals listed. If so, then do three in class as examples.

Materials

encyclopedia or other reference book

Procedures and observations

The table below lists some other examples of the invertebrates studied in Chapter 15. Use encyclopedias and other reference books to find the missing information needed to complete the table. Some of the more difficult answers have been provided.

Some annelids appear to have radial symmetry at first, but close examination reveals that they have bilateral symmetry.

	Animal	Phylum	Symmetry: radial or bilateral	Parasite: yes or no	Type of food
1.	Redbeard Sponge	*Porifera*	*radial*	*no*	*filters particles from water*
2.	Portuguese Man-of-War	*Cnidaria*	bilateral	*no*	*marine organisms*
3.	Box Jellyfish (sea wasp)	*Cnidaria*	*radial*	*no*	*marine organisms*
4.	Anemone	*Cnidaria*	*radial*	*no*	*marine organisms*
5.	Brain Coral	*Cnidaria*	*radial*	*no*	*microscopic marine organisms*
6.	Liver Fluke	*Platyhelminthes*	bilateral	*yes*	*parasite of animals*
7.	Marine Flatworm (Turbellarian)	*Platyhelminthes*	*bilateral*	*no*	small marine organisms
8.	Hookworm	*Nematoda*	*bilateral*	*yes*	*humans*
9.	Vinegar Eel	*Nematoda*	bilateral	*no*	*fungus in cider/vinegar*
10.	Leech	*Annelida*	*bilateral*	*yes*	*human and animal blood*
11.	Sandworm	*Annelida*	*bilateral*	*no*	*small marine organisms*
12.	Lugworm	*Annelida*	*bilateral*	*no*	*organic matter in sand*
13.	Fanworm ("feather duster")	*Annelida*	bilateral	*no*	*filters particles from water*

Name ____________________
Date ________ Hour ________

16–Invertebrates II: Mollusks, Arthropods, and Echinoderms

Ideas 16a

Mollusks

Directions: Read the following descriptions and decide whether a clam, octopus, or snail is being described. In the space by each statement, place *C* if it describes a clam, *O* if it describes an octopus, and *S* if it describes a snail. Some descriptions will have more than one answer.

cos 1. Exceptionally soft body

o 2. Suction discs

cs 3. Has shell(s)

c 4. Filters food from water

o 5. Color changes with mental state

s 6. Univalve

o 7. "Smoke screen"

c 8. Bivalve

co 9. Siphon

cos 10. Food for humans

Ideas 16b

Insect Life Cycles

Consider reviewing the Thinking Critically facet: Life Cycles (Chapter 3, page 49 in the textbook).

Students will find the term nymph *in Figure 16B-5 on page 250 of the text.*

Egg cases are not shown in these diagrams.

Directions: Below are diagrams of the two types of metamorphoses commonly found in insects. On the lines below the diagrams indicate which type of metamorphosis is being illustrated. Add arrows to the curved lines to show the order in which metamorphosis occurs. Then label the stages of metamorphosis on the lines provided.

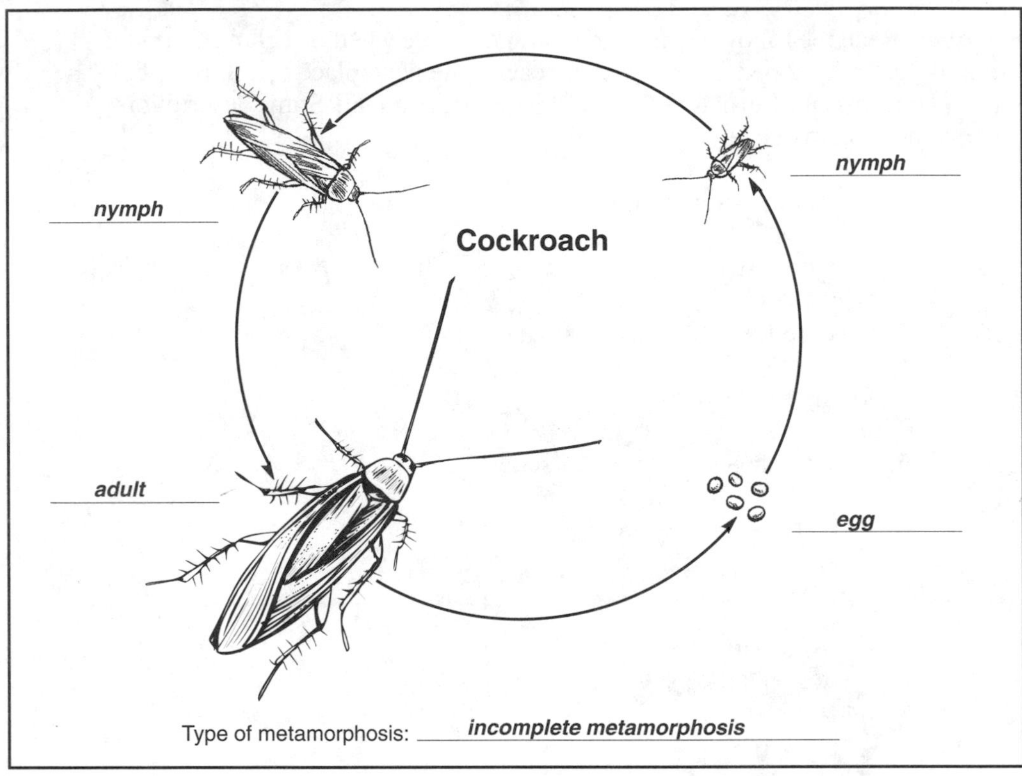

Type of metamorphosis: ***incomplete metamorphosis***

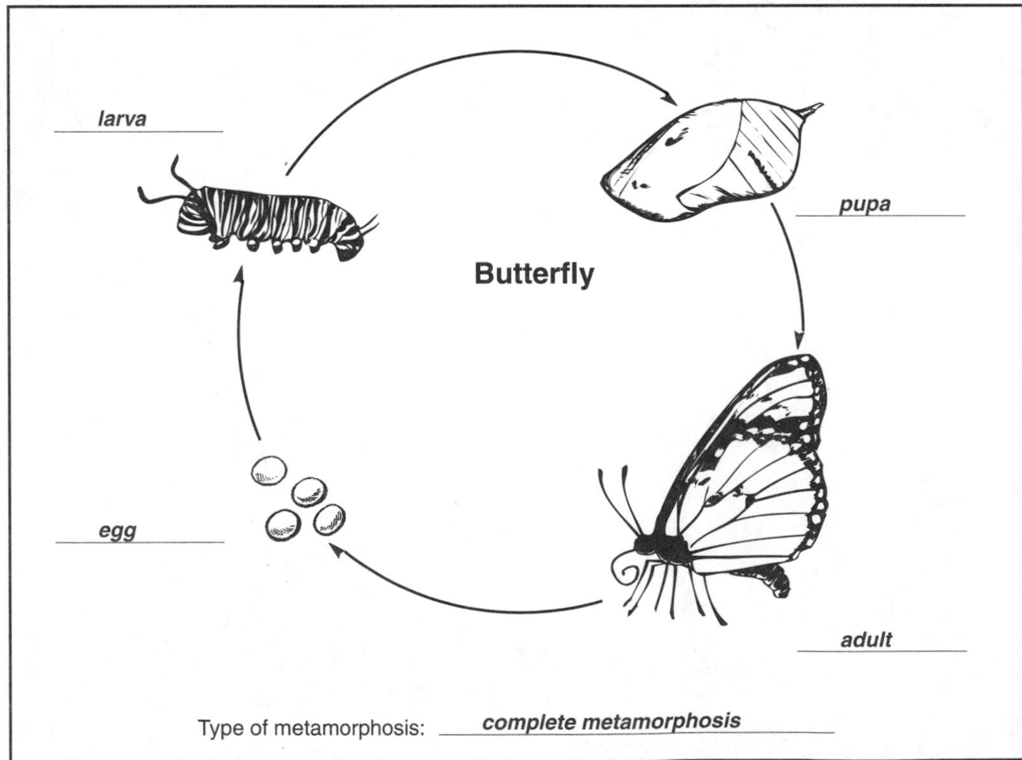

Type of metamorphosis: ***complete metamorphosis***

Name ______________________

Date ____________ Hour ____________

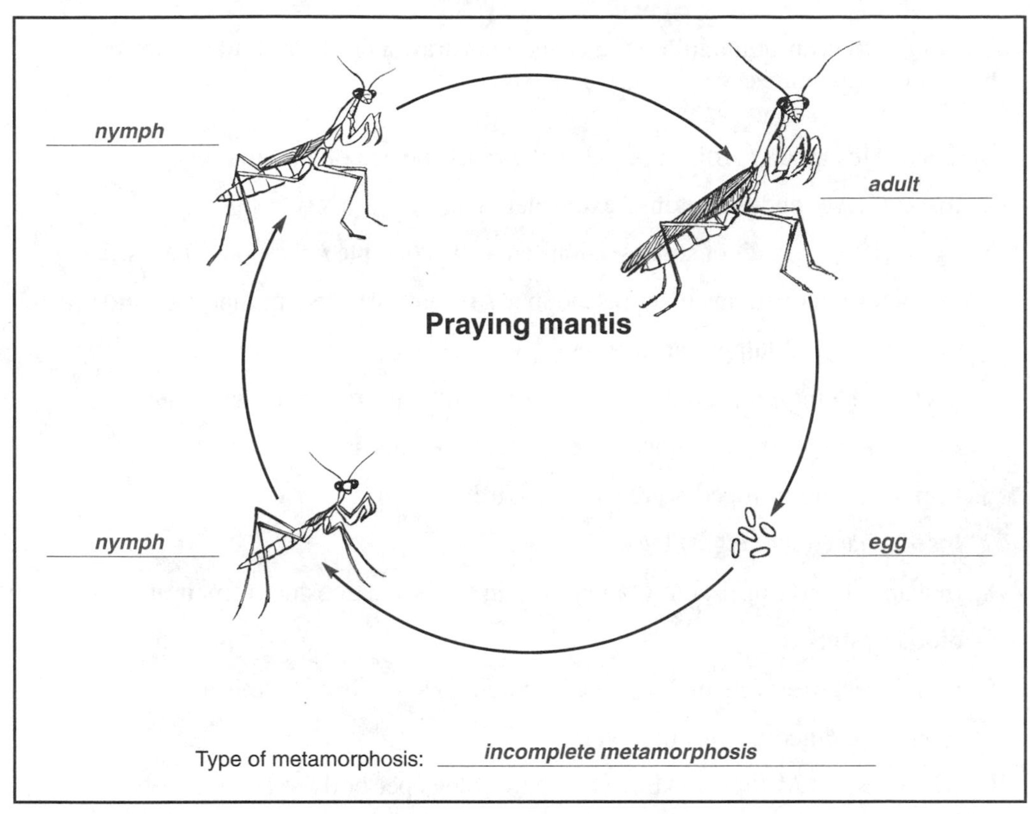

nymph
adult
Praying mantis
nymph
egg
Type of metamorphosis: incomplete metamorphosis

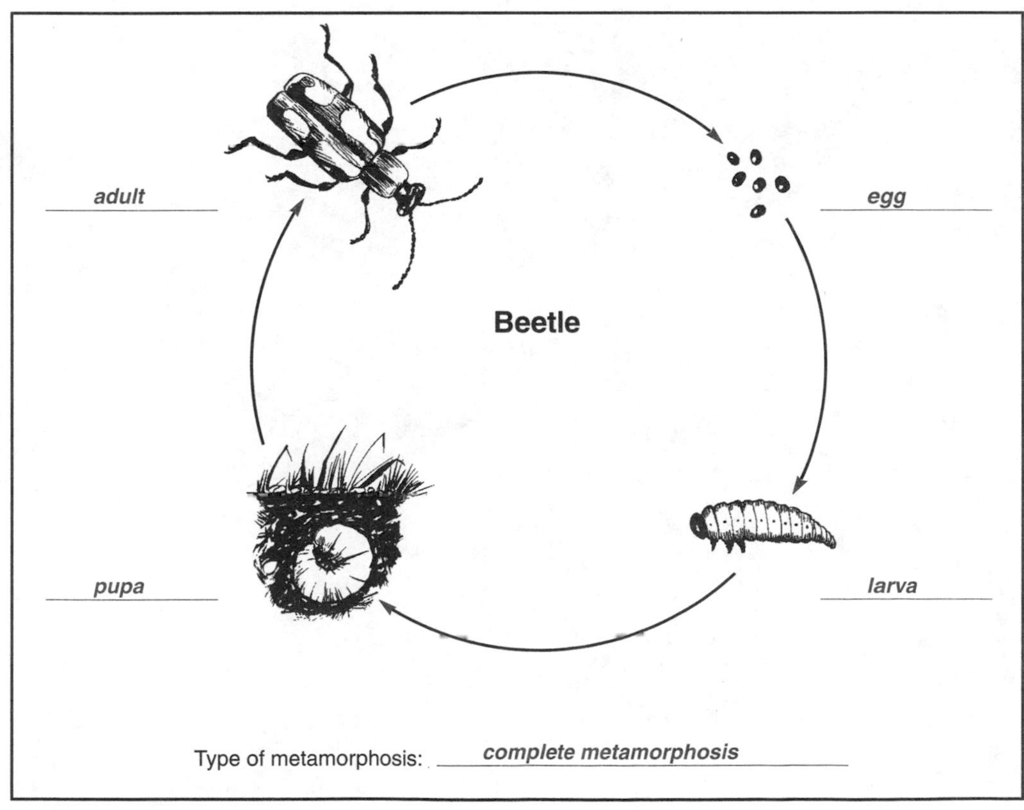

adult
egg
Beetle
pupa
larva
Type of metamorphosis: complete metamorphosis

Ideas 16c

Arthropods

Directions: In each of the following statements draw a circle around the correct choice in the parentheses.

1. Class (Hexapoda / Arthropoda) has the most species of any animal class.
2. Insects have (endoskeletons / exoskeletons).
3. Eyes with thousands of small sections are called (simple / compound) eyes.
4. Spiracles are openings in a grasshopper's respiratory system that lead into the (tracheas / Malpighian tubules).
5. Insects that molt repeatedly and become a little more mature with each molt exhibit (complete / incomplete) metamorphosis.
6. Barnacles and millipedes are (insects / arthropods).
7. Insects have (six / eight) legs.
8. In a/an (closed / open) circulatory system the blood does not remain in blood vessels.
9. If an insect life cycle includes a caterpillar, then the life cycle is a/an (complete / incomplete) life cycle.
10. (Centipedes / Millipedes) have one pair of legs per body segment.

Name ____________________
Date ____________ Hour ____________

Review

Directions: Below is a list of scrambled words. Unscramble the words and write them on the lines to the right of the words. Then match them to the clues given below by writing the proper letters in the blanks by the clues.

a. lettacens — *tentacles*

b. dilpelmie — *millipede*

c. texosleonek — *exoskeleton*

d. bute tefe — *tube feet*

e. phonis — *siphon*

f. hidemoecrns — *echinoderms*

g. creathas — *tracheas*

h. dopmucno — *compound*

i. livesvab — *bivalves*

j. aupp — *pupa*

k. ltmo — *molt*

l. moelpect / ratmmossihoep — *complete metamorphosis*

b 1. Arthropod that has two pairs of legs per body segment

c 2. A hard outer covering that supports and protects

a 3. The long, flexible, armlike structures of an octopus

d 4. Structures that help starfish move and hold on to things

g 5. Breathing tubes in insects

i 6. Clams, scallops, and mussels; but not snails

f 7. Starfish and sea urchins

l 8. Life cycle that includes a cocoon, chrysalis, or puparium

h 9. The eyes of an insect

e 10. Part of the jet propulsion system of an octopus

k 11. To shed and replace an exoskeleton

j 12. Resting stage of metamorphosis

Name ______________________
Date ____________ Hour ______________

Research Investigation 16a

Sea Monsters, Fact or Fiction?

The classic story *Twenty Thousand Leagues Under the Sea* follows the adventures of Captain Nemo and his submarine the *Nautilus* as they travel the seas. Published in 1869, this story was futuristic science fiction. It incorporated the newest technology of the day, submarines and electricity for example. Jules Verne, the author, showed great insight into what modern technology would develop. But how would Jules Verne deal with the topic of sea monsters? In the late 1800s people believed that sea monsters existed. He took what was known and filled in what was unknown with his imagination. Sometimes he guessed right, sometimes wrong.

Materials

encyclopedia or other reference book

Directions: Read the following excerpt from Chapter 18 of *Twenty Thousand Leagues Under the Sea*, which records a description of a giant cuttlefish they were about to battle. (A cuttlefish is a type of mollusk similar to squid and octopus.) Then, consult encyclopedias and other reference books to determine which parts of Verne's description of the cuttlefish could be true and which parts are false. Use the table on the next page as a guide.

I looked in my turn, and could not repress a gesture of disgust. Before my eyes was a horrible monster, worthy to figure in the legends of the marvellous. It was an immense cuttle-fish, being eight yards long. It swam crossways in the direction of the *Nautilus* with great speed, watching us with its enormous staring green eyes. Its eight arms, or rather feet, fixed to its head, that have given the name of cephalopod to these animals, were twice as long as its body, and were twisted like the furies' hair. One could see 250 air-holes on the inner side of the tentacles. The monster's mouth, a horned beak like a parrot's, opened and shut vertically. Its tongue, a horned substance, furnished with several rows of pointed teeth, came out quivering from this veritable pair of shears. What a freak of nature, a bird's beak on a mollusc! Its spindle-like body formed a fleshy mass that might weigh 4,000 to 5,000 lbs. The varying colour changing with great rapidity, according to the irritation of the animal, passed successively from livid grey to reddish brown. What irritated this mollusc? No doubt the presence of the *Nautilus,* more formidable than itself, and on which its suckers or its jaws had no hold. Yet, what monsters these poulps are! what vitality the Creator has given them! what vigour in their movements! and they possess three hearts! Chance had brought us in presence of this cuttle-fish, and I did not wish to lose the opportunity of carefully studying this specimen of cephalopods. I overcame the horror that inspired me; and, taking a pencil, began to draw it.

Description	True? Yes/No	If False Give Correct Description
Eight yards long	*No*	*maximum reported length is 35 inches*
Fast swimmer	*Yes*	
Green eyes	*possibly*	*eyes can change color*
Eight arms	*Yes*	*8 arms and 2 retractable tentacles*
Arms twice as long as body	*Yes*	
250 air holes on inner surface of tentacles	*No*	*tentacles have no air holes*
Beaked mouth	*Yes*	
Horned or toothed tongue	*Yes*	
4,000 to 5,000 lbs.	*No*	*at 35 inches, the maximum weight would be no more than 40 lbs.*
Can change color	*Yes*	
Suckers (on arms)	*Yes*	
Three hearts	*possibly*	*has three separated heart chambers*

Name ______________________
Date ____________ Hour ____________

Class Investigation 16b

Butterfly Metamorphosis

Goals

- Observe the stages of complete metamorphosis.
- Learn about the life cycle of a butterfly.

Materials

containers for growing larvae and hatching butterflies, painted lady butterfly larvae, suitable food source

Note: This investigation is written for use with the painted lady butterfly (*Vanessa cardui*), a small common butterfly that is available from biological supply companies. If you use other species of butterflies, you may need to alter the directions.

Procedures and observations

Raise the larvae

1. Place several larvae in a container with a suitable food source. In the wild, these caterpillars would pull the edges of a leaf together with themselves inside and would then begin eating the leaf. If you have purchased your caterpillars, they probably have come with a food source. Thistles are a favorite food of painted lady butterfly caterpillars.
2. Place the container in a well-lighted, warm area. The caterpillars should not be in direct sunlight, and the temperature should not go above 25°C (77°F).
3. Observe your caterpillars daily and record your observations on a separate sheet of paper. Note such things as changes in size, shape, and activity.
4. After a time of feeding and growing, the caterpillars will climb to the top of the container and will hang from it. They will then form a chrysalis.

Observe the chrysalis

1. How many days did you observe the caterpillars before the first one formed a chrysalis? ***It takes five to ten days at normal room temperatures.***
2. Describe the shape, size, color, and other characteristics of the chrysalis. ***Answers will vary. It looks like a brownish piece of twig hanging by a thread.***
3. How many days did you observe the caterpillars before the last one formed a chrysalis? ***Answers will vary.***
4. Take the chrysalises and place them in a larger container.
5. How many days did you observe the chrysalises before any adults emerged? ***The pupa stage lasts about seven to ten days.***
6. Once an adult comes out, observe the other chrysalises carefully. Try to observe a butterfly emerging from a chrysalis. On a separate sheet of paper describe the process. Tell what part of the butterfly came out first,

The painted lady butterfly was chosen because its life cycle is short and because it can feed on an artificial medium. This artificial medium is available from the biological supply company where you obtain the larvae. By using the artificial medium, you will not need to hunt the proper food source for your caterpillars.

Thistles are a favorite food of painted lady butterfly caterpillars in the wild.

You may want to stop the investigation soon after the adults emerge. Keeping the adults in a cage or a terrarium that is large enough for them and keeping the plants in good condition in the cage is often difficult.

Place the chrysalises in a large terrarium with a screen or tightly fitting cloth top. Be sure there are some twigs or pieces of crumpled paper for the butterflies to climb on in the terrarium.

Most biological suppliers will send more complete instructions with the larvae. Adults should be fed with a 5% sugar solution (dissolve 5 g in 100 ml of water). The plant material is needed for the laying of eggs.

Larvae may form chrysalises in about an hour.

how long the butterfly took to come out, and how long it was out before it tried to fly.

Raise the adults

1. The adults will feed on a weak sugar solution placed in a bottle with a wick of paper towel sticking out of it. Place leaves, stems, or seedlings of mallow or hollyhock in the containers.
2. If these materials are supplied for them, the adults will mate and begin to lay eggs on the plant leaves within about a week.
3. The eggs are small, light green balls with lines on them. They will hatch in about a week.

Summing up

What did you learn about butterfly metamorphosis by observing this process that you did not know before? ***Answers will vary.*** ______

______

______

______

______

______

______

Which observation was the most fascinating to you? Why? ***Answers will vary.***

______

______

______

______

______

______

Name ______________________

Date __________ Hour __________

17–Vertebrates I: Fish, Amphibians, and Reptiles

Ideas 17a

Vertebrate Digestive System

Directions: Label the following drawings by supplying the missing term or definition, and then draw a line from each term to the proper structure in the drawing.

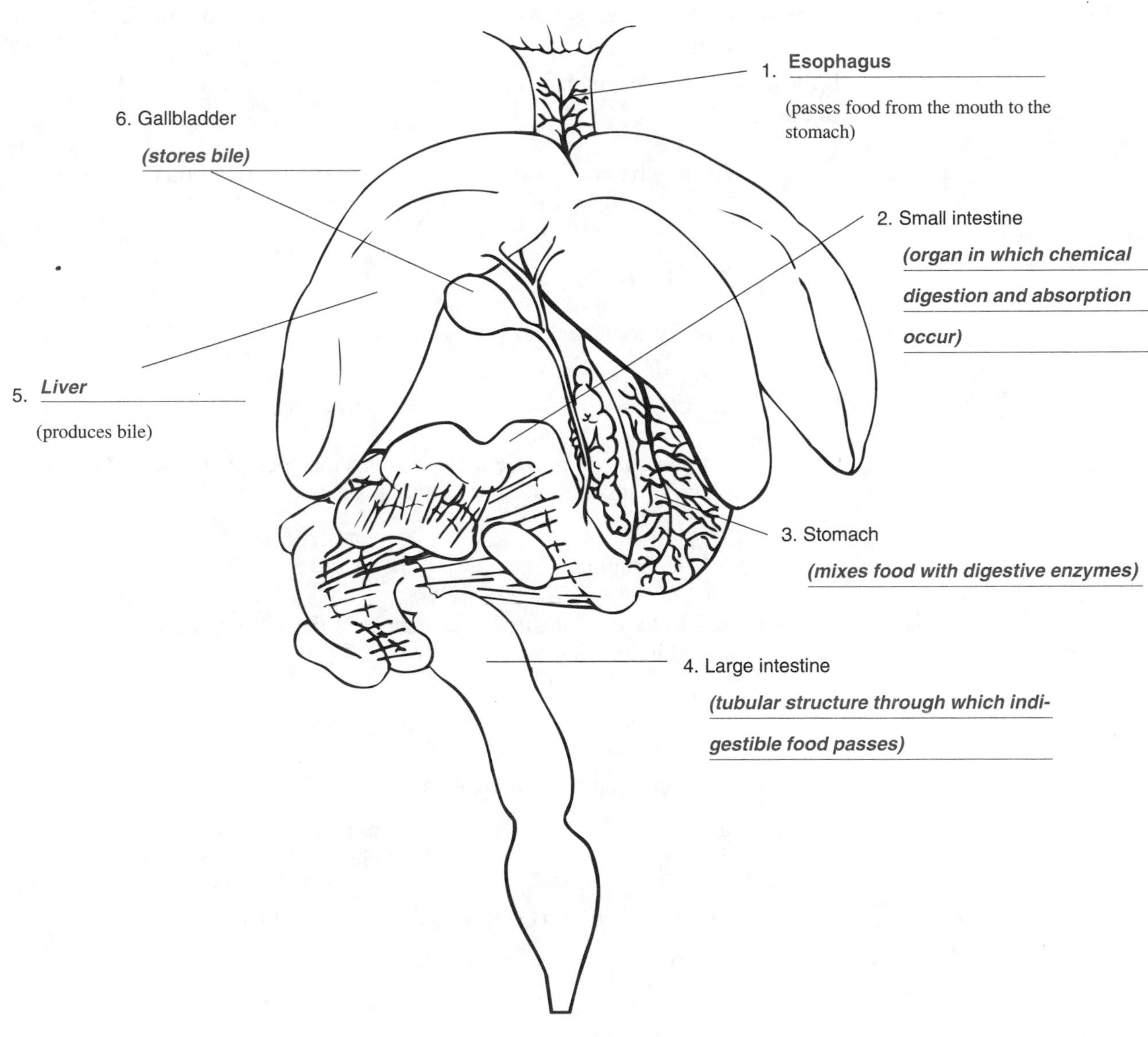

Ideas 17b

Body Systems in Vertebrate Animals

Directions: Choose the best answer to complete each of the following statements and record your choice in the blank by the number. Then use the letters of your answer (*a, b, c,* or *d)* with the key below to plot a trail on the map. If all your answers are correct and you correctly plot the trail, your trail will end in the state that answers the question below the map.

Key:

If the answer to a statement is *a,* draw a line 5° northward from your last stopping point.

If the answer to a statement is *b,* draw a line 5° southward from your last stopping point.

If the answer to a statement is *c,* draw a line 5° eastward from your last stopping point.

If the answer to a statement is *d,* draw a line 5° westward from your last stopping point.

a_____ 1. The air chambers inside an animal's body where blood can get oxygen and give off carbon dioxide are

a. lungs. c. nephridia.
b. spiracles. d. flame cells.

c_____ 2. Blood vessels that take the blood to the heart are called

a. capillaries. c. veins.
b. arteries. d. aortic arches.

b_____ 3. A dome-shaped muscle that separates the chest from the abdomen in many animals and in humans is the

a. mesoderm. c. ventricle.
b. diaphragm. d. air sac.

c_____ 4. A fluid tissue that carries substances both in its cells and dissolved in its liquid is

a. bile. c. blood.
b. enzymes. d. urine.

c_____ 5. Blood containing little oxygen is

a. yellow. c. red.
b. blue. d. clear.

b_____ 6. The central nervous system includes the brain and

a. skull. c. sensory receptors.
b. spinal cord. d. sensory organs.

d_____ 7. A structure between the atrium and ventricle that allows blood to go only one way is a(n)

a. artery. c. vein.
b. capillary. d. valve.

Name ______________________

Date ____________ Hour ____________

b ______ 8. Blood that carries an abundant amount of oxygen is

a. deoxygenated.
b. oxygenated.
c. unoxygenated.
d. thin.

d ______ 9. Spinal nerves branch off the

a. vertebrae.
b. brain.
c. muscles.
d. spinal cord.

a ______ 10. The normal process of forcing air into and out of the lungs is called

a. breathing.
b. sneezing.
c. coughing.
d. swallowing.

d ______ 11. Blood vessels that take the blood away from the heart are called

a. atriums.
b. veins.
c. capillaries.
d. arteries.

d ______ 12. The respiratory structures that have capillaries close to their surfaces to exchange oxygen and carbon dioxide in water are the

a. lungs.
b. tracheas.
c. air sacs.
d. gills.

a ______ 13. Tiny blood vessels that allow substances to pass between the blood and body tissues are called

a. capillaries.
b. veins.
c. arteries.
d. aortic arches.

d ______ 14. Bile aids in the digestion of

a. minerals.
b. carbohydrates.
c. proteins.
d. fats.

a ______ 15. The part of the heart that receives blood from the veins and collects it for a short period of time is the

a. atrium.
b. artery.
c. vein.
d. valve.

d ______ 16. Blood that has had most of its oxygen given to the body's cells is called

a. diluted.
b. oxygenated.
c. dissolved.
d. deoxygenated.

b ______ 17. The number of chambers in a fish heart is

a. one.
b. two.
c. three.
d. four.

d ______ 18. Undigested foods leave the digestive tract through the

a. kidneys.
b. small intestine.
c. urinary bladder.
d. anus.

b 19. Upon leaving the stomach, food normally moves to the

a. esophagus.
b. small intestine.
c. gallbladder.
d. liver.

c 20. The structures that filter wastes from the blood in vertebrates are the

a. flame cells.
b. urethras.
c. kidneys.
d. urinary bladders.

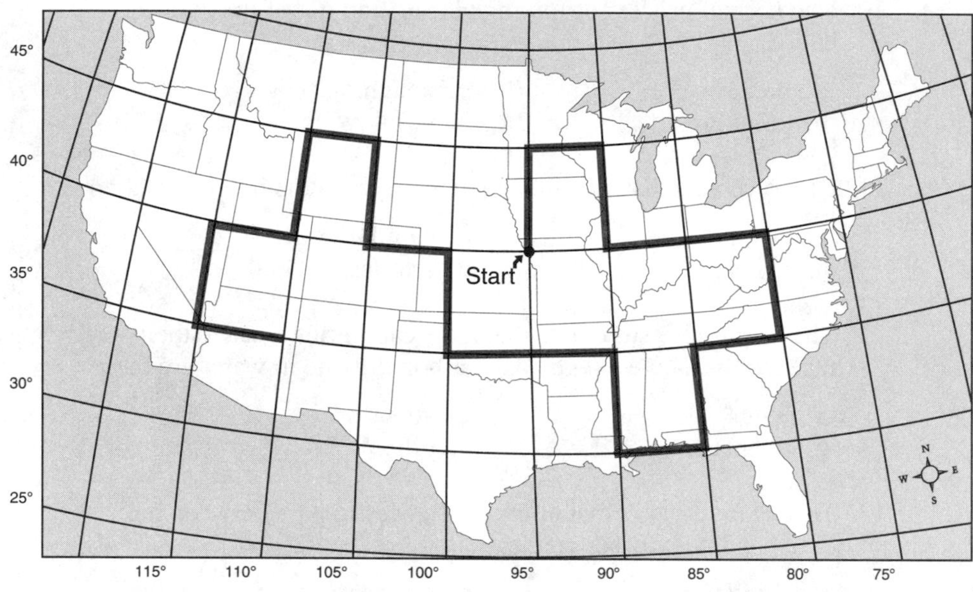

Which state has the largest number of poisonous reptile species? *Arizona*

Name ____________________
Date __________ Hour __________

Ideas 17c

Fish

Directions: Read the following statements. In the space provided, write *True* if the statement is true and *False* if the statement is false and draw a line through the word or words that make the statement false. In the space in the margin, write the word or words necessary to make the statement true.

False 1. Fish are ~~invertebrates~~. *vertebrates*

True 2. Fish are cold-blooded.

False 3. A fish's scales ~~are shed~~ as the fish grows larger. *grow larger*

True 4. If a fish had a defective lateral line, it would not sense its environment as well as it should.

False 5. A fish has a ~~three~~-chambered heart. *two*

True 6. The lamprey is a jawless fish.

True 7. Sharks do not have swim bladders.

False 8. Sharks and rays are ~~bony~~ fish. *cartilage*

False 9. If a shark stops swimming, it will ~~float~~. *sink*

False 10. In bony fish, gill flap movement moves water in through the ~~gills~~ and out the ~~mouth~~. *mouth, gills*

Ideas 17d

Amphibians

Directions: Choose the best word from the list below to complete each sentence. Write the word in the blank provided. A word may be used once or not at all.

Appalachian	estivation	moist
Asian	front	single
back	hibernation	spiracles
coastal	incisors	skin
double	maxillary	tailed
dry	metamorphosis	tailless

1. The name *amphibian* literally means *double* life.
2. The process that changes an amphibian from a gilled organism to one with lungs is called *metamorphosis*.
3. Amphibians must return to *moist* places to lay their eggs.
4. *Estivation* is a period of inactivity during hot, dry spells.
5. Frogs and toads are *tailless* amphibians.
6. A frog's tongue is attached to the *front* of its mouth.
7. Frogs have *maxillary* and vomerine teeth.

8. Salamanders and newts are ___tailed___ amphibians.
9. Most amphibians can exchange gases through their ___skin___.
10. The ___Appalachian___ region has the most salamander species.

Ideas 17e

Reptiles

Directions: Record your responses in the spaces provided.

1. Why do reptiles not have to return to water to lay their eggs? *Their leathery eggshells protect them from drying out.*

2. What sense organ do humans have that snakes do not have? *ears*

3. Are most snakes poisonous or nonpoisonous? *nonpoisonous*

4. Why are snakes capable of eating prey larger in diameter than themselves? *Their jaws are doubly hinged and not firmly attached to each other at the front, and their throats can stretch.*

5. How can a large alligator approach its prey and yet be almost completely hidden? *Except for its nostrils and eyes, it can remain underwater.*

6. How do sea turtles, tortoises, and terrapins differ? *Sea turtles live in the ocean, tortoises live on land, and terrapins live in fresh water but may venture onto land.*

7. Below is a drawing of an American alligator and an American crocodile. Label each correctly.

alligator

crocodile

Name ______________________

Date __________ Hour ______________

Class Investigation 17a

Fish Respiration Rates

Goals

- Observe the respiration of a fish.
- Determine the effects of temperature on the respiration rate of a fish.

Materials

a live fish, a small aquarium, ice, plastic bags, hot water, thermometer

Setting up

Place a live fish in a small aquarium. The water in the aquarium should be the same as the water to which the fish is accustomed. Place a thermometer in the aquarium.

A goldfish would be a good fish to observe. It should be at least 5 to 8 cm (2 to 3 in.) long. If it is much smaller, students will not be able to see the movements of the operculum easily. If it is a strong, healthy fish, it will recover from these temperature changes; if it is not, it will probably suffer stress and become weakened.

Procedures and observations

1. Locate and observe the operculum. The operculum is the flap that covers the gills of fish. Fish move this flap back and forth to cause water to circulate over the gills. Gases are exchanged in the gills between the water and the blood.
2. Carefully count the number of times the operculum beats in fifteen seconds. Multiply this number by four to find out how many times it moves in one minute. Repeat the observation four times. Record your findings below.
   - Temperature: ______
   - Number of movements of the operculum in one minute:

Use a relatively small aquarium for this investigation. The larger the aquarium, the longer the water will take to heat and cool. A 3.8-L (1-gal.) glass tank about three-fourths full works well.

Be prepared to do other things while you are waiting for the water to change temperatures.

First count ______________ Second count ______________

Third count ______________ Fourth count ______________

- Average number of movements per minute: ______

You may want to do this exercise as a demonstration. If you do, you should have four different students making observations of operculum movements at the same time. By having several students near the aquarium observing the temperature of the water, you can continue lecturing or doing other classroom activities while the water temperature is changing.

3. Place several cups of hot water in a plastic bag and close it tightly. Slowly, so as not to disturb the fish, lower the bag into the aquarium. Wait for the aquarium water to increase five degrees. Then slowly remove the bag of hot water.
4. Repeat your observations of the operculum's movements.
   - Temperature: ______
   - Number of movements of the operculum in one minute:

You should probably try this experiment a few days in advance on the type of fish you are going to use. Some fish may show little change within a ten-degree span. You may need to extend the temperature changes a few degrees.

First count ______________ Second count ______________

Third count ______________ Fourth count ______________

- Average number of movements per minute: ______

5. Record any observations you make at this temperature that are different from those at the previous temperature. ***Answers will vary. The fish should be more active.***

6. Place several ice cubes in a plastic bag and close it tightly. Slowly, so as not to disturb the fish, lower the bag into the aquarium. Wait for the aquarium water to cool five degrees below the original temperature. You may need to replace the ice. Slowly remove the bag of ice.
7. Repeat your observations of the operculum's movements.

   Temperature: ______

   • Number of movements of the operculum in one minute:

First count	____________	Second count	____________
Third count	____________	Fourth count	____________

   • Average number of movements per minute: ______

Since you already have the fish in the classroom, consider observing its capillaries. Wrap the fish in moist tissue and place it on a microscope slide (if it is small enough). Make sure its tail (caudal fin) is spread out. Focus the microscope on the capillaries in the thinnest part of the tail fin.

8. Record any other observations you make at this temperature that are different from those at the other temperatures. ***Answers will vary. The fish should move more slowly and may even be resting on the bottom of the tank.***

9. Let the aquarium water return slowly to its normal temperature.

Summing up

1. When was the fish's operculum the most active? (Check one.)
   ☒ high temperature ☐ medium temperature ☐ low temperature
2. When was the fish's operculum the least active? (Check one.)
   ☐ high temperature ☐ medium temperature ☒ low temperature
3. How did the rate of operculum movements compare to the amount of activity of the fish? ***The rate of the operculum movements should have corresponded directly to the activity of the fish. The fish moved its operculum more as it became more active.***

4. Based on these observations, when was the fish's respiration rate the highest? (Check one.)

   ☒ high temperature ☐ medium temperature ☐ low temperature
5. Based on these observations, when was the fish's respiration rate the slowest? (Check one.)

   ☐ high temperature ☐ medium temperature ☒ low temperature
6. Is this fish a warm-blooded or a cold-blooded animal? ☐ warm-blooded ☒ cold-blooded Explain how the results of this investigation support your answer. ***The amount of respiration carried on by the fish depended on the temperature of the fish's environment.***

Name ______________________________

Class Investigation 17b

Date ______________ Hour ______________

Frog Dissection (part 1)

Goals

- Identify the organs of a frog.
- Prepare for a study of human organs by studying frog organs.

Materials

forceps, dissection pan, dissection pins, latex gloves (optional), preserved frog, probe, ruler, scalpel, scissors, thin straw

You can use the closed activity approach for this investigation.

You can use one frog for a group of five students and have the students take turns doing the activities. Providing one frog for every two students is better; one frog for every student is best.

BJU Press carries a dissection kit that includes the specimens as well as the tools and instructions needed to dissect a frog, an earthworm, a crayfish, and a perch. A videocassette is also available from BJUP that shows the dissection of these four animals. Actual dissection by the student is preferable.

Procedures and observations

Examine the external structures of the frog

1. Feel the frog's skin. Describe the texture. *Answers will vary. The frog's skin is smooth and slippery.*
2. Remove a small section of skin from the frog's back. Look on the underside of the skin and notice the blood vessels located there. Why would the frog's skin need to have a rich supply of blood? *The frog exchanges gases through its skin.*
3. Find the following structures: eyes, mouth, nostrils, and tympanic membrane.
4. Notice the difference in size between the frog's forelegs and hind legs.

   How long are the forelegs? ______________________________

   How long are the hind legs? ______________________________

   Do you think this difference in size has anything to do with the different ways the frog uses its legs? ☒ Yes ☐ No

   What is the function of the forelegs? *Provide support and cushion falls*

   What is the function of the hind legs? *The frog uses its hind legs for jumping.*
5. Determine the sex of your frog. Examine the innermost toes ("thumbs") on the forelegs. The innermost toes are enlarged in males. Is your frog a ☐ male or a ☐ female?

Examine your frog's mouth

1. Open the mouth of your frog and notice the grooves and ridges along the edge of the jaws. These grooves and ridges allow the mouth to close tightly.

   Why does the frog's mouth need to close tightly? *A frog breathes by swallowing air. If its mouth did not close tightly, the frog could not breathe.*

   Does the frog have lips? ☒ Yes ☐ No
2. Move your finger along the upper jaw and feel the frog's tiny teeth.

   What are these teeth called? *These are the maxillary teeth.*

   How does the frog use them? *It uses them to hold prey.*

3. Locate the frog's vomerine teeth at the front of the roof of the mouth.
4. Gently pull the tongue until it extends from the frog's mouth.

   Where does the tongue attach to the jaw? *It attaches at the front of the mouth.*

   How is the free end of the tongue shaped? *It is notched.*

   Normally when the frog is alive, a part of the tongue is sticky.

   Why is this characteristic important to the frog? *Frogs catch insects with their sticky tongues.*

Open the frog's body cavity

1. Place the frog on its back in your dissection pan.
2. Beginning above the anus, place your scissors to the left of the whitish or reddish line that runs down the middle of the frog.
3. Break through the body wall with the point of your scissors and cut toward the mouth. Make sure you cut only the skin and muscles.
4. Continue cutting until you reach the frog's neck region. You will have to cut through the bone in the chest region.
5. Make additional cuts across the top and bottom of your first cut. Pull back the cut sections and pin them to the dissection pan.

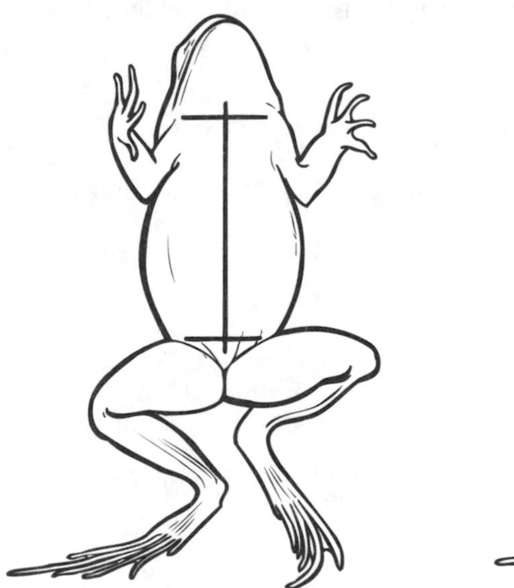

Examine the frog's heart

1. Describe what the heart looks like. *a triangular, reddish-brown mass of muscle*
2. Cut the heart in half so that there is a front half and a back half.

   How many atriums does the frog's heart have? *two*

   What is the function of an atrium? *It receives blood that flows into the heart.*

   How many ventricles does the frog's heart have? *one*

   What is the function of a ventricle? *It pumps blood out of the heart to the body.*

Name ______________________

Date ____________ Hour ____________

Find the frog's lungs

1. To help locate these organs, open the frog's mouth and place a thin straw through the opening that leads to the trachea. Gently blow through the straw. As the lungs fill with air, they will become more noticeable to you.
2. Where are the lungs located in relation to the heart? ***They are behind the heart.***
3. When the frog was alive, how did air enter its lungs? ***The frog took air into its mouth and then forced the air into the lungs.***

Find the organs belonging to the digestive system

1. The liver

   Where is the liver located in relation to the heart? ***It is on each side of the heart.***

   What color is it? ***The liver is reddish-brown.***

   What does the liver produce? ***It produces bile.***
2. The gallbladder

   The gallbladder is a small greenish sac located between the lobes (sections) of the liver.

   What is the function of the gallbladder? ***The gallbladder stores bile.***
3. The esophagus

   To find the esophagus, open the frog's mouth and place a probe into the hole leading to the digestive system.

   Describe the esophagus. ***The esophagus is the short, tube-shaped section just before the stomach.***
4. The stomach

   Move the left lobe of the liver to find the stomach.

   What color is the stomach? ***The stomach is pink.***

   Does it feel hard or soft? ***It feels hard.***

   What is the function of the stomach? ***It mixes the food with digestive enzymes.***
5. The small intestine

   The small intestine is the small, tube-shaped organ continuing from the stomach.

   Cut the tissues that hold the small intestine in place (but do not cut the small intestine).

   How long is the small intestine? ***Answers will vary.***

   What color is it? ***The small intestine is pink.***

   What does the small intestine do to the food that the frog eats? ***It digests and absorbs the food.***
6. The large intestine

   The large intestine is a larger tube-shaped organ that continues from the small intestine.

   How long is the large intestine? ***Answers will vary.***

Give two differences (other than length) between the large and small intestine. ***(1) The large intestine is thicker than the small intestine. (2) The large intestine is darker in color than the small intestine.***

7. The pancreas

   The pancreas is a yellowish organ that is thin and flat. It is located in the thin membrane that is attached to the stomach and small intestine. (You may have difficulty locating this organ.)

   What does the pancreas produce? ***It produces insulin and digestive enzymes.***

Remove the digestive system

1. Cut across the esophagus and the lower section of the large intestine.

   Carefully lift and remove the digestive system out of the body cavity. The heart will come with the digestive system.
2. Cut open the stomach and look inside.

   Is there any food in the stomach? ☐ Yes ☐ No

   Can you recognize any of it? ☐ Yes ☐ No

   If so, what did you find? ***Answers will vary.***
3. Rinse out the stomach and study the stomach's muscular walls.

   How do these walls help digestion? ***They contract to help mix the food.***

Study the excretory and reproductive systems

Find the following structures.

1. Kidneys

   The kidneys are oval-shaped organs that are positioned against the frog's body wall.

   How many kidneys does the frog have? ***It has two kidneys.***

   What color are they? ***They are reddish-brown.***

   What do the kidneys do? ***They filter wastes from the blood.***
2. The urinary bladder

   The urinary bladder looks like a small deflated balloon at the bottom of the body cavity.

   What does the urinary bladder store? ***It stores urine.***
3. The reproductive structures

   If your frog is a male, locate the testes. These are two small organs attached near the kidneys.

   If your frog is a female, locate the ovaries. If there were large masses of dark eggs filling the body cavity of your frog, you removed the ovaries when you removed the eggs. Ovaries with few or no eggs, however, are located near the kidneys.

   When you complete this investigation, carefully wrap your preserved frog in moist paper towels and place it in a plastic bag. You will need your frog again for Investigation 17c.

Name ______________________

Date ____________ Hour ____________

Class Investigation 17c

Frog Dissection (part 2)

Follow the same procedures you used for Investigation 17b, Frog Dissection, part 1.

Goals

- Locate and identify the parts of the frog's nervous system.
- Prepare for a study of the human nervous system by becoming familiar with the frog's nervous system.

Students should dispose of their frogs after this investigation. Some teachers may want to have students remove the skeleton from their frogs. This may be a profitable activity when studying the human skeletal system (Chapter 24). If you wish to save the frogs for that type of activity, have the students return them to the preservative that they came in and store them in a cool place. Although removing a frog's skeleton can be a fun activity, students can spend a great amount of time doing this without learning much from it. In that type of exercise, the dexterous and patient students usually do good work, but the others seem to become frustrated.

Materials 

forceps, dissection pan, latex gloves (optional), preserved frog (same as in Investigation 17b), probes, scissors, scalpel

Procedures and observations

Observe the frog's sensory organs

1. Examine one of the frog's eyes.

   Does the frog have an upper eyelid? ☒ Yes ☐ No

   Does the frog have a lower eyelid? ☒ Yes ☐ No

   The frog has a thin, transparent membrane that it can spread over its eye. Why do you think this kind of protection would be necessary for the frog? ***When the frog is underwater, this third eyelid protects the eye and still allows the frog to see.***

2. Examine one of the frog's tympanic membranes.

   What type of stimulus does the tympanic membrane receive? ***It receives sound waves.***

   Press your finger against one of the tympanic membranes. Describe what happened. ***It moved back and forth.***

Examine the frog's brain and cranial nerves

1. To expose the frog's brain, carefully scrape away the skin from between the frog's eyes to reveal the frog's skull. Use the handles of your scissors to crack the skull. Carefully pull away pieces of the skull with forceps and scissors. Be careful not to destroy the lobes of the brain.
2. Describe the brain.

   What color is the brain? ***It is yellowish-white.***

   What shape is the brain? ***Answers will vary. It is long and has several different sections (lobes).***

3. Can you see any cranial nerves? If so, which ones? (You may carefully use your probe to move the brain around slightly.) ***Answers will vary. If they are careful, students may see various cranial nerves.***

   The cranial nerves are part of which division of the nervous system? ***They are part of the peripheral nervous system.***

Examine the frog's spinal cord and spinal nerves

1. Place your frog on its back so that you can see into its body cavity. Look at its backbone. Locate the whitish-yellow cords running out of the backbone and into various parts of the frog's body. These are spinal nerves.

   To which body area do most of the spinal nerves go? ***Most of them go to the hind legs.***

   Why do so many of the spinal nerves go to this area? ***Answers will vary. The frog uses its hind legs for most of its movements. A great deal of control is necessary.***

   The spinal nerves are part of which division of the nervous system? ***They are a part of the peripheral nervous system.***

2. Carefully use your scalpel to scrape away some of the muscle and backbone that cover the spinal cord. Be careful not to damage the spinal cord.

   What color is the spinal cord? ***It is yellowish-white.***

   The spinal cord is part of which division of the nervous system? ***It is a part of the central nervous system.***

Name ______________________
Date __________ Hour __________

18–Vertebrates II: Birds and Mammals

Ideas 18a

Warm-blooded, Cold-blooded

Directions: Below are listed several words and statements that relate to being warm-blooded or cold-blooded. In the space by each word or phrase, write *W* if it relates to warm-bloodedness and *C* if it relates to cold-bloodedness.

C ______ 1. Amphibians

W ______ 2. Birds

C ______ 3. Body temperature same as surroundings

W ______ 4. Can be active regardless of temperature

C ______ 5. Cannot control body temperature by internal means

C ______ 6. Fish

C ______ 7. Insects

W ______ 8. Mammals

W ______ 9. May have fur or feathers

W ______ 10. May sweat

W ______ 11. Relatively constant body temperature

C ______ 12. Reptiles

Ideas 18b

Birds

Directions: Complete the crossword puzzle.

Across

2. Much energy and _______ must be available to flight muscles during flight.
4. Birds have wings and _______.
5. A bird's _______ are filled with oxygen-rich air when it inhales and exhales.
6. Usually birds build nests and _______ their eggs.
8. The _______ is a food storage organ.

Down

1. Birds with _______ beaks probably eat meat.
3. Birds' lightweight bones are reinforced by a ______ structure.
7. Birds must _______ their eggs regularly so that normal development will not be disrupted.

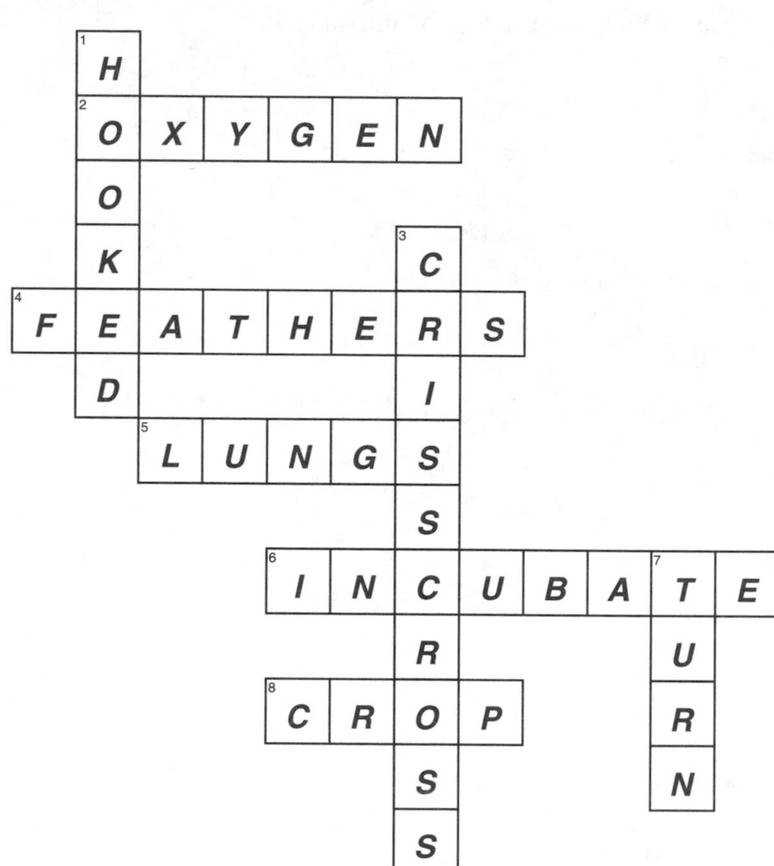

Name ____________

Date ________ Hour ________

Ideas 18c

Allow the students to use the textbook. Give credit for any correctly connected concepts and bonus points for correctly connecting all concepts.

Mammals

Directions: Use the concept words from the list below to fill in the chart showing the relationships between the concepts. Words on the arrows show the relationships. Each concept word(s) is used only once and *there is only one correct way to use all the concept words* in this chart. Three words have already been placed in the chart to get you started.

Concept Words

~~eggs~~	monotremes
~~hair~~	opossum
horse	placenta
mammals	placental mammals
mammary glands	platypus
marsupials	pouches
milk	~~umbilical cord~~

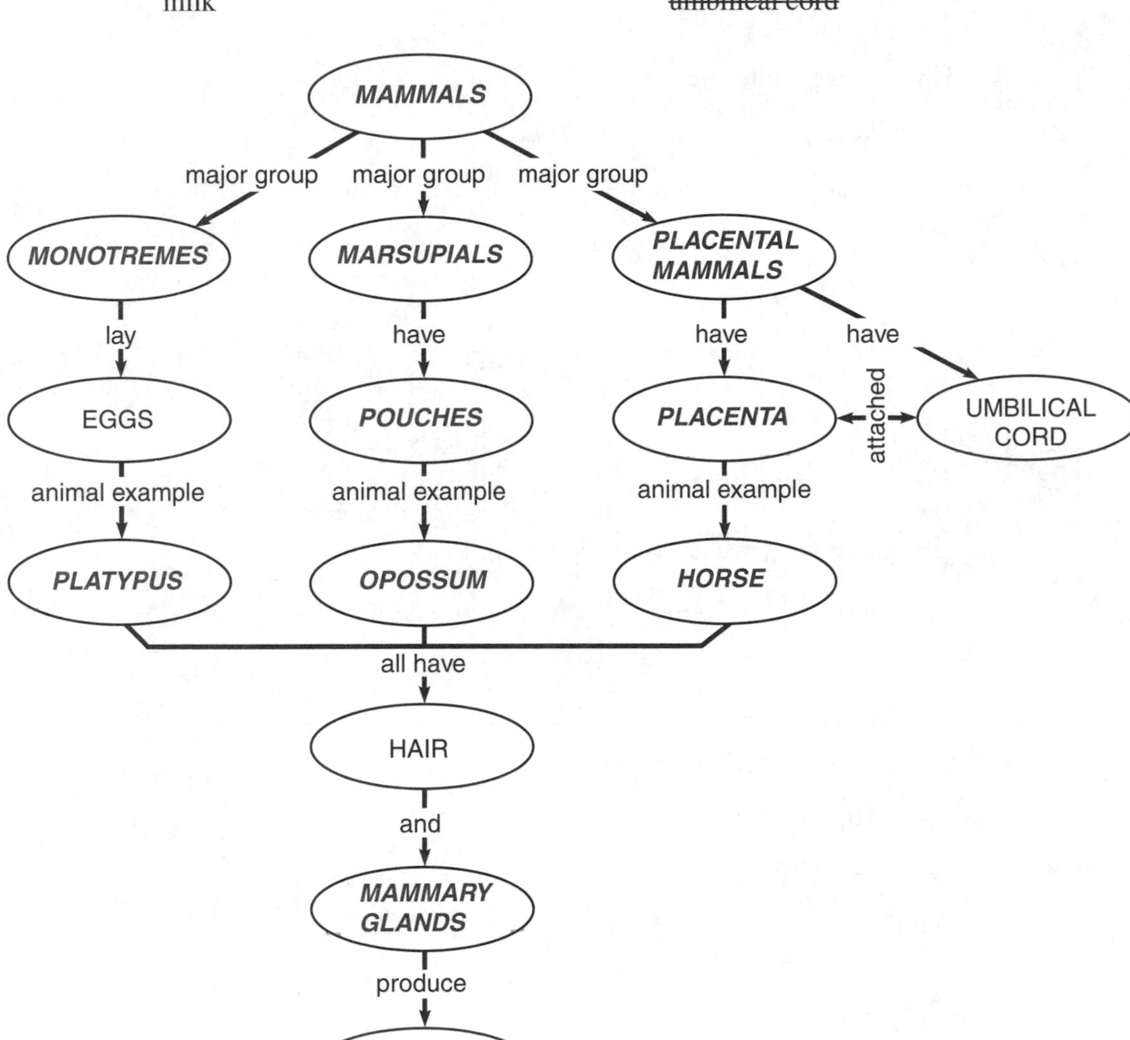

Review

Directions: In the spaces provided tell how each pair of terms are similar; then tell how they are different.

The answers given here are the most logical. Students, however, may devise other good answers.

If this seems too difficult for your students, then let them find only the similarities or only the differences. You may wish to specify which choice to answer for each number.

1. warm-blooded / cold-blooded

   similar: ***Both refer to regulation of an animal's body temperature.***

   different: ***Warm-blooded animals maintain a relatively constant body temperature by internal means. Cold-blooded animals cannot control their temperature by internal means.***

2. sweating / panting

   similar: ***Both are ways that warm-blooded animals may cool themselves.***

   different: ***Sweating occurs on the skin, while panting uses the lining of the mouth and throat.***

3. yolk / egg white

   similar: ***Both are parts of bird eggs.***

   different: ***Yolk is the food reserve. Egg white provides a liquid environment in the egg.***

4. incisors / canines

   similar: ***Both are types of teeth found in mammals.***

   different: ***Incisors are used for cutting. Canines are used for tearing.***

5. monotremes / marsupials

   similar: ***Both are groups of mammals.***

   different: ***Monotremes lay eggs; marsupials give birth to live young and rear them in pouches.***

6. placenta / umbilical cord

   similar: ***Both help provide food and oxygen to and remove wastes from developing mammals while inside the mother.***

   different: ***The umbilical cord connects the developing mammal to the placenta.***

7. hair / milk

   similar: ***Both are produced by mammals.***

   different: ***Hair is a body covering produced in the hair follicles of skin. Milk is produced in mammary glands and is a food for newborn offspring.***

Name ______________________
Date ____________ Hour ____________

Class Investigation 18a

Conserving Body Heat: Wool vs. Down

Find out if any of your students are allergic to wool, down, or pet hair (if used) before you begin this investigation.

Goal

- Compare the effectiveness of fur (wool) and down (feathers) as insulators.

Materials

down (feathers), freezer, three containers with lids (cups or glasses), three lab thermometers, wool

Substitutions: *Down from a down pillow is fine to use, and it can be returned to the pillow when finished.*

Wool yarn or shredded wool cloth will work fine.

Procedures and observations

1. Fill one container with wool and another with down. The containers should have equal amounts of the material to be tested. Label the containers. Label the empty container as *control.*
2. Put lids on all three containers and insert a thermometer through the hole in each lid. The thermometers should be positioned so that the thermometer bulb is about midway in the container. Do not allow the thermometer bulbs to touch the bottom or sides of the containers.
3. Record the temperatures of all three containers on the table below; then put all three in the freezer. (Note: All three should be approximately the same starting temperature.)
4. Record the temperatures of all three containers at five-minute intervals.

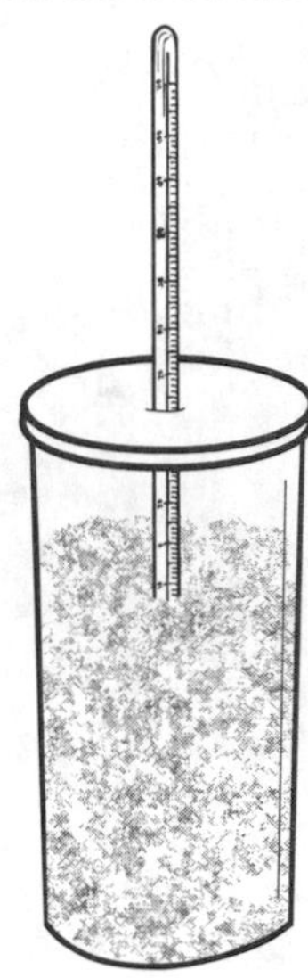

Time	Control, °C	Down, °C	Wool, °C
start			
5 minutes			
10 minutes			
15 minutes			
20 minutes			
25 minutes			

You could use hair brushed from pet dogs or cats instead of wool. However, be sure to guard against parasites. You might supply latex gloves or require hand washing.

Lab thermometers are best to use here because they are long enough to have the bulbs in the insulated space while having the temperature scale exposed.

Summing up

1. Which container had the most rapid temperature change (from start to finish) in this experiment? ***the control container***
2. Which container had the smallest temperature change in this experiment? ***Answers will vary. Either the down or the wool container will have the smallest change.***
3. Are down and wool insulators? How do you know? ***Yes, they allowed less temperature change than the control group during this experiment.***

Twelve- to twenty-two-ounce beverage containers with lids with straw holes (from fast-food restaurants) are perfect for this investigation. The three containers should be identical. Do not use Styrofoam or other insulated cups.

Use either equal weights or equal volumes.

It may be necessary to tape the thermometer in place in the control container.

There may be some temperature variation between different locations in the freezer. Also, repeated opening and closing of the freezer door may affect the temperature.

Any number of variables will affect the insulating value of the wool and down including the following: how densely it is packed, how the wool was processed, kind of bird down used, and so forth.

Consider having the students graph their results (temperature vs. time) before they answer the questions. The "Thinking Critically" facet in Chapter 13 (p. 198) of the text may be helpful as you explain how to make the graph.

4. Which of the materials tested in this experiment is the best insulator? ____
Answers will vary.

5. What role do down and wool serve warm-blooded animals? ***They help maintain a constant body temperature by conserving body heat during cold periods.***

6. Explain how down and wool could be a *disadvantage* to warm-blooded animals? ***In hot climates warm-blooded animals would need to lose body heat rather than conserve it.***

Name ______________________
Date ____________ Hour ____________

Class Investigation 18b

Feathers are available from farms and craft stores.

Observing Feathers and Hair

Substitutions: *You can make your own slides of animal hairs by simply taping them to the slide (view the non-taped portion).*

Goals

- Compare types of feathers.
- Observe the fine structure of feathers and hair.

Materials

contour (wing or tail) feather, down feather, hand lens, microscope, microscope slide of animal hairs

Procedures and observations

1. Observe the contour feather. Bend it. Is it stiff? ___*yes*___ Examine the quill. Is it solid or hollow? ___*hollow*___ Separate some barbs from the other barbs. Can you refasten them? ___*no*___ Separate a barb and examine it with the hand lens or microscope. What can you see on the barb? ___*tiny hooks*___ Why do you think these are important? ___*They hold the barbs together.*___
2. In the space below make a drawing of the contour feather as seen with your hand lens or microscope.
3. Observe the down feather with the hand lens. Is it stiff? ___*no*___ Can you fasten the barbs together? ___*no*___ Make a drawing in the space below of the down feather as seen with your hand lens or microscope.

4. Examine the microscope slide of animal hairs. Describe what the hairs look like as seen through the microscope. *Answers will vary but should indicate the scaly nature of hairs.*

5. In the space below, draw the microscopic views of the hairs of three different animals. Your drawings should show how the animal hairs differ.

Summing up

1. Which do you think are most important in flight, contour feathers or down feathers? *contour feathers*

2. Why do hairs not need to hold together like contour feathers do? *Hairs are not used for flying.*

3. What is the function of down feathers? *for insulation to keep warm*

Name ______________________
Date ____________ Hour ____________

19–Animal Behavior

Ideas 19a

Innate and Learned Behaviors

Part 1

Directions: Answer the following questions in the space provided.

1. How are reflexes and instincts similar? *Both are innate behaviors which animals have when they are born.*

2. How are reflexes and instincts different? *Reflexes are simple responses to some change in the environment. Instincts are complex reactions that often require longer periods of time to complete than reflexes do.*

3. What do you think would happen to an animal if its reflexes and instincts did not function properly? *It would probably die.*

4. Give an example of a learned behavior intentionally taught to an animal by man. *Answers will vary: animal tricks, seeing-eye dogs, and so on.*

Part 2

Directions: Each of the Scripture passages listed in the table below mentions or describes an animal doing something. Find each passage in your Bible; then complete the table by naming the animal, describing what the animal does, and writing whether the action is innate or learned.

Dogs' eating and begging in Matt. 15:27 are innate. Loitering near the table is a learned behavior.

Passage	Animal	The animal's action	Innate or learned?
Deut. 22:10	*ox*	*plowing*	*learned*
	ass (donkey)	*plowing*	*learned*
Deut. 28:42	*locust (cricket)*	*eating*	*innate*
Deut. 32:11	*eagle*	*protecting and training young*	*innate*
Esther 6:8	*horse*	*carrying a rider*	*learned*
Matt. 15:27	*dog (pups)*	*begging table scraps/loitering near table*	*both*
Luke 13:34	*hen*	*protecting young*	*innate*
John 10:4	*sheep*	*following shepherd*	*learned*
II Peter 2:22	*dog*	*returning to vomit*	*innate*
	sow	*wallowing in mire (mud)*	*innate*
Rev. 9:5	*scorpion*	*striking (stinging)*	*innate*

Name ______________________

Date ____________ Hour ____________

Ideas 19b

Review 1

Directions: Read the following examples and decide which of the various levels of behavior are being described. Then indicate your answers by writing the proper letters in the blanks provided.

a. innate-reflex
b. innate-instinct
c. learned
d. intelligent

Point out to students that if their answer is innate, they must tell whether the innate behavior is an instinct or a reflex.

b ______ 1. When given the proper materials, a bird kept isolated for its entire life builds a nest typical of its species.

c ______ 2. During dinner a dog sits under the chair belonging to the family member who often gives the dog bites of food.

c ______ 3. After watching the older lions in its pride, a young lion cub stalks its first prey.

c/d ______ 4. A monkey uses a long stick to get to food that is beyond its reach.

a ______ 5. When a bird becomes cold, its feathers stand up, and it begins to shiver.

c ______ 6. A guard dog attacks a prowler who comes into the yard but does not attack the owner who similarly enters the yard.

b ______ 7. A honeybee collects pollen from flowers to produce honey.

b ______ 8. Canada geese leave Canada and migrate to the United States.

a/b ______ 9. When frightened, a de-scented pet skunk raises its tail and turns its back to the thing that frightened it.

c ______ 10. At a security checkpoint, dogs sniff the packages of travelers. When a dog smells drugs, it barks and claws at the package.

c ______ 11. After twenty tries, the rat can run the maze in less than one third of its original time.

b ______ 12. Screeching loudly, the mockingbird swoops down toward you as you walk by the tree where its nest is.

Review 2

Directions: Write clues that relate to animal behavior for each of the crossword answers below.

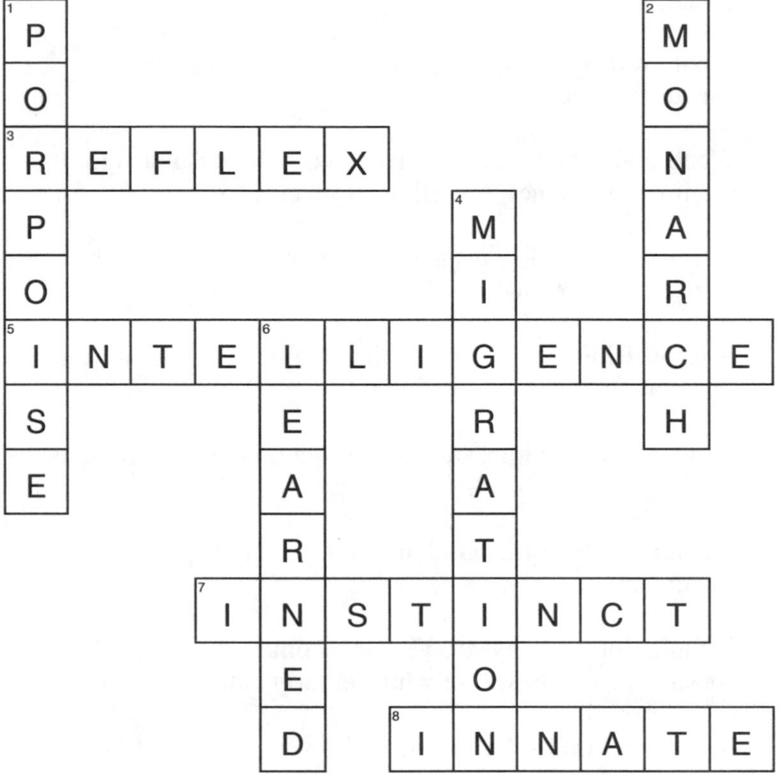

Answers will vary.

Across

3. *Simple, immediate response to some change in the environment*

5. *The ability to reason out a solution to a problem*

7. *Complex, inborn reaction*

8. *Type of behavior an animal has when it is born*

Down

1. *One of the most intelligent animals*

2. *Famous butterfly migrator*

4. *Long-distance, seasonal movement of animals*

6. *Type of behavior demonstrated by a talking parakeet*

Name ____________
Date ________ Hour ________

Class Investigation 19a

Myrmecology (The Study of Ants)

Goals

- Become familiar with ants.
- Observe relationships within an ant colony.

Materials

ant microcosm chamber, ants, eyedropper, food (corn flakes, wheat or barley seed, potato), sand

Setting up

A microcosm is a small area that simulates, as closely as possible, the situation in a larger area. Scientists often use microcosms to study organisms. Myrmecologists (scientists who study ants) use ant microcosms to study ant behavior. An ant microcosm chamber is a thin, clear container that people use to observe the actions of ants. If the container were thick, the ants would construct their tunnels in the middle of the sand or dirt, and you would not be able to see them. Since ant microcosm chambers are thin, you can observe the tunnels that the ants build. You can build an ant microcosm or purchase a specially designed one.

1. Place sand or some other medium in the ant microcosm chamber and fill the chamber about halfway.
2. Add water to make the sand moist but not soggy.
3. Obtain your ants.
   - You can collect your own ants by placing a stick in front of a group of ants and permitting them to crawl up the stick and then placing them in your microcosm. You can also dig up an anthill and collect a mass of ants all at once, perhaps even a queen. If you collect your own ants, *collect them from only one colony.* If you put ants from different colonies in your ant farm, they will kill each other.
   - You can obtain ants from biological supply houses. Carefully put your ants into the ant chamber. Be ready with sticks and various other devices to direct the ants into the chamber. Placing a paper funnel into the opening of the ant chamber often works well to direct the ants into the chamber. Do not injure the ants.
4. Place a piece of food into the chamber. A tiny portion of a corn flake is good to use.

Procedures and observations

Care for your ant colony

1. Add several drops of water (more if your microcosm is large) every two or three days.
2. Add a small piece of food every three or four days. The major problem with keeping ant microcosms is overfeeding. If you put in too much food, it will begin to rot and will cause the ants to die. If food is not consumed before it begins to mold, remove the food. Removing the food can be difficult if the ants have taken their food deep into the colony. The best solution is to feed the ants very small amounts. If the ants ignore the food you introduce, do not feed them for several days.

You may want to set up several ant microcosms in the classroom. This will allow the students to compare them and will also allow many students to make observations at the same time. If you decide to use only one ant microcosm and you have a large class, consider purchasing a larger microcosm chamber. You can purchase ant microcosm chambers under the brand name Giant Ant Farm through BJU Press. Normally they come with a certificate to be mailed in for a supply of ants. Ant microcosm chambers can be made out of glass plates (or Plexiglas), metal strips, and aquarium sealer. They should be constructed tightly enough to prevent the escape of ants but should contain small ventilation and drainage openings.

Purchased ant farm microcosm chambers come with sterile, sandlike media. If you use your own sand, you should boil it thoroughly before you set up your ant microcosm. Various fungi and bacteria will quickly take over the microcosm if you use regular, untreated garden soil. Sand is recommended. It is less messy and is easier for the ants to work with. If you do this investigation during the proper season, you may collect your own ants. Normally, however, ordering a supply will be far easier.

Home School Tip

An inexpensive ant farm can be constructed from a 3 L plastic soft-drink bottle. Use the kind that does not have a black plastic base. Crush (flatten) the middle of the bottle along its vertical axis (the sides should be a half-inch to an inch apart). Add a few rocks to take up some of the volume in the uncrushed base. Secure this flattened shape by attaching clothespins. Use a small straight pin to make ventilation and drainage holes. Fill the bottle with sand to about an inch or two above the flattened middle. Be careful not to add too much food since it will be difficult to remove the excess.

If you live in an area where fire ants are known to occur, caution your students not to collect these.

Seeds of barley or wheat are good foods that spoil less easily than fresh fruits and vegetables. If you introduce items that may spoil quickly, you should keep them on a string so that you can remove them easily. A good pair of long forceps is a good investment.

In certain species of ants, the workers will sometimes produce eggs. Those eggs will produce male ants. Only a queen will produce new workers and new queens.

In the absence of the queen, ants sometimes establish a "mayor" who dabs pheromones onto the other ants. This action permits the entire colony to have the same odor. When an outsider with a different odor is detected, he is quickly surrounded, killed, and disposed of.

Ants will often establish a "cemetery" in which they will place dead bodies. Actually this "cemetery" is a trash heap where the ants will put any unwanted substance. Since there is relatively little foreign matter in the ant microcosm, the trash heap looks more like a cemetery. The establishment of a permanent trash heap depends upon the order of the colony and the size of the area the ants have to work with. Small areas are constantly being reworked, and trash heaps are often torn down and relocated. As your students conduct their observations, encourage them to notice social relationships. Discuss the social relationships that the students observe.

Supplementary reading: "Stalking the Mighty Ant." Reader's Digest, *July 1990, pp. 139-42. (general discussion about ants; has an evolutionary slant); "Hot Ants."* Scientific American, *Sept. 1992, p. 23. (describes the unusual habits of a genus of desert ant; has an evolutionary slant)*

3. Keep your ant farm in a well-lighted area. Do not put it in direct sunlight or in very strong light. The strong light will cause the temperature inside the ant farm to rise so high that it will kill the ants.
4. Keep your ant farm steady. If you must move it, move it carefully and slowly. Ants are sensitive to movement.

Observe your ant microcosm often

1. Record your observations. Although you may want to observe the ant farm several times a day, record your observations only once or twice a day.
2. Make your recorded observations at the same time every day.

Myrmecology Notes

A normal ant colony has female workers and a queen. The queen lays hundreds of eggs a day that develop into the workers that build and protect the colony. Usually once a year the queen lays eggs that develop into males and other queens. The males and potential queens have wings, and they fly away from the colony. They mate in the air and then land. Once on the ground they soon lose their wings, and the males die. The new queens then establish new colonies.

Unless special arrangements have been made, the ants you have in your ant microcosm are all workers. The queen usually remains deeply underground, and you would need to dig carefully to obtain her. If you purchased your ants, you will not have a queen since shipping queens is illegal. (Shipping ant queens has been made illegal to prevent unwanted ants from being introduced to various parts of the country. Workers alone cannot produce a new colony.)

Even without a queen the ants in your colony will still carry on most of their normal functions. This is possible because their actions and reactions are not regulated by a queen. What are the ants' actions and reactions based on? Ant workers, if properly cared for, can live for a year in an ant microcosm. For various reasons they often live for only a few months.

Observe the various activities occurring in your ant microcosm

1. What are the ants doing? Where are they tunneling? Where are they stacking sand? Where are their chambers?
2. As they work on various projects, ants will work in large groups, in small groups, or sometimes alone. Indicate the size of the group that is working on each ant project you observe.
3. What do the ants do with the food?
4. What do the ants do when water is introduced?
5. Are all the ants working? Where are the ones that are not working? Is there any difference between those that are working and those that are not?
6. When an ant dies, what do the other ants do?

Summing up

After you have observed the ant microcosm for several weeks, write a brief summary of what you saw the ants do. Include the ants' reactions that you observed.

Name ______________________________

Date ______________ Hour ______________

Field Investigation 19b

An Animal's Response to Its Environment

Goal

- Observe and categorize an animal's reactions to stimuli in its environment.

All animals constantly respond to their environment. We may not always be able to determine what stimulates the responses. Often, however, we can determine what the animal is responding to if we observe carefully and think about our observations.

Find some active animal in a large area. A squirrel in a yard or park, a dog in a yard, a bird near a bird feeder, a rabbit in a meadow, or a zoo animal in a large enclosure would be good to observe. If you cannot observe an animal in a large space, you can use an active animal in a smaller space: a fish in an aquarium or a bird, chameleon, guinea pig, or hamster in a cage. Observe this animal for three five-minute periods. These five-minute periods should be separated by several minutes.

While you are watching the animal, record every reaction to a stimulus you observe. Note the stimulus and the reaction. In order to do this, you may need to use a tape recorder, videocassette recorder, or a friend or two to record your observations. Animals will not wait for you to write down notes. You may even want to have a friend recording his own observations of the same animal at the same time you are. You could then compare notes and compile a more accurate list of the animal's reactions.

Compile your list of reactions. Then indicate whether each reaction was a reflex, an instinct, a learned reaction, or an intelligent behavior. Compute the percentage of the reactions in each group. Bring your list of observations, your decisions regarding the type of behaviors that you observed, and your percentage figures to class. Present your findings to the class for discussion.

This exercise is best done as a small group activity. The entire group, however, will need to meet together outside of school to do their observations, list compilations, and determine behavior levels.

If you have classroom pets, these observations can be done on them. It is wise, however, to have only about five students doing an observation of a single pet at one time.

You may want to give the students an example of what they should be observing.

In class you may want to discuss the various observations the students have made. Especially go over the classification of the reactions. Point out to the class that some of the reactions they observed may have been caused by things that the animals saw or heard but that the students did not detect.

Home School Tip

Not all students will be able to make reliable observations on their own. Help them make observations yourself, or let your student cooperate with another home school student on this investigation.

You may need to explain how to calculate percentages.

Supplemental resource:

Animal Behavior Science Projects, *by Nancy Woodard Cain, (ISBN 0-471-02636-0) is an excellent source of instructions for animal behavior observations. The observations suggested are relatively easy to make, and sufficient background information is provided to allow meaningful explanation.*

Name ______________________
Date __________ Hour __________

20–Sexual Reproduction in Animals

Ideas 20a

Meiosis, Gametes, and Fertilization

Directions: In the space provided describe the difference between the terms given.

Answers will vary.

1. ovaries / testes *Ovaries form eggs and testes form sperm.*

2. eggs / sperm *Eggs are the gametes produced by females, and sperm are the gametes produced by males.*

3. eggs / zygotes *Eggs are unfertilized female gametes. Zygotes are the diploid cells that result from fertilization (or fertilized eggs).*

4. fertilization / zygote *Fertilization is the uniting of an egg and a sperm. The zygote is the diploid cell that results from fertilization.*

5. haploid / gametes *Haploid describes a cell that has only one of each kind of chromosome normally found in the cells of that organism. Gametes are a special type of haploid cell designed to transfer or receive chromosomes.*

Ideas 20b

External and Internal Fertilization

Directions: In each of the following statements, draw a circle around the correct choice in the parentheses. On the lines provided explain why the incorrect choice is not acceptable.

1. (Male / female) salmon produce milt. ***Milt contains sperm and is produced by the male salmon.***

2. Salmon reproduce by (spawning / nesting). ***Salmon do not build nests.***

3. A baby animal develops within an egg during a period of time known as (incubation / gestation). ***Gestation refers to development within a uterus, not an egg.***

4. When egg and sperm are united inside the female's body, (internal / external) fertilization will take place. ***External fertilization occurs outside the body.***

5. (Yolk / albumen) is the primary stored food that a developing chick will use to grow. ***Albumen is secondary compared to the yolk.***

6. An eggshell has tiny pores to allow (water / gases) to pass. ***The developing organism would drown if water entered the egg.***

7. Crocodiles incubate their eggs by (the heat of rotting plants / sitting on them). ***Birds incubate their eggs by sitting on them.***

8. The umbilical cord carries (amniotic fluid / blood). ***The amniotic fluid surrounds the embryo.***

Name ______________________________

Date ______________ Hour ______________

Ideas 20c

Chick Embryology

Directions: Match the statements below with the correct terms. Place the letter of the answer on the blank of the appropriate statement. One of the terms is not used.

a. albumen
b. allantois
c. amniotic fluid
d. chorion
e. egg tooth
f. shell
g. yolk
h. yolk sac
i. zygote

g ______ 1. Primary source of nutrients for the developing chick embryo

a ______ 2. Supplies water, vitamins, and minerals to the chick embryo

f ______ 3. Supplies calcium to the chick embryo

c ______ 4. Cushions the chick embryo

b ______ 5. Membrane that stores wastes and helps with gas exchange

e ______ 6. Helps a chick break out of its shell

i ______ 7. Formed by union of a sperm and an egg

h ______ 8. Membrane that surrounds the yolk

Review

Directions: All of the scrambled words listed below deal with sexual reproduction in animals. Unscramble the words and write them in the blanks. For some of the words a definition has been supplied. For those that lack a definition, you must write one in the space provided.

1. teelanxr tetiiaifoznrl — *external fertilization* — The union of ova and sperm outside an animal's body
2. tilm — *milt* — *Fluid containing fish sperm*
3. butoiicnna — *incubation* — Period of growth inside an egg
4. lenntira eilafzrtotiin — *internal fertilization* — *Union of an ovum and sperm inside the female parent*
5. tetogansi — *gestation* — Period of time an embryo spends inside the womb
6. yomber — *embryo* — *Unborn organism*
7. balnume — *albumen* — Egg white
8. geg — *egg* — *A zygote enclosed by a shell*
9. nnomia — *amnion* — The fluid-filled sac around an embryo
10. liilcuamb droc — *umbilical cord* — *Structure with blood vessels connecting the embryo to the mother*
11. getaprnn — *pregnant* — Condition of an animal with an unborn offspring
12. wpasginn — *spawning* — *External fertilization carried on by a fish*
13. remsp — *sperm* — Gametes produced by the male
14. okly — *yolk* — *Stored food that an unhatched chick uses to grow*
15. yavor — *ovary* — Organ that produces ova
16. rayammm danlgs — *mammary glands* — Structures that produce milk for the newborn
17. ritbh — *birth* — Normal end of pregnancy
18. caatelnp — *placenta* — Structure that is attached to the wall of the uterus and provides nourishment and oxygen for the embryo

Name ______________________
Date __________ Hour __________

Class Investigation 20a

Why Did God Create Sexual Reproduction?

Encounters between animals armed with fangs, razor-sharp claws, strong muscles, and mean tempers can be deadly. Yet sexual reproduction often requires such encounters. Why would God create a method of reproduction which could be deadly if something went wrong?

Sexual reproduction offers one clear advantage that asexual reproduction (or cloning) does not offer—variation. Organisms produced by sexual reproduction are similar to, but not exactly like, their parents. In Chapters 7 and 8 of your text, you can read how this variation occurs. In this investigation you are going to verify that animals produced by sexual reproduction can have certain characteristics which are different from their parents.

The SPCA, ASPCS, American Humane Association (Humane Society), or local pound is a good source for a large litter of kittens or puppies. Be sure to select a litter that demonstrates variation in coat pattern. Focus on pattern in the coats since color differences are sometimes due to juvenile/adult differences. You may be able to get only one animal parent. Be sure to get a litter of at least three.

Materials

a litter of kittens or puppies and at least one of the parents

Procedure and observations

Describe the fur coat pattern of each animal.

mother ______________________

father ______________________

offspring #1 ______________________

offspring #2 ______________________

offspring #3 ______________________

offspring #4 ______________________

offspring #5 ______________________

offspring #6 ______________________

offspring #7 ______________________

offspring #8 ______________________

Home School Tip

Rather than bringing a litter to your home, make the necessary observations on a visit to the SPCA (or such organization) or visit a friend with a litter.

1. How many of the offspring had fur coat patterns identical to the mother's or father's? *Answers will vary.*

2. How many different kinds of fur coat patterns were found in the litter? *Answers will vary.*

3. How many different kinds of fur coat patterns were demonstrated by the parents? *one or two*

4. If the offspring were genetically identical to one parent, would the pattern of their fur coats be different from that parent? *no*

Summing up

1. Other than fur coat pattern, list five traits in which wild animals could vary from their parents.
   a. *Answers will vary. size*
   b. *color*
   c. *temperament*
   d. *fur/hair length*
   e. *tail length*

2. How could having different patterns of fur coats help an animal species survive for thousands of years? *Answers will vary. Certain patterns might be better camouflaged at different geographical areas or times of the year.*

Variation insures that there will be some individuals of a species capable of surviving unusually difficult conditions or events.

Evolutionists erroneously use variation as evidence for the theory of evolution. As creationists we view variation as a God-designed way to aid the survival of a kind.

3. [Thinking Question] Why would not having variation be harmful to a species? *If every individual of a species were exactly the same, a natural event (predator, disease, climatic condition) that could efficiently eliminate one due to a particular inherited trait could eliminate all.*

Name ______________________

Date ____________ Hour ______________

Research Investigation 20b

Animal Reproduction Worksheet

The underlying goal here is not to memorize facts about the reproduction of specific animals. The goal is to reinforce the concepts of incubation and gestation, and to show that different kinds of animals produce different numbers of offspring at one time and care for them in different ways.

Goal

- Compare the various ways that animals reproduce.

Materials

encyclopedia or other reference books

Procedures and observations

Use encyclopedias and other reference books to find the missing information needed to complete the table. Some sample answers have been provided.

Animal name	How long is incubation or gestation?	Live bearer or egg layer?	Number of eggs or young at one time	Parents provide care? yes or no
black widow	*14-30 days*	*eggs*	*250-750*	yes
blue crab	*2 weeks*	*eggs*	up to 1 million	*yes*
lobster	*11-12 months*	eggs	*5,000-10,000*	*no*
scorpion	a few weeks	*live*	*20-40*	*yes*
guppy	*4 weeks*	*live*	*10-100*	*no*
trout	*40-60 days*	*eggs*	*200 (10,000/yr)*	no
sea horse	*8-45 days*	*eggs*	up to 200	*yes*
bull frog	*1 week*	*eggs*	*10,000-25,000*	*no*
Surinam toad	*80 days*	*eggs*	60	*yes*
box turtle	over winter	*eggs*	*2-8*	*no*
Gila monster	*1 month*	*eggs*	*3-15*	no
snapping turtle	3-6 months	*eggs*	*20-40*	*no*
bald eagle	*6 weeks*	eggs	*1-3*	*yes*
brown pelican	*29-30 days*	*eggs*	*1-4*	*yes*
emperor penguin	*2 months*	*eggs*	*1*	yes
common cuckoo	*12½ days*	*eggs*	*1*	*no*
brown rat	*3 weeks*	*live*	*8-9*	yes
cottontail rabbit	*26-30 days*	live	*4-5*	*yes*
Asian elephant	*645 days*	*live*	1	*yes*
orangutan	275 days	*live*	*1*	*yes*

Do not require a single student to complete the whole table. Assign five animals to each student and then complete the chart in class. Assign the summary section after they have completed the chart.

You may need to adjust the list depending on what reference books are available.

Parental care ranges from protecting or incubating eggs to providing food for several years.

Allow some variation in numerical answers. These vary from source to source.

Home School Tip

A single student should be required to find the data for only five animals.

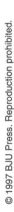

Summing up

1. What is the difference between incubation and gestation? *Incubation is the period of time during which an animal develops inside an egg. Gestation is the period of time during which an animal that is born live develops inside the mother.*

2. Which of the animals above do you think has the most unusual reproduction? Why? *Answers will vary.*

3. What type of care might an animal provide for its young? *food, warmth, protection, training/teaching*

Name ______________________

Date ____________ Hour ____________

21–The Ecosystem

Ideas 21a

Ecosystems and the Physical Environment

Part 1

Directions: Listed below are three common relationships in ecosystems. Below the list are examples of relationships in ecosystems. In the blanks by the examples, write the letter of the relationship that is being described. You will use each letter more than once.

Common Relationships in Ecosystems

a. Organisms affected other organisms.
b. The nonliving factors affected organisms.
c. Organisms affected the nonliving factors.

b______ 1. To keep from becoming too hot, the lizard spent the hottest part of the afternoon in the shadow of a rock.

c______ 2. The earthworm dug deep holes in the soil.

a______ 3. The squirrel scampered up the tree, sat on a limb, and began eating a pecan.

c______ 4. The roots of the tree had grown into the cracks of the rock. As the roots continued to grow, the rock slowly crumbled.

a______ 5. The leech attached itself to the turtle's flipper and obtained a meal of blood.

b______ 6. Scientists have discovered that birds navigate their migrations by the stars.

a______ 7. The wrasse is a small fish that cleans parasites off the head and gills of larger fish.

b______ 8. The warm soil and the abundant moisture triggered the seed to sprout.

c______ 9. When it rains, the plants growing on hillsides prevent the water from running down the hill quickly and carrying the soil with it.

b______ 10. A year of drought caused an oak tree to produce few acorns.

Part 2

Directions: In the spaces provided describe the difference between the terms.

Answers will vary.

1. ecology / ecosystem ***Ecology is the study of relationships within an ecosystem. An ecosystem is an area in which living and nonliving things interact.***

2. physical environment / biotic community ***The physical environment consists of all the nonliving things in an ecosystem. The biotic community consists of all the living things in an ecosystem.***

3. intensity of light / duration of light ***The intensity of light is the brightness of light. The duration of light is the length of time it is present.***

4. humus / substrate ***Humus is the decaying plant material in the soil. The substrate is the material found under the soil.***

5. evaporation / precipitation ***Evaporation is the process by which water escapes into the atmosphere. Precipitation is water falling out of the atmosphere.***

6. run-off water / ground water ***Run-off water is water that flows off the surface of the ground. Ground water is water that seeps into the soil and then collects to form the water table.***

Name ______________________

Date ____________ Hour ____________

Ideas 21b

Succession on a Volcano

Remind students to explain why the incorrect choice is not acceptable. They may have difficulty accurately and clearly explaining their reasons. You may not want to grade their reasons.

Directions: In each of the following statements, draw a circle around the correct choice in the parentheses. On the lines provided explain why the incorrect choice is not acceptable.

1. The plants and animals that lived on Mount Saint Helens in Washington before its 1980 eruption included pine and fir trees, grouse, foxes, hares, deer, bobcats, bears, and mountain lions. Populations of these organisms made up the (natural biotic community / climax vegetation) of Mount Saint Helens. ***Climax vegetation refers only to plants.***

2. When Mount Saint Helens erupted in 1980, almost all living things on the mountain were destroyed. This is an example of the (biotic community affecting the physical environment / physical environment affecting the biotic community). ***Volcanoes are part of the physical environment.***

3. In some areas, all life was destroyed. But, within a few months of the eruption, plants, such as pearly everlasting and fireweed, were found growing in these areas. These had sprouted from windblown seeds. Such plants are examples of (pioneer organisms / climax vegetation). ***Climax vegetation appears at the end of succession.***

4. Pine and fir seedlings cannot grow on the fresh volcanic surface of Mount Saint Helens because they require soil. Several generations of other plants will build the soil necessary for pines to grow. Soil building is an example of the (physical environment affecting the biotic community / biotic community affecting the physical environment). ***Soil is part of the physical environment.***

5. As this soil is built, the first plants will give way to other plants. Once again, pine and fir trees will grow on Mount Saint Helens if there are no more eruptions. These predictable changes in the biotic community are called (succession / Krakatoa). ***Krakatoa is another volcano where succession has been observed.***

6. The appearance of pine and fir trees on Mount Saint Helens does *not* represent the final climax community, since other major species changes (will yet occur / will not occur). ***If major changes are yet to occur, it would not be the climax community.***

7. The community surrounding Mount Saint Helens immediately before the 1980 eruption was not a climax community. It was still recovering from an 1857 eruption. A hemlock-fir forest community is the climax community for mountains in that area. If no more eruptions occur, Mount Saint Helens will reach its climax community (before / (after)) the year 2103.

Since the climax community had not recovered in the 123 years following the previous eruption, there is no reason to believe that it will recover to the climax within 123 years following the most recent eruption.

Ideas 21c

The Water Cycle

Directions: In the illustration below, draw arrows to show the water cycle. Draw label lines from the terms around the illustration to what they describe in the picture.

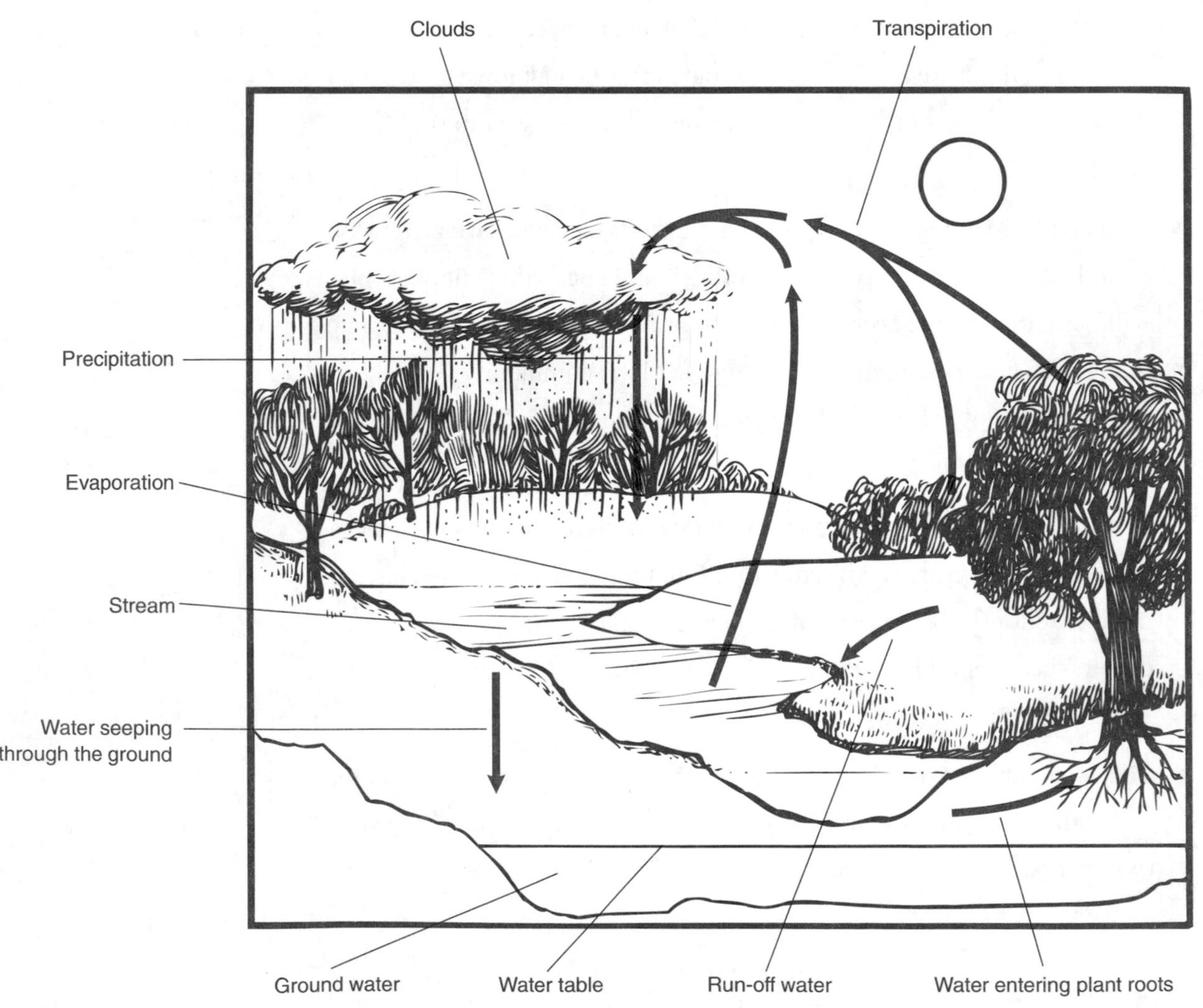

Name ____________________

Date __________ Hour __________

Ideas 21d

Rhythms in the Ecosystem

Directions: Unscramble the words and fill in the chart. For some of the words a definition has been supplied. For those that lack a definition, you must write one in the blank provided.

	Scrambled	Word	Definition
1.	hthymrs	*rhythms*	Changes that take place on a regular basis
2.	alnoesas	*seasonal*	*Occurs at a certain time of the year*
3.	tunrlacno	*nocturnal*	Active at night
4.	aidyl	*daily*	Rhythms that happen every twenty-four hours
5.	dlruian	*diurnal*	*Active during the day*
6.	rodycnam	*dormancy*	*A period of inactivity*
7.	rodtmna / dbu	*dormant bud*	*A bud that is not growing*
8.	nilesepnra	*perennials*	Plants that grow year after year
9.	nnaauls	*annuals*	*Plants that grow and die within a year*
10.	nrebhiatoni	*hibernation*	*Winter dormancy in some animals*
11.	tinnerla / ckclo	*internal clock*	Idea that internal factors control rhythms in many organisms

Review

Directions: Record your responses in the spaces provided.

1. List the major factors of the physical environment that are found in most ecosystems. ***Light, temperature, soil, substrate, and wind or current are major factors. (Students may also include fire, air, and topography.)***

2. List several materials that are cyclic in an ecosystem. Why is it essential that these materials cycle in an ecosystem? ***Water, oxygen, carbon, and nitrogen are cyclic materials. If these materials did not cycle, they would soon be used up.***

3. Choose an ecosystem. How does your choice qualify as an ecosystem? ***Selections will vary. The ecosystem should have living and nonliving things interacting in a limited area.***

4. List several factors of the physical environment that are significant in the ecosystem you chose in question 3. ***Answers will vary.***

5. List several populations that would be found in the ecosystem you chose in question 3. Indicate which of these populations are producers and which are consumers. ***Answers will vary.***

6. What are the differences between a winter-resident bird, a summer-resident bird, and a permanent-resident bird? ***A winter-resident bird comes to a particular area only in the winter. A summer-resident bird comes to the area only in the summer. A permanent-resident bird remains in the area throughout the year.***

Name ______________________
Date ____________ Hour ____________

Research Investigation 21a

Our Environment (part 1)

Do not assign all of the projects in this investigation. For many areas of the country, some of the projects outlined will not apply. Depending on your particular area, you may wish to add or expand certain projects or combine some of them into a single project. The projects outlined should serve as springboards for student work. You should supply additional direction before allowing the students to begin their work.

We suggest that you supply the notebook, properly labeled and divided. You should also select and provide good notebook paper and drawing paper. Tell the students that this notebook will be kept and used as reference material for future classes. Perhaps you could add the notebook to the school's library. This may help students to feel that they are doing something of value and not just another report.

You could consider doing sections of the notebook this year and adding sections to it in future years. This could be a good procedure to follow if your classes are small. You may want to have each class do certain projects (such as looking up information about organisms [project 3] and making food webs [project 5])but let different classes do some of the more difficult projects during different years.

If you teach several sections of the same class, you may want all the sections to work together to make one notebook.

Materials

encyclopedia or other reference book

Procedures and observations

If you are like most people, you probably know very little about the area in which you live. You may be able to find your way around well, but you probably have never carefully observed those surroundings that characterize your environment. This investigation, along with certain investigations in the next three chapters, is designed to help you and your classmates discover what your environment was like before people started living in the area. You will also discover the various changes that humans have made in the area.

This project will require several weeks to complete and will consist of many assignments. Sometimes you will work alone; other times you will work in groups. Your entire class will keep a notebook so that you can find out what your classmates are learning about your environment and they can benefit from what you find out. This notebook will contain the reports and other materials prepared by your class. When completed, it will describe many aspects of your environment.

In order to form a neat, organized notebook, your class will follow the outline presented in the box below. To keep your notebook neat and organized, follow the instructions in the box below when submitting a report for the notebook.

> **Note:** This investigation has three parts; it continues in Investigation 22a and Investigation 23a. These investigations are divided into sixteen different projects that cover some part of the ecology of your area. Some of the projects will be done by everyone in your class; other projects will be done by groups. Your teacher may omit a few of the projects if they do not apply to your area or may add some projects for special situations in your area.

Outline for the *Our Environment* Notebook

I. The natural environment
  A. Location
  B. The physical environment
  C. The Biotic Community
    1. Producer organisms
      a. Annuals
      b. Nonwoody perennials
      c. Woody perennials
    2. Consumer organisms
      a. Invertebrates
      b. Fish
      c. Reptiles
      d. Amphibians
      e. Birds
      f. Mammals
      g. Others (mushrooms and other fungi)
  D. Relationships between organisms
    1. Relationships within populations
    2. Relationships between populations
    3. Succession

II. Man's use of the environment
  A. The physical environment
    1. Water sources and uses
    2. Energy sources and uses
    3. Pollution
    4. Sewage and trash
  B. The biotic community
    1. Agriculture
    2. Extinct and endangered organisms
    3. Game, game management, and hunting
  C. Other human activities
    1. Conservation
    2. Future development

You may want to do a couple of reports yourself. Show them to the students (either on the bulletin board or in handouts) to show them what you are expecting from them. Some of the projects in later investigations can become complicated, and the information can be difficult to find. You may wish to do reports for some of the more complicated projects and then explain how you did them. This will help the students feel that this is a group project in which you are also involved.

One of the keys to success with some of the more complicated projects is finding the information yourself before assigning the project to the class. This is essential for several reasons. First, you will need to know whether the students have found the correct information or if they have found information that pertains to some other areas of the country. Second, you will often need to direct the students' research. The type of information necessary for this investigation is not usually found in encyclopedias. Third, some organizations or individuals have the information or are logical sources of the information but are not friendly to young students who are asking a lot of questions. Some sources may not be friendly to private Christian schools or home schools. You need to be aware of this type of problem before you send the students out to look for information.

Be careful that a large group of students does not repeatedly call or visit the same source. An individual who may have been a good reference could become uncooperative if pestered.

You will need to coach students on how to ask for information, how to represent themselves graciously, and how to thank a person, agency, or company for favors.

Preparing Reports for the *Our Environment* Notebook

Using your own paper and pen, write the report.

At the end of the report, list the sources you used to find the information for your report. Use the bibliography form that your teacher suggests for books, magazines, and pamphlets.

If you interviewed someone to find the information, list the person's name, his position, the date he was interviewed, and the person who interviewed him. (Example: Mr. Harold Smith, Director of Farming Research at Wayne County Agricultural Station in Pumpkintown, Massachusetts: November 15, 1997; interviewed by Erin Harris and Tal Looper)

Below the list of sources write, "This report was prepared by . . . ." On the lines underneath, list in alphabetical order the names of the people who prepared the report.

Give the report to your teacher. Your teacher will read it and, if necessary, will comment on it. If the report is not acceptable, your teacher will return it to you to rewrite.

If the report is acceptable, your teacher will return it to you with blank paper attached to it. Using blue or black ink, neatly copy your report onto the paper that your teacher gives you. Use only the front side of the paper.

If you include pictures (photographs or pictures cut from magazines and other sources) in your report, include them with the report when you first hand it in to your teacher. Your teacher will give you paper on which to mount these pictures.

If you are making drawings for your report, include rough sketches on your own paper when you first hand in your report to your teacher. Your teacher will give you paper on which to make your drawings.

Give any finished report and any drawings or pictures that you have to the classmates who are responsible for keeping the notebook. They will place the report in the notebook.

Project 1 for the Our Environment Notebook

Where Are We?

Before you can begin to describe an area, you have to know what area you are talking about.

Determine which biome you live in. A biome is a large geographical area that contains a particular group of plants and animals and has a specific physical environment. The map on page 348 of your text may give you some idea of the biome in which you live, but it is too small to give you specific information. You will need to consult other texts to determine your area's biome.

Biomes are divided into smaller areas that have particular characteristics. Determine the type and size of the area you live in. Some areas may include several states. Sometimes three or four different areas may be present in a single state. (This often happens if the state has mountains in one area or if it borders the ocean.) If members of your class come from different areas, determine which area your class will use for its notebook. If the area you live in is quite large (several states), you may want to limit yourself to a smaller area.

A student who is good at drawing can prepare a series of maps. He should first draw your continent and shade in your biome. He should then outline the state in which you live. On another map he should enlarge the state, shade the area of the biome you are using for your study, and outline the county in which you live. On this map he should include major bodies of water, such as rivers and large lakes.

Name ______________________________

Date ____________ Hour ______________

If possible, obtain a topographical map of your county from a library or county government agency. Topographical maps include information about the land (hills, valleys, streams, lakes, and so forth). Choose a student to draw a simplified county map for your notebook. In the drawing, he should include bodies of water and any other significant topographical features. He should also include major roads and cities. If the area you are studying does not fill the entire county, someone should indicate this by drawing the county limits on your map.

For variety, consider having the students do much of their writing on a computer or word processor. They could then turn the written portion of their projects in as computer disks or as a neat printout. This will function to improve their computer literacy.

Project 2 for the Our Environment Notebook

The Physical Environment

At various times your area probably receives rain, sunshine, cold weather, and warm weather. How do these and various other factors combine to make up the physical environment of your area? Different students or groups of students can prepare reports on each of the following factors.

- *Temperatures.* In your area, what is the average daytime high temperature for each month? What is the average nighttime low temperature for each month? What is the average temperature for each month? Plot this information on a graph. Are there any significant or unusual aspects about the temperatures in your area?
- *Precipitation.* In your area, what is the average precipitation for each month? Plot this information on a graph. Are snow, ice, hail, sleet, or fog common or significant factors in your area? Are there any significant or unusual aspects about the precipitation in your area?
- *Bodies of water.* What bodies of water are found in your area? If they are flowing water, how fast do they flow? How much seasonal difference is there in the amount of water they carry? How large are the standing bodies of water? How deep are they? What seasonal differences do they experience?
- *Sunlight.* How many daily hours of sunlight does your area average during each month? Plot this information on a graph. Are there any significant factors that affect the number of hours of sunlight that your area receives? Are cloudy days common in your area? If so, during what seasons?
- *Soil and substrate.* What kind of soil is found in your area? How deep is the topsoil. What is under the topsoil?
- *Winds.* In which direction are the prevailing winds in your area? Are they different during different seasons? What is the average speed (mph) of the winds for each month? Are storms common during a particular season? What are the winds like during the storms? Does your area have hurricanes or tornadoes? If so, how often?

Information about soil and substrate will probably be available from county agents. Since you may need to contact a county agent later for other projects, you may want to combine all the requests you have for him and seek his help only once rather than repeatedly.

You may want to visit with someone at a small local airport rather than a large metropolitan airport.

Sometimes local newspapers have this type of information in their files.

Some farmers can provide much of this information. Do not rely on a farmer's memory or guesses; ask for his sources.

To find this information you will probably need to do research in a library. You may need to ask the librarian for help in locating local statistics. Another source of information is the weather bureau for your area. Some of the information will also be available from county or state agencies. Sometimes this information is available at airports. Airplane pilots may have access to this information or may be able to tell you where to look for it.

Project 3 for the Our Environment Notebook

The Biotic Community

What organisms make up the natural biotic community of your area? Use field guides that deal with the organisms in your area. There are field guides to the trees, wildflowers, ferns, mushrooms, insects, fish, birds, reptiles, amphibians, mammals, and many other groups for virtually every area. Compile lists of significant organisms found in your area.

Most of the information called for will be available from the field guides. You may obtain some keys to the plants and animals of your area. (These should not be used as keys—an awesome project for a seventh grader.) Keys often contain a great deal of information about organisms. Students can use the index to look up the organisms.

Several large publishers have large, colorful books with titles such as Wildflowers of the Eastern United States, Mammals of North America, Birds of the Western States, *and* Mushrooms of the United States. *These types of books make excellent sources of information about the organisms. The students will enjoy using them.*

From these lists, you and your classmates should choose organisms that you would like to prepare reports about. Your teacher will determine the number of reports that each student should do. Each person should report on some large organisms and some small organisms. Do not report on an organism if it is found only in small numbers or if it is one of a large group of similar organisms in your area. For example, if there are ten different types of wrens in your area, you may want to deal with all of them as a group or with only one, but do not write a different report for each wren.

As much as possible follow the outlines given below for your reports. Sometimes you may not be able to find all of the information for the organisms you are researching. If your teacher does not feel that you have included enough information, she will return the report to you with a note saying that you need to continue your research.

Animal

Name: *(common and scientific)*

Description: *(size, color, physical characteristics)*

Food: *(what the animal prefers, what it will eat if the preferred food is not available, and what it eats during different seasons)*

Range: *(the areas of the country in which this organism is found)*

Habitat: *(the area in which this organism lives, feeds, builds its nest, den, etc.)*

Daily activity: *(diurnal or nocturnal)*

Seasonal activity: *(migration, dormancy, hibernation)*

Picture: *(photograph or drawing, if possible)*

Plant

Name: *(common and scientific)*

Description: *(size, type of stem, leaves, flowers, fruits, etc.)*

Range: *(the areas of the country in which this plant grows)*

Habitat: *(area that provides the conditions necessary for this plant to grow)*

Seasonal: *(when it flowers, bears fruit, is dormant, sprouts, etc.)*

Picture: *(photograph or drawing, if possible)*

Project 4 for the Our Environment Notebook

The Seasons

Consider giving this project to the creative individuals in your class. Have them write flowing descriptions of the environment and the changes that are occurring. Make sure they base their reports on fact and not fancy.

Establish several large groups in your class. Each group will be responsible for a different season. Depending upon your area of the country, you may wish to divide spring into early spring and late spring and divide autumn into early autumn and late autumn. In some areas of the country, there will be only three, and in some cases two, seasons. Using the information gathered in projects 2 and 3, write descriptions of your area during the various seasons.

You may want students to do this project orally in class. Ask the students to describe each of the seasons. You may want to ask a student to take notes and then copy the notes for the notebook.

You may want to write your descriptions as those of a typical day during the season that you are dealing with. A sample you might like to follow is the description of the dawn on page 323 of your textbook. There are other methods you could use to describe your area during the various seasons. Be sure to include information about the physical environment and the biotic community.

Name ______________________________

Date ____________ Hour ______________

Class Investigation 21b

The Biotic Community of the Soil

Goals

- Collect and identify the organisms in a soil sample.
- Demonstrate that a wide variety of organisms live in soil.

Materials

hand lens, incandescent light bulb (60-100 watts), isopropyl alcohol (optional), large funnel, nutrient agar plate (optional), ring stand and iron ring, sample of topsoil, slice of bread (optional), small jar or 250 ml beaker, wire screen (¼ inch mesh)

Many equipment substitutes are possible in this investigation. The basic design is to have a soil sample suspended over a container and to force organisms out of the soil and into the container using heat and light from an incandescent light bulb.

Procedures and observations

1. Collect about 1 L of topsoil. Include any organic debris on the surface. Avoid areas which have been treated with insecticide, such as lawns, or recently cultivated areas, such as gardens. Forest soil is excellent for this investigation.
2. Assemble a Berlese funnel. This is a large funnel with a wire screen set inside it. Support the funnel with a ring stand and iron ring as shown. The wire screen should be cut or bent into a disc which fits the funnel about halfway down the fluted portion.
3. Place part or all of your soil sample on the wire screen in the Berlese funnel. Place the portion of the soil that has the most organic material (leaves, stems, twigs, etc.) on the screen first. It will help to keep the remainder of the soil from falling through the screen. The soil layer should be about 5 cm deep.
4. Position the funnel over a jar or beaker containing isopropyl alcohol to collect the organisms that fall through. You may substitute water for alcohol, but some organisms may then escape.
5. Suspend an incandescent light over the funnel about 4 in. above the soil. Turn on the light for about 24 hours. Organisms in the soil will burrow deeper to avoid the heat, light, and drying. As they do, they will fall through the screen and into the collection jar or beaker.
6. Use a hand lens (or stereomicroscope) to observe the collected organisms. Identify and count the organisms. Your teacher will help you identify them. Record your observations in the table on the next page.
7. (Optional) Put a small amount of soil on a nutrient agar plate or on a piece of bread moistened with water. Incubate this in a warm, dark area for 1-2 days. Observe the organisms that grow and include your observations in the table on the next page.

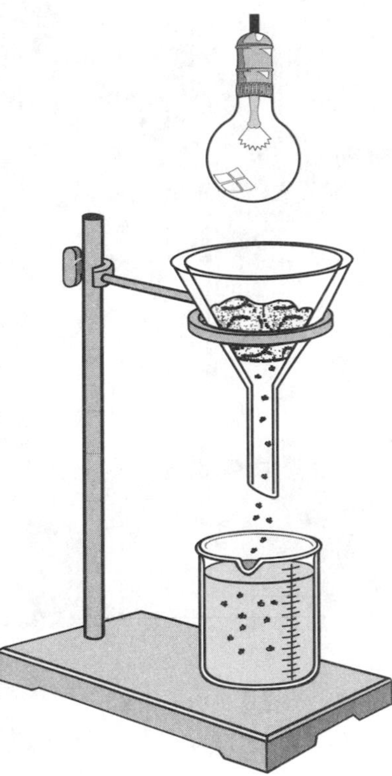

Identification may be general or specific.

Type of organism	How many?	Notes and observations

Summing up

1. How many different types of organisms did you find in the soil? *Answers will vary.*
2. What type of organism was most numerous in the soil? *Answers will vary.*
3. If you did the optional soil incubation, what type of organisms did you find? *fungi and bacteria* Could there be more of these in the soil than of the larger organisms? *yes*
4. Do you think there are organisms that you did not find in the soil sample? *yes* If so, what do you think they are? *Answers will vary but may include small seeds, other species of a kind of organism found, and other microscopic organisms.*

Go a step further

Repeat your observations using soil samples from different areas (meadow, swamp, riverbank, deeper in the ground, etc). Record your findings and determine what differences in the biotic community of the soil exist between these areas.

Name ______________________

Date ____________ Hour ______________

Field Investigation 21c

Back Yard Ecosystems

An ecosystem is a limited area in which living and nonliving things interact. Thus a back yard, a school yard, or a park is an ecosystem. Each of these areas has a biotic community (made up of various populations of living organisms) and a physical environment (made up of nonliving factors). You observe these ecosystems every day. But what specific organisms and factors make up these ecosystems?

Choose an area and list the various factors of the physical environment that are present in it. Be sure to list the factors that man controls. For example, mowing the lawn, watering, and planting certain plants are all physical environmental factors that are not natural to the area but are important parts of the ecosystem.

List the populations that make up the biotic community of the ecosystem you are studying. Include not only the plant populations but also the visible and "invisible" (such as earthworm and ant) animal populations. Be as specific as possible. In other words, do not just list "birds," but list the specific kinds of bird populations in the ecosystem. Include the various populations that may be "out of season" (such as grasshoppers and daffodils). Do not forget that if pets use the area, they are a part of the ecosystem—even though they may not be in the ecosystem all the time.

Bring your list to school and be prepared to discuss your observations.

You may want to do this as a group project. If you can use your school yard for a study, divide the class into groups and have each group compile a list of certain components of the ecosystem. Natural factors of the physical environment, man-controlled factors of the environment, plant populations, and animal populations are logical groups to form.

This investigation may serve as the first part of Investigation 22e. You may want to do these two investigations together.

You could ask students to name a certain number of factors and populations in given areas. As a class, combine these into one complete list for the area.

Home School Tip

Select two or three factors for your student to research.

Name ______________________
Date ____________ Hour ____________

22–Relationships Between Organisms

Ideas 22a

Energy Exchange Between Organisms

Directions: In each of the food chain examples given below, write the organisms in the proper level of the ecological pyramid provided. Then answer the questions to the left of the pyramid. Sometimes you may need to write *none* in the blank. Empty blanks are considered to be wrong answers.

Food chain (in alphabetical order): clover, hawk, rabbit

1. Name the producer(s) in this food chain. *clover*
2. Name the consumer(s) in this food chain. *hawk, rabbit*
3. Name the decomposer(s) in this food chain. *none*
4. Name the herbivore(s) in this food chain. *rabbit*
5. Name the carnivore(s) in this food chain. *hawk*
6. Which population in this food chain contains the most energy? *clover*
7. Which population in this food chain contains the least energy? *hawk*
8. Give an example of a predator-prey relationship in this food chain. *hawk (predator) and rabbit (prey)*

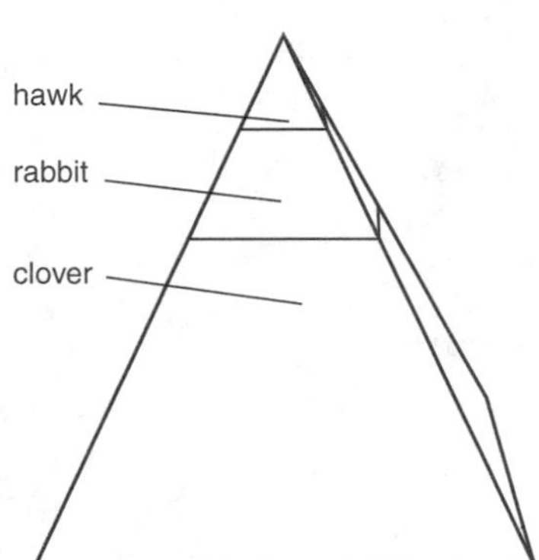

Food chain (in alphabetical order): frog, grasshopper, snake, wheat

1. Name the producer(s) in this food chain. *wheat*
2. Name the consumer(s) is this food chain. *frog, grasshopper, snake*
3. Name the decomposer(s) in this food chain. *none*
4. Name the herbivore(s) in this food chain. *grasshopper*
5. Name the carnivore(s) in this food chain. *frog, snake*
6. Which population in this food chain contains the most energy? *wheat*
7. Which population in this food chain contains the least energy? *snake*
8. Give an example of a predator-prey relationship in this food chain. *snake (predator) and frog (prey) or frog (predator) and grasshopper (prey)*

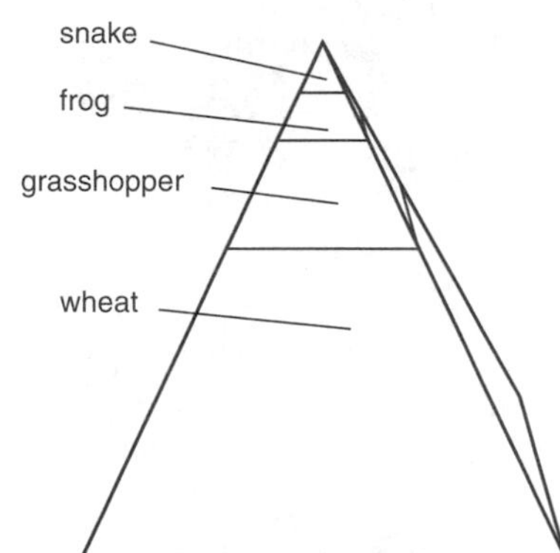

Answers can be one set of organisms or the other.

Ideas 22b

Food Chains—Food Webs

Directions: Draw arrows to represent the flow of energy between the various organisms in the food web illustrated below. Then on the blank by each organism place one letter from Column 1, telling whether the organism is a producer or a consumer. If the organism is a consumer, place a letter from Column 2 beside the *C,* telling which kind of consumer the organism is.

Drawing all the possible arrows can get quite confusing, messy, and difficult to grade. Simply check to see that the students have drawn a complicated food web and perhaps spot check a few of the arrows.

Column 1

P - Producer

C - Consumer

Column 2

C - Carnivore

H - Herbivore

D - Decomposer

O - Omnivore

T - Detritus feeder

Food Web of a Meadow

Name ______________________
Date ____________ Hour ____________

Ideas 22c

Relationships Between Organisms of the Same Species

Directions: Below is a list of several examples of relationships between organisms of the same species. Each example is followed by two blanks. In the first blank, name an organism that has the kind of relationship described. Use the organisms listed below. In the second blank, name another organism that has that kind of relationship. You will need to provide the second set of examples yourself.

Organisms

ant	buffalo
bald eagle	praying mantis
sea gull	tuna
wolf	

1. Independent organism	*praying mantis*	*Answers will vary.*
2. Mates for life	*bald eagle*	
3. Social insect	*ant*	
4 Lives in a school	*tuna*	
5. Lives in a herd	*buffalo*	
6. Nests in a flock	*sea gull*	
7. Lives in a pack	*wolf*	

Ideas 22d

Relationships Between Different Populations in an Ecosystem

Directions: Below is a list of several types of relationships between organisms of different species. Each type is followed by two blanks. In the first blank, name a pair of organisms that are involved in that kind of relationship. Use the organism pairs listed below. In the second blank, name another pair of organisms that are provided in that kind of relationship. You will need to provide the second set of examples yourself.

Organism Pairs

Flies that look like bees
Lions and vultures
Mosquitoes and dogs
Cows and protozoans that digest cellulose in cows' stomachs
Tigers and tall, brown grass
Hawks and mice
Grasshoppers and rabbits

1. Competition ***Grasshoppers and rabbits*** ***Answers will vary.***
2. Predator-prey ***Hawks and mice***
3. Parasite-host ***Mosquitoes and dogs***
4. Commensalism ***Lions and vultures***
5. Mutualism ***Cows and protozoans that digest cellulose in cows' stomachs***
6. Camouflage ***Tigers and tall, brown grass***
7. Mimicry ***Flies that look like bees***

Name ____________________
Date __________ Hour __________

Ideas 22e

Review

Directions: Write the proper terms next to the following definitions and descriptions. Then find and circle the terms in the word puzzle on the next page. The terms may appear horizontally, vertically, or diagonally and may be forward or backward.

predator 1. An animal that eats another animal

prey 2. An animal that is eaten by another animal

competition 3. Relationship between two organisms that are using the same factor in the environment

commensalism 4. Relationship in which one organism is benefited and the other organism is not helped or hurt

independent 5. The type of organism that does not live with others of its same species

social 6. The type of organism that does live with others of its same species

scavenger 7. An organism that eats dead, decaying bodies

cyclic 8. Used over and over again

epiphyte 9. A plant that grows on another plant but does not receive nourishment from the plant it grows on

flock 10. Society for the birds

mutualism 11. The type of relationship that profits both organisms involved

camouflaged 12. An organism is ______ when it looks like its surroundings.

warning coloration 13. An organism with bright colors that inform other organisms of its presence has ______.

mimicry 14. A relationship in which an organism appears very similar to another organism

parasite 15. An organism that feeds off another living organism

host 16. A living organism that supplies materials to another organism

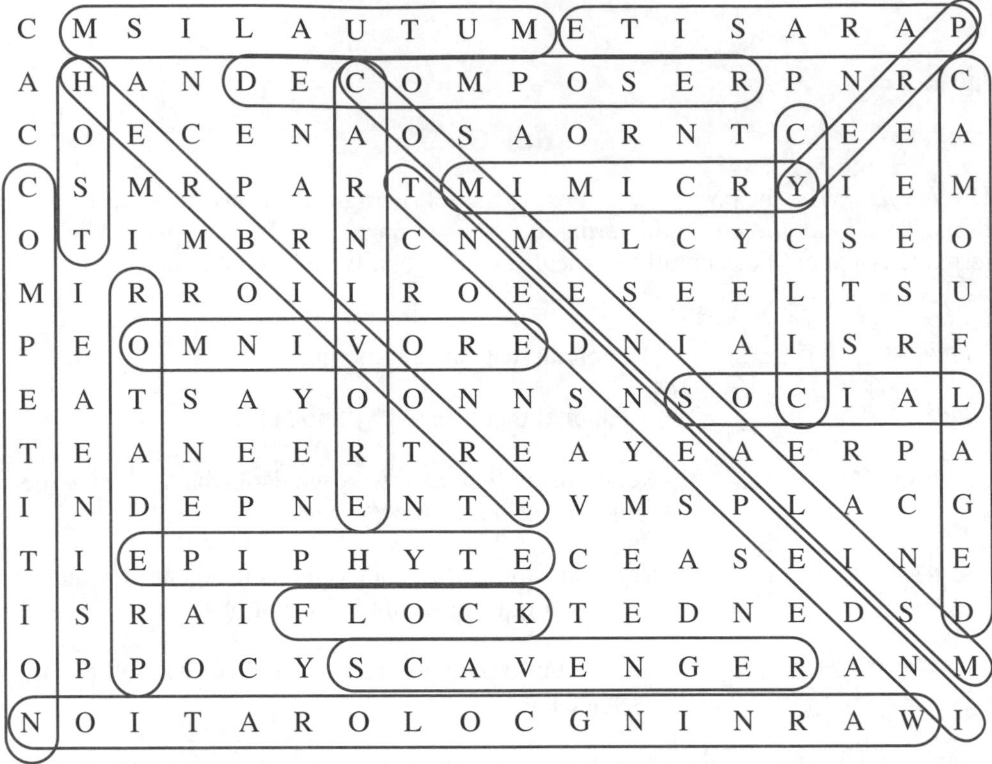

In the word puzzle are four additional words that describe different types of consumers. Find them and list them below.

17. *decomposer*

18. *herbivore*

19. *carnivore*

20. *omnivore*

Name ______________________________

Date ______________ Hour ______________

Research Investigation 22a

Our Environment (part 2)

See Investigation 21a for instructions for this project.

Project 5 for the Our Environment Notebook

Food Webs

Prepare diagrams of food webs that take place in your area. Use the organisms that your class wrote reports about in the notebook. Be sure that each food web applies to a particular season and a particular area. In other words, do not diagram squirrels eating both wild strawberries (a spring fruit) and apples (a fall fruit). You may need to prepare reports on more organisms in order to draw good food webs.

When you prepare the food web diagram, use names, not pictures, of the organisms. Place the diagram under "Relationships Between Populations" in the notebook.

You may want each student to include a minimum number of organisms in a food web. You may also want to list certain organisms that each student must include in his food web diagrams.

Project 6 for the Our Environment Notebook

Relationships Within Populations

The relationships among organisms of the same kind in a particular environment can be interesting. Choose an animal that lives in a flock, herd, school, or some other social group in your area. In various books, research the social relationships within the animal's group. Write a brief report telling of the social structure involved in the group.

Some organisms that live in groups have a very loose social structure or a social structure that has not been studied. You may want to preview the literature that is available to your students before you assign a particular organism for them to research.

You can do this project in conjunction with project 7. Various groups could study social organisms while others are studying nonfood relationships.

You may want the class to do this investigation in groups. Choose several organisms that live in societies. Have each group of students research one of these organisms and write a brief report on it.

Project 7 for the Our Environment Notebook

You may want the class to do this investigation in groups. Assign one type of relationship to each group and ask each group to provide examples of the relationship. Providing examples for some relationships may be difficult. You may wish to assign the easier relationships to large groups of average students and assign some of the more difficult ones to smaller groups of sharp students.

You can assign this project in conjunction with project 6. See the teacher's notes for project 6.

Nonfood Relationships Between Populations

Some of the nonfood relationships between organisms include commensalism, mutualism, camouflage, warning coloration, and mimicry. What examples of these nonfood relationships can you find in your area?

Define a relationship and then list organisms (from your area) that are involved in that relationship. Briefly tell how each example you give illustrates the relationship. Use a separate sheet of paper for each of the relationships. Look for pictures that illustrate these relationships among the organisms you are describing. Include them in your report.

Project 8 for the Our Environment Notebook

For many areas, information about succession is readily available. For some areas it is not.

Some areas are "fire limited." They have a natural disaster periodically and almost constantly go through succession without reaching the climax community. This type of occurrence could be interesting to research.

In large areas several different successions may occur. For example, succession in a beaver pond and succession after a forest fire are quite different, but they may occur in the same area. You may be able to assign these various types of succession to different students or groups of students.

Succession

Assume that a natural disaster destroys a twenty-acre section of the area your class is studying and all the plants and animals of the natural biotic community in that section are killed. What will happen now? The area will go through succession to reach its climax community again.

Go to a library or interview a knowledgeable person to find out what the stages of succession in your area are like. What are the pioneer organisms? What organisms will begin to live and grow in the area after the pioneer organisms? How many major stages are in the succession to the natural biotic community? How long will it take for the area to reach its climax community?

Write a report answering these questions. Include any other interesting or significant material you learn about succession in your area.

Name ______________________
Date __________ Hour __________

Personal Investigation 22b

Your Food Chain

Humans are consumer organisms. Every time you eat, you are a link in a food chain. But what food chains are you involved in?

Record the foods you eat during an entire day. You may need to divide some of the foods into various categories. For example, you should consider a sandwich made of bread, cheese, and ham as bread, cheese, and ham—not simply a sandwich.

Determine which organisms your food came from and which link you are in the food chain. List the organisms that are involved in the food chain for each of the foods you ate. If you eat plants or plant products, you are a herbivore and are the second link in the food chain. If you eat meat or animal products (such as milk or cheese), you are a carnivore and are the final link (hopefully) in a three- or four-link food chain. By eating some foods you may become the last link in a four- or five-link food chain. Put a *2* in the column if you were the second link in a particular food chain, a *3* if you were the third, and so on.

Most of our foods are either producers (plants) or herbivores. Some fish that man eats are true carnivores. Pork could be considered as an omnivore meat. When we eat cheese and similar milk products, we become the fourth link in a food chain (if we consider the bacteria or fungi responsible for the formation of these foods). By eating certain fish and exotic foods, we become the fifth or even higher link of the food chain.

You may want to suggest foods for which the students should determine the food chain. Occasionally students will eat only foods that are plants or herbivores.

You may want to do this investigation as an oral class project for a part of a class period.

Students may suggest their favorite foods for consideration. You may collect pictures of meals from magazines and then have the students analyze the pictured foods rather than recording their foods for a day.

Foods I have eaten	I am link #	Organisms in the food chain leading to the food I ate

1. As a herbivore, the foods I ate were ***Answers will vary.***

2. As a carnivore, the foods I ate were ***Answers will vary.***

3. List the organisms in a food chain that includes you, but not as the final link. ***Answers will vary. Direct the students away from unlikely scenarios such as cannibalism or lion attack. The use of predator/parasites such as mosquitoes, chiggers, or ticks will suffice as will including decomposers.***

Name ______________________

Date ____________ Hour ______________

Class Investigation 22c

Overcrowding

This investigation could be started on a Thursday or Friday, and the bean seeds could be left unobserved over the weekend. You may want to have the students observe the pots every other day.

Goal

- Observe the effects of overcrowding on bean seedlings.

Materials

thirty-three bean seeds, potting soil, two flower pots about 10 cm (4 in.) in diameter

Rather than having two pots for every student, you may want to do this investigation with small groups of students.

Procedures and observations

1. Fill the pots with potting soil to about 2.5 cm (1 in.) below the rim. Do not add any fertilizer or plant food to the soil.
2. Place three bean seeds in one pot and thirty in the other pot. Cover the seeds with about 1 cm (0.5 in.) of soil. Water each pot thoroughly and set them in a warm, well-lighted area where they will have identical conditions (temperature, light).
3. Record the date that you planted your seeds: ______________________
4. Regularly water the pot with three seeds with enough water to keep the soil moist but not soggy. The pot with thirty seeds should be watered with the same amount of water as the first pot regardless of how much water it appears to need.
5. Once the seeds sprout, do not move the pots. If some seedlings in the crowded pot get more light than others, that is a consequence of overcrowding and should not be changed.
6. Observe the pots daily. Begin recording your observations on the chart below when the seeds sprout. In the columns that ask for observations about the sprouts, record data about the height, color, number of leaves, and general condition of the plants.

Home School Tip

If you have a garden and the weather is warm, you could do this investigation in your garden and thus omit the need for pots and potting soil.

Any seeds that germinate rapidly can be used in this investigation. However, if you extend the observations for several weeks, perennials (especially trees such as sweet gum, oaks, maples, and pines) may exhibit self-thinning in which some crowded seedlings will quickly die.

The seeds in the pot with three seeds should be spaced evenly apart in the pot.

Date	Pot with three seeds		Pot with thirty seeds	
	No. of sprouts	Observations	No. of sprouts	Observations

You could do this investigation as a demonstration, discussing the observations rather than having the students make the observations. You should still have the students record the observations on the chart and answer Summing Up questions.

7. After you have completed your observations for a week or two, unpot the seedlings and carefully remove the soil from them. Do this by putting the seedlings in a large dish of water and gently moving them.

8. Record your observations of the differences between the root systems of the plants in the two pots. ***Overcrowded roots are usually thinner and longer than normal roots.***

You can achieve the same experimental results using smaller pots and fewer seeds. The number of seeds in the overcrowded pot should completely cover the surface area of the soil.

9. As an alternative to procedure 8 above, you could allow the seedlings to grow for 4-6 weeks before making your final observations. Depending on a number of factors, the seedling differences may be more obvious after an extended time period.

Summing up

Write a paragraph comparing and contrasting the bean sprouts in the two pots. ***Answers will vary.***

Name ______________________

Date ____________ Hour ____________

Class Investigation 22d

Lichens

Goal

- Observe the mutualistic relationship of lichens.

Materials

coverslips, eyedropper, glass slides, lichen specimens, microscopes, prepared microscope slides of lichens

Setting up

- Using field guides, find the types and locations of lichens that are common in your area.
- Obtain samples of several different lichens. Be sure to obtain permission from the people who own the land where you collect your specimens. Be careful not to destroy other living things while you collect specimens.
- Using a field guide, try to identify your specimens.
- Bring your specimens to class.

Procedures and observations

Observe the various lichen specimens in your classroom

In the spaces below, describe what you see. From the person who collected the specimens, find out where the lichen came from. Include that information in your description.

1. lichen name ______________ description ______________
2. lichen name ______________ description ______________
3. lichen name ______________ description ______________
4. lichen name ______________ description ______________
5. lichen name ______________ description ______________

You may want to collect the lichen specimens yourself and have them ready to observe in class.

You may want to omit the teased wet mount of fresh lichen. If you have the right type of lichen and make the slide during the growing season, it can be profitable. If the season or the lichen is wrong, however, you will see little. Be careful not to place bark or other substrate on your slide.

This investigation can be very profitable if you purchase good prepared lichen slides. You may want to set up one or two microscopes and let the students observe the slides on them.

You may wish to observe the slides before class begins and find out what the algal and fungal parts of the lichen look like. You can then offer your students descriptions of each. By describing these parts you can help the students understand what they are seeing.

You may do individual parts of this investigation rather than doing the entire exercise.

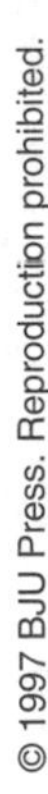

Prepare a slide of a lichen and observe it through a microscope

1. Place a tiny piece of lichen in a drop of water on a glass slide.
2. Using probes, tear the lichen into small shreds. This process is called teasing.
3. Place a coverslip on top of the teased lichen.
4. Observe this slide through a microscope.
5. Describe what you see. *Answers will vary. Often you can see filaments of fungi. You can recognize the algae by the presence of chlorophyll.*

Observe a prepared slide of a cross section of a lichen

1. Focus the prepared slide of a lichen.
2. Find the cells of the algae and fungi.
3. Describe what you see. *Answers will vary depending upon the slides you are using.*

Summing up

1. What is a lichen? *A lichen is algae and fungi that are living together.*
2. How does a lichen exhibit mutualism? *Mutualism occurs when two organisms live together and both benefit. In the lichen the algae provide food for the fungi, and the fungi provide support and protection for the algae.*
3. Why can lichens grow in places where other organisms cannot grow? *They can grow in such places because of the mutualism. Lichens can grow in places where the fungi could not otherwise obtain food and where the algae could not otherwise receive protection and support.*

Supplementary reading

"Kaintuck Hollow, Missouri." *Natural History,* Sept. 1991, pp. 74-77.

"In Praise of the Lowly Lichen." *International Wildlife,* Nov./Dec. 1991, pp. 30-33.

Name ______________________
Date __________ Hour __________

Field Investigation 22e

Observing Relationships

Organisms are constantly interacting with each other. With even a casual observation of a natural setting, you can see dozens of interactions if you know what to look for.

The relationships discussed in Chapter 22 of your text are listed below. Beside each of these relationships is a point value. On a sheet of paper make a separate column for each of these relationships. Then go to a field, a forest, a meadow, or some other natural area where you can observe both plants and animals.

At the top of your paper record the date(s), time(s), and place(s) in which you made your observations. List in the proper columns the names of the organisms involved in the relationships you observed. Try to earn fifty points. You may earn points for only five of each kind of relationship listed below.

Predator and prey (2 points)

Parasite and host (5 points)

Scavenger and its food (4 points)

Decomposer and its food (1 point)

Independent organisms (1 point)

Couples that are mated for life (4 points)

Social organisms in a group (3 points)

Competition between animals (same species) (3 points)

Competition between plants (same species) (1 point)

Competition between populations (3 points)

Commensalism (5 points)

Mutualism (5 points)

Camouflage (4 points)

Warning coloration (5 points)

Mimicry (5 points)

You may want the students to do this investigation in small groups rather than individually. If you have a large school yard or a partially wooded area, you can do this investigation during a class period or after school.

You may wish to have students orally suggest examples of each of the relationships that they may see while they are doing their field work. This will help some students to understand what to look for.

Establish the number of points needed for each grade level and announce this scale to the students before they begin the assignment. A scale of 44-50 points for an A, 37-43 points for a B, 30-36 points for a C, and 21-29 points for a D is suggested. Depending upon your area and the season, you may need to adjust the scale.

Home School Tip

Not all students will be able to make reliable observations on their own. Help them make observations yourself, or let your student cooperate with another home school student on this investigation.

Major Biomes of the World

Directions: Complete the crossword puzzle.

Across

1. A shallow, standing-water biome
3. Plants that store water
4. A hoofed animal found on African grasslands
6. Biome in which buffalo live
11. Area near land where the ocean is shallow (two words)
14. Precipitation
16. Continent
19. Disk operating system
20. Type of tundra on mountains
22. A daily task
23. A product made by trees that serves as food for many animals in deciduous forests
24. A plant organ
25. A type of vegetation in American deserts
26. ______ down.
27. An ostrichlike bird found on grasslands of South America
29. Type of freshwater biome that includes rivers and streams
30. Opposite of young
32. A large, marine predator
37. Land formations that may have several different biomes within a relatively small area
40. Traveling around the world visiting all the biomes would be ______.
41. Children who are too young to walk well are sometimes called tiny ______.
42. A salt-water ecosystem
43. Half of two
44. Vertebrate nekton organism
46. Abbreviation for road
48. Biome that has the least amount of rainfall
50. A beverage made from certain leaves soaked in hot water
51. Biome with scattered trees on a grassland
53. An ostrichlike bird found on grasslands of Australia
55. *Felis*
56. An organism that is in the phylum Echinodermata and is commonly found in tide pools
57. Abbreviation for the explosive trinitrotoluene
59. A type of coniferous tree
60. Prefix meaning "not"
63. Masses of coral may accumulate to form a coral ______.
64. Name of the area that is covered by water at high tide and exposed during low tide (two words)
65. A small doglike carnivore

Name ______________________________

Date ______________ Hour ______________

Down

2. A large tree-dwelling primate found in tropical rain forests
3. "Yes ______," said the private.
5. A type of bread
7. Too
8. "As far as the eye can ______ "
9. Biome with trees that lose their leaves for a season during the year (two words)
10. Type of animal that migrates into and out of water
11. Biome with a dry summer and a wet winter
12. A type of biome on land
13. Biome that usually has rain once a day during at least one season of the year (three words)
15. A short rest
17. Type of freshwater biome that includes swamps and lakes
18. Type of tundra near one of the earth's poles
21. Organism that swims
28. A large, antlered herbivore often found in coniferous forests
31. An herbivore commonly found in a deciduous forest
33. Organisms that live on the bottom of bodies of water
34. Those plants that are found in a biome at the end of succession (two words)
35. The old man often needed a ______ to help him walk.
36. Area in the tundra's soil that does not thaw
38. Biome that is frozen most of the year
39. Substance in which plants grow
45. Organisms that float in bodies of water
48. There is no typical aquatic ecosystem. They are more ______ than terrestrial biomes.
49. Television
50. A large-beaked, fruit-eating bird that lives in tropical rain forests
52. Bird's home
53. Trees that grow above the canopy in a tropical rain forest
54. The Gila monster is one of the few poisonous ______.
58. Layer formed by trees that grow together, blocking out the sunlight in a forest
59. A regularly occurring physical environmental factor that is destructive yet necessary in certain environments.
61. Covers seventy percent of the earth's surface
62. Structure that falls periodically from deciduous trees

1 SWAMP
2 APE
3 SUCCULENTS
3 SIR
4 ZEBRA
5 RY
6 GRASSLAND
7 ALSO
8 SEE
9 DECIDUOUSFOREST
10 TRANSIENT
11 CONTINENTALSHELF
11 CHAPARRAL
12 TERRESTRIAL
13 TROPICALRAINFOREST
14 RAIN
15 NAP
16 ASIA
17 STANDING
18 ARCTIC
19 DOS
20 ALPINE
21 NEKTON
22 CHORE
23 NUT
24 ROOT
25 CACTI
26 SIT
27 RHEA
28 ELK
29 RUNNING
30 OLD
31 DEER
32 SHARK
33 BENTHOS
34 CLIMAXVEGETATION
35 CANE
36 PERMAFROST
37 MOUNTAINS
38 TUNDRA
39 SOIL
40 FUN
41 TOTS
42 MARINE
43 ONE
44 FISH
45 PLANKTON
46 RD
48 DESERT
48 DIVERSE
49 TV
50 TEA
50 TOUCAN
51 SAVANNA
52 NEST
53 EMU
53 EMERGENT
54 LIZARDS
55 CAT
56 STARFISH
57 TNT
58 CANOPY
59 FIR
59 FIRE
60 NON
61 OCEAN
62 LEAF
63 REEF
64 INTERTIDALZONE
65 FOX

Name ____________________
Date __________ Hour __________

23–Natural Resources

Ideas 23a

Renewable and Nonrenewable Resources

Directions: Below are listed several materials that are considered to be natural resources. In the space by each material, place an *R* if it is a *renewable* resource or place an *N* if it is a *nonrenewable* resource.

N	gold	*R*	soil	*R*	wool
R	trees	*R*	deer	*N*	petroleum (oil)
N	coal	*N*	aluminum	*N*	diamonds
R	lumber	*R*	water	*R*	cotton

Ideas 23b

Agriculture and the Soil

Directions: Below are several groups of words. In each group, three of the four words (or phrases) are related to one another. Draw a line through the unrelated word and then write a sentence using the remaining words. Your sentence should show how the words are related. You may slightly change the form of the word in your sentence (for example, *legumes* to *legume, fertilizer* to *fertilizing*).

Answers will vary. Students will devise other good sentences that involve three of the four words in each group.

1. agriculture / livestock / crops / ~~soil~~ ***Agriculture is the science of growing crops and livestock.***

2. ~~fertilizer~~ / harvest / land grants / fertility ***A few years after moving into wilderness land grants, people found that soil lost its fertility and harvests decreased.***

3. humus / ~~irrigation~~ / depletion of minerals / soil fertility ***Lack of humus and depletion of minerals can cause a loss of soil fertility.***

4. fertility / depletion / ~~agriculture~~ / decompose ***If plants are removed and not allowed to decompose, soil will be depleted and lose its fertility.***

5. clover / ~~humus~~ / legumes / nitrogen ***Some plants, such as clover and other legumes, add nitrogen to the soil.***

6. depletion of minerals / fertilizer / legumes / ~~irrigation~~ ***Adding fertilizers and planting legumes are methods of preventing the depletion of minerals in the soil.***

7. crop rotation / field / crop / ~~fertilizer~~ ***Crop rotation is growing a different crop in a field each year.***

Ideas 23c

Man, the Steward

Directions: In each of the following examples, decide whether man is acting as an ecological consumer, an ecological manager, or both. Then indicate your answer by writing the proper letter in the space provided. You will use each letter three or four times.

C - Ecological consumer
M - Ecological manager
B - Both an ecological consumer and manager

C ______ 1. Bob and Krissi are picking wild blackberries.

M ______ 2. Farmer Brown plowed his field to plant potatoes.

M ______ 3. To control flooding, the government built a dam on the river.

C ______ 4. Uncle George went duck hunting.

C ______ 5. Dick filled the tank of the car with gasoline.

M ______ 6. During the summer, Bill's job was to mow and water the lawn.

B ______ 7. Each day the shepherd led the sheep to a hillside to graze.

B ______ 8. Bob dammed a stream to irrigate his corn.

B ______ 9. The Collins boys raised minks to help pay for their education.

M ______ 10. Foresters used aerial spraying to kill gypsy moths.

Name ______________________

Date __________ Hour __________

Ideas 23d

Man's Role in the Ecosystem

Directions: Unscramble the words and write them in the blanks. For some of the words a definition has been supplied. For those that lack a definition, you must write one in the space provided.

	Scrambled	Answer	Definition
1.	xpnoeenaitl owthgr	*exponential growth*	Constant rate of increase
2.	traethrib	*birthrate*	*Rate at which individuals enter a population*
3.	namhu tionlaupop	*human population*	Number of people on the earth at one time
4.	pupoalnoit inrcasee	*population increase*	A condition that occurs when the birthrate of a population is larger than the death rate
5.	brtnaoio	*abortion*	*The killing of unborn children*
6.	dthea rtea	*death rate*	Rate at which individuals leave the population
7.	noitlaopup crdeaese	*population decrease*	*Condition that occurs when the death rate of a population is greater than the birthrate*
8.	ueiaaathns	*euthanasia*	*The killing of very old or very sick people*
9.	yasdmdoo	*doomsday*	Time when man destroys the earth by abusing it
10.	srvacnontioe	*conservation*	*The careful use of natural resources*

Ideas 23e

Pollution

Directions: Complete the words missing in the following statements by filling in the necessary letters. The circled letters form words that complete a sentence at the bottom of the exercise.

1. Today aluminum is cheaper to RECYCLE than to mine.
2. Gases and tiny particles form the major components of AIR POLLUTION.
3. Substances that the environment can recycle are called BIODEGRADABLE substances.
4. The final stage of sewage treatment that removes chemicals from the water is called TERTIARY treatment.
5. A solid, liquid, or gas may be a SUBSTANCE pollutant.
6. Chemicals and heat released into streams and lakes are common forms of WATER POLLUTION.
7. One of the most abundant components of air pollution is the deadly gas CARBON MONOXIDE.
8. Solid unwanted or unusable materials are called TRASH.
9. SULFUR compounds are the second most abundant type of air pollutant.
10. An area where cities used to dispose trash was the city DUMP.
11. The sewage treatment that reduces the amount of biodegradable materials is called SECONDARY treatment.
12. Although too much pollution can be bad, not all pollution is HARMFUL to an environment.
13. A dump that has layers of soil placed over it is called a SANITARY LANDFILL.
14. Unwanted products potentially harmful to man or the environment are called HAZARDOUS WASTES.
15. The two major types of pollutants are substance pollutants and ENERGY pollutants.
16. By law, many NEWSPAPERS are made of recycled paper.

In the environment man is both an ECOLOGICAL CONSUMER and a MANAGER.

Name ____________________
Date ____________ Hour ____________

Research Investigation 23a

Our Environment (part 3)

See Investigation 21a for instructions for this project.

Project 9 for the Our Environment Notebook

Water Resources and Uses

Water is one of our three most important natural resources. In your area, where does the water that humans use come from? For this project you may wish to limit yourself to one city or to a section of your area. Find the answers to the following questions.

- What are the primary sources of water for human use? How much water is used per day? How much of the water is used for industrial purposes? For agriculture?
- Is the water treated before it is sent to the homes of the area? If so, what is done to it? Is the drinking water in your area hard or soft? If it is hard, what chemicals in the water make it hard?
- Where is the water stored? Are there any reservoirs in your area? Are there water tanks?
- Are there any private wells in the area? How many homes supply their drinking water by private wells? How often are these wells inspected for water quality? In the past five years, how many wells contained water that was deemed unfit for human consumption? Why was it considered unfit? Is there a water shortage in the water table during certain seasons of the year?
- Is there any danger that your area will not have enough water within the next few years? What water sources are being considered for meeting the needs of the future? Does your area supply water for other areas? If so, how much water does it supply? To which other areas does it supply this water?

The answers to these questions may be found in a public library. Your city or county water department should be able to answer these and any other questions you may have about your water resources.

Write a brief report answering these questions and telling any other interesting information you learned about your area's water supply.

You may wish to divide the class into eight groups and have each group do a different project from this investigation. If, for some reason, you decide not to do all eight projects, you can then divide the class into a smaller number of groups. Many of the projects will require information from the same sources. You may need to coordinate and guide the outside research so that a single government agency or other source is not bombarded by dozens of students requesting information.

Quite frequently a government agency or other source will supply you with booklets, brochures, copies of releases, and the like, which will give you the information your students need. Students may use these brochures and other materials to prepare to contact the sources and ask intelligent questions. This project is best done by an individual or a small group. An individual or small group can phone or visit the water department and obtain answers to the questions.

A field trip to a water-treatment facility can often be interesting. Visit the facility in advance. If the facility is large and is set up to instruct visitors, it may be a good place for a class field trip. If not, it may be a good place for an after-school trip for the individual or group working on this project. Usually all the questions in this project can be answered at such a facility.

Project 10 for the Our Environment Notebook

Energy Sources

What energy sources are available in your area? Does your area produce coal, oil, or natural gas? Are there hydroelectric dams in your area? Is solar power used much in your area? Does your area have an abundant amount of forests? If so, is any of the wood used privately or commercially as an energy source? Is wind energy or geothermal energy used significantly in your area? Does your area depend upon other areas to supply you with energy?

If your area does produce its own energy, prepare a report telling the extent to which these various energy sources are used.

If your area uses some unusual energy resource, such as geothermal or wind energy, an investigation of this resource may be very profitable—even if the resource is used on a limited basis.

Project 11 for the Our Environment Notebook

If your area produces great quantities of different agricultural products, you may want your students to study only the most common ones.

Common information sources for this investigation are the chamber of commerce or other agencies responsible for encouraging business in your area.

Agriculture

What farm products are produced in your area? Farm products include not only fruits, vegetables, and the typical "farm animals" but also products such as honey and animal fur. How much of each of these products is produced? In your report, do not include the products that are grown in back yard gardens for the gardener's personal use. Instead, research the products that are grown for market.

Make a list of the agricultural products that your area produces and sells. Also indicate how much of each product is produced. If possible, indicate how much this amount of product is worth each year. What are some of the special problems that farmers growing these products face? Do unseasonably cold, hot, wet, or dry spells endanger crops? Are there certain insects or other pests that greatly threaten the farmers' crops in your area?

This information may be available in libraries or from county agents.

Project 12 for the Our Environment Notebook

Explain to the students that you are not interested in the dinosaurs or other antediluvian organisms that may have once roamed your area. Students should report on organisms that have lived during the past two hundred years.

Information needed for this project and Project 13 may be found in the same sources. You might wish to combine these two projects or gather the information for them at one time.

Extinct and Endangered Organisms

In many areas of the United States wolves, bald eagles, turkeys, bison, and other animals were common in days gone by. But now development, hunting, and various other human activities have forced these animals out of many of the areas in which they once lived. Other animals, like the passenger pigeon and the Carolina parakeet, were once common in areas of the United States but are now extinct.

What animals or plants were once common in your area but are now no longer found there? What caused them to leave or die out? In what areas are these animals or plants now found?

Are any of the animals or plants now extinct that were once in your area? If so, name them.

Are there any endangered species found in your area? If so, what are they, how many of them are supposedly in your area, and where are they found? What is being done to protect these organisms?

You can find the answers to these questions in libraries or through state, regional, or national wildlife agencies. Sometimes this information will be available from game management agencies. Prepare a report answering these questions and telling any other interesting material you discovered about extinct or endangered organisms.

Project 13 for the Our Environment Notebook

You may wish to combine this project with Project 12 and/or Investigation 23b. Some students who enjoy hunting will find this investigation considerably more interesting than finding out about the sources of electricity in their areas.

Some students may have access to most of this information through their parents or through local sportsman supply stores.

Game and Game Management

When people in your area go hunting or fishing, what do they bring home? How many of each game animal are believed to be in your area? Are any migratory? In your area, how many of each game animal are believed to be taken by hunters or fishermen each year?

When are the seasons for hunting the various game animals in your area? How many of each game animal may an individual kill? Are there any other restrictions that hunters must follow? What sizes or sexes of game animals may or may not be killed?

What do the game management authorities do to insure an abundance of game animals in your area? Do the game management authorities also manage nongame animals? If so, what animals do they control and how do they care for these animals?

Name ______________________

Date __________ Hour ____________

Are there official bounties on any animals in your area? If so, what are they, and why are these animals considered harmful? How many of the bountied animals were taken last year?

You can find the answers to these questions in libraries or through the wildlife or game management authorities in your area. After you have found the information, prepare a report telling the answers to these questions and including any other interesting information you found out about game and game management in your area.

If your area has many different game animals, you may want your students to limit themselves to only a few of the major animals.

Project 14 for the Our Environment Notebook

Pollution

What problems does your area have with pollution? Find out the answers to the following questions.

- What are the major sources of air pollution in your area? Are there laws that restrict the pollution of the air in your area? What types of pollution do these laws deal with? Is the air cleaner, more polluted, or about the same as it was five years ago? Is your area prone to thermal inversions, acid precipitation, smog, or other problems as a result of air pollution? If so, how often do these problems occur, and how severe are they?
- What are the major sources of water pollution in your area? Are there laws restricting the pollution of water in your area? What types of pollution do these laws deal with? Are there areas that are no longer suitable for swimming or fishing because of water pollution? Are the streams, rivers, and lakes in your area cleaner, more polluted, or about the same as they were five years ago? Has the water in any wells been deemed unfit for drinking because of pollution? What substance was found in the water? From where did this substance probably come?
- Are there any other major forms of pollution that affect your area? If so, what are they, and what is being done about them? Are there any hazardous waste dumps that a government agency is cleaning up? Are any of these federal Superfund sites?

You may need to offer special guidance to the students who are working on this project. Often the best sources of information will be newspapers. Unfortunately, most newspapers lack indexes and are thus difficult for students to use. You may need to keep a file of articles about local problems so that your students will know where to begin their research.

Project 15 for the Our Environment Notebook

Sewage and Trash

What type of treatment is given to sewage in the city where you live? What happens to the sewage after it is treated? What happens to the water that remains after the sewage is treated?

If your area uses septic tanks, use an encyclopedia and other books in a library to find out what a septic tank is and how it works. Write a brief report about septic tanks. Be sure to include problems that may result from the use of septic tanks.

What does your city do with the trash it collects? Are any of the materials in your trash recycled? Are any of them burned? Are any of them composted? If your city uses a sanitary landfill, where is it located? How long can your city continue to use the landfill before it is filled up? What will your city do then? Does your area dispose of trash for other areas?

By calling the various agencies responsible for these municipal functions, students should be able to gain the necessary information for this investigation. In large cities the agencies may be so large that students will have difficulty getting the information.

Project 16 for the Our Environment Notebook

Conservation and Development

Consider beginning this project with a discussion. Ask students to name the developments that are planned for your area and to list the areas that have been set aside for conservation. You may need to suggest some areas to help start the discussion. Be careful not to consider projects that are too small. Divide the class into groups and have each group discuss one section of the investigation.

A field trip to a national or state park or forest can be a valuable activity. If your entire class cannot go, consider having a group go and report back to the others.

Are there sections of your area that serve as wildlife refuges, wilderness areas, national or state parks or forests? If so, how large are these areas? Why have these areas been set aside? What are the purposes and uses of these areas? If possible, visit these areas and see what they are like. Find out from the rangers or from other people who are responsible for the area what they do to maintain the area.

Are any areas being considered for conservation? If so, how large are they and why are they being considered?

What developments are planned for your area? Are major government projects being considered? Are dams, tourist attractions, major industrial complexes, nuclear energy plants, utilization of natural resources (mines, oil wells, or the like), landfills, waste dumps, or other developments being considered for your area? Why are these developments needed? Are there objections to these developments? What are they? Were any studies done to determine what impact these developments would have on the environment? If so, what did they reveal?

Personal Investigation 23b

Hunting with a Camera

You may combine this investigation with Investigation 23a, Project 13. This investigation is ideal for a student who is interested in hunting or photography but has difficulty with school work. You may want to add certain requirements from Investigation 23a, Project 13, to his report.

Hunting is not always easy. Knowing where to look, when to look, and what to look for can be a challenge. Even experienced hunters can spend long hours in the field and come back with nothing but tired feet.

You should make sure that a novice or nonhunter who is doing this investigation is supervised by a qualified hunter/adult.

Go on a hunting trip yourself. But rather than taking a gun, take a camera and photograph the game you find. You can then show your pictures to your classmates. Be sure that you are well aware of the proper safety procedures for hunting the game in your area. Make sure that you secure the proper permission to be in the area. Take pictures of the game you see, the area in which you looked for game, and any nongame animals you see. Prepare a report about your trip. Include the pictures you took while you were "hunting."

The single-use cameras now available are perfect for this project. They are inexpensive enough that damage by students should not be of much concern. They are simple to use and regular, panoramic, and telephoto versions can be used, depending on how close the student plans to get to the game animals.

For obvious safety reasons it is not advisable to do this investigation during a regular hunting season.

Some game animals that could be photographed by students include deer, squirrels, rabbits, geese, ducks, and doves.

If students are "hunting" with a camera only, some procedures that normally are illegal may be acceptable. For example, the students may be able to "hunt" at a salt lick or feeding station. Check with a local game warden.

Name ______________________
Date ____________ Hour ____________

Personal Investigation 23c

Estimates

Chapter 23 made the amazing claim that over one hundred million (100,000,000) tons of trash are produced by Americans per day. How can we know that number is correct? Would different people produce different amounts of trash? Would we produce different amounts of trash on different days? Did someone weigh all the trash in America on a particular day? With a population of over 250 million people, how long would it take to weigh all of our trash?

That amount of trash is an *estimate*. Estimates are neither guesses nor accurate counts. One way to make an estimate is to count (or measure or weigh) *samples* of the subject in question. A sample is a small portion of the subject. Once the sample is counted, it is multiplied by the number of samples that could have been taken.

By "the number of samples that could have been taken" we actually mean the total number of disjoint (non-overlapping) samples necessary to cover the subject once.

To arrive at the claim of one hundred million tons of trash per day, someone weighed the trash produced by people living in different parts of the country. This weight was divided by the number of people who produced the trash to give an average weight. The average was multiplied by the number of people in the United States to give the final total. Of course, the accuracy of the people weighing varies a little bit, and one sample varies from another. Since the accuracy and samples vary, one hundred million tons is not exactly correct, but it is better than a guess; it is an estimate.

Lead the students in making the estimate suggested below. Students should be able to make estimates given a representative sample and population of the United States. Other things that could be estimated are the number of hairs on the forearm, the number of letters in a book, the number of leaves on a tree, the number of scales on a fish, or the number of grass plants in a lawn.

Estimates are useful when it is impractical or impossible to count the things in question. Estimates have been used to report the number of people in a crowd, the number of trees in a forest, and the number of bacteria in the air. Have you ever made an estimate?

Goals

- Understand how estimates are made.
- Estimate how much waste paper American people produce per day.

One third to one pound (0.2 to 0.5 kg) are typical waste paper weights per person per day.

Materials

a scale or balance (Bathroom scales will work.)

Procedures and observations

There may be some items in the trash that you may not want the students to see (confidential letters, financial statements, personal hygiene products, etc.). Alert the parents to remove any such items before the students collect the waste paper.

1. Collect and weigh all the waste paper produced by your family in one day. Include newspapers, paper towels, candy bar wrappers, envelopes, and waste paper that your parents produce at work and that you produce at school. ______ kg or lb.
2. Collect and weigh paper products that are discarded once a year by your family. Include paper calendars, catalogs, and perhaps magazines. Divide this weight by 365 to find the weight that should be included with the daily weight. ______ kg or lb.
3. Next, add the weights from #1 and #2 together and then divide by the number of people in your family. This is the average weight of waste paper produced by a person in your family per day. (Your teacher may want you to include the weights of waste paper of your classmates' families and then divide by the total number of people represented.) ______ kg or lb. (average waste paper per person per day)

4. Multiply the average waste paper weight for your family members (or class family members) by the population of the United States. The population is around 250 million. The product is your estimate of the weight of the waste paper produced by people in the United States per day. _______ kg or lb. (waste paper produced per day in the United States)

God does not need to estimate. He is omniscient (all-knowing). Even the hairs of your head are numbered (not estimated). See Matthew 10:30.

A representative sample is similar to that of the entire population. How then can you know that it actually is similar to the population without weighing everyone's trash? When scientists sample something, they count several samples from different locations or times, and they take the samples at random. By taking several samples, rather than just one, they increase the likelihood that they are representative. Random samples are usually chosen mathematically. This separates a person's ideas (bias) about the area from the data collection. In making the estimate in this investigation, it is not necessary to choose several random samples unless your teacher instructs you otherwise.

Name ______________________
Date ____________ Hour ______________

Class Investigation 23d

Recycling Paper

Goals

- Demonstrate how paper is recycled.
- Make recycled paper.

Materials

paper to be recycled (newspaper), blender, water, piece of cloth (or blotting paper), mesh screen (window screen), clothes iron (optional), large sponge, large dishpan, wood frame, staple gun with staples, heavy object such as a phone book (optional)

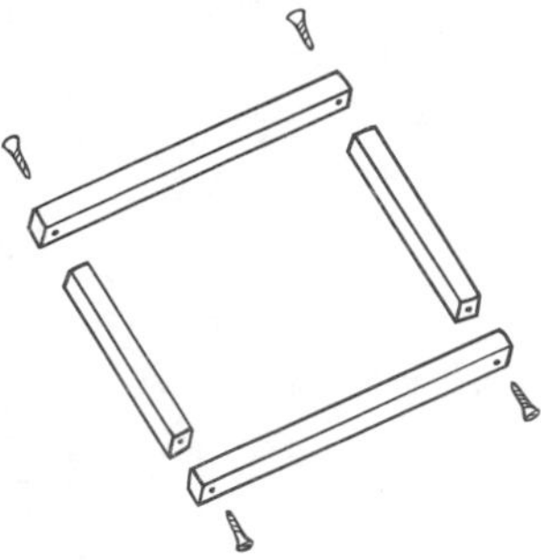

The dishpan should be of sufficient size to permit the screen frame to fit horizontally in it. The pieces of cloth should be larger than the screen frame.

Procedures and observations

1. Construct the screen frame as shown in the diagram. Your teacher may have already done this in advance. The screen frame should be smaller than the dishpan.
2. Cut or tear an amount of paper equal to a single page of a newspaper into pieces approximately 2 cm wide and long.
3. Place the torn paper into a blender with 1000 ml (1 qt.) of water, and blend it until it becomes a slurry rather than wet, stringy bits of recognizable paper (15-30 seconds). This recycles the paper back into pulp.
4. Pour the pulp into the dishpan. Continue making pulp until the dishpan is filled to within 8 cm (3 in.) of the top.
5. Stir the pulp in the dishpan with your hands. (Roll up your sleeves.) You may need to add water if the pulp seems thick.
6. Hold the screen frame with both hands (screen side towards you). In one motion, lower it vertically into the pulp in the dishpan and then position it horizontally in the pulp. (See diagram.)
7. Holding the screen frame horizontally, lift it straight up out of the pulp. Wiggle the frame slightly while lifting to evenly distribute the pulp on the screen. A layer of pulp will be deposited on the screen. Steps 6 and 7 should take 10-30 seconds depending on how much pulp is in the water and how thick you want your paper to be.
8. Allow the screen to drain over the dishpan for 15-30 seconds. You may tilt it slightly to help the water drain.
9. Flip the screen frame upside-down and place it on a piece of cloth. (The layer of pulp should be between the cloth and screen.)

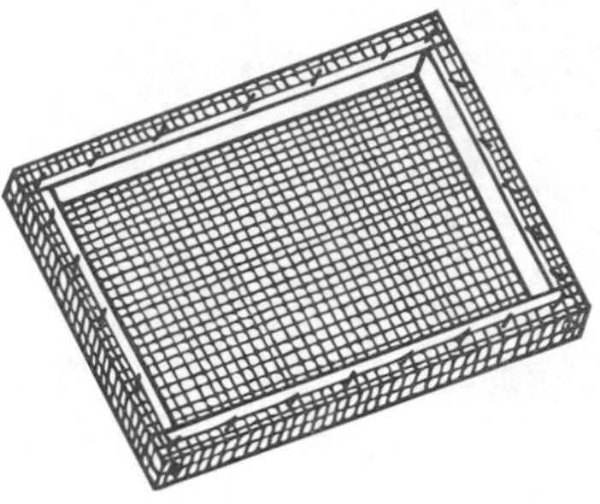

It is not essential that the paper be completely reduced to pulp. Thus, using an electric mixer or egg beater or even much stirring by hand will suffice. Some "recipes" simply call for soaking the torn pieces for 2-3 days.

Some recipes include starch in the pulp for a stronger paper.

After making several pieces of paper you may need to add more pulp to the dishpan.

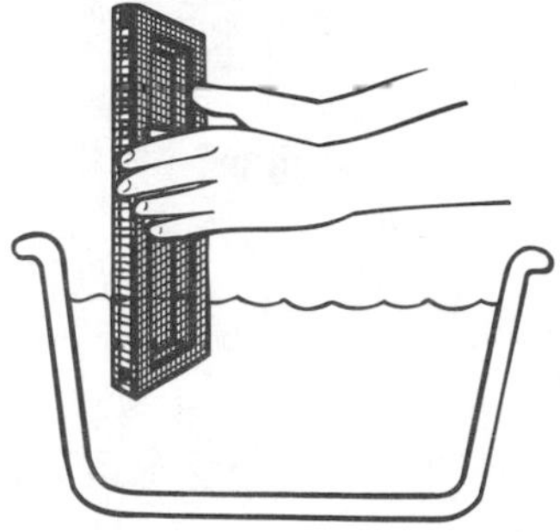

10. Press down on the screen with the sponge to absorb water from the recycled piece of paper.
11. Carefully lift the screen frame from the recycled paper. The paper should adhere to the cloth instead of the screen. Then carefully peel the paper from the cloth.
12. There are two general ways to dry your recycled paper.
    A. Sandwich your paper between two pieces of dry cloth. Put a heavy weight such as a phone book on top and let the paper dry for a day or two. Several such sandwiches can be stacked together and weighted by the same heavy weight.
    B. Iron your paper with a clothes iron on an ironing board. Be certain *not* to use the steam setting on the iron.
13. When cleaning up, do not pour leftover pulp down the drain. Pour it through the screen frame or a sieve to remove most of the pulp from the water. This pulp can be saved for later use or discarded.

Summing up

1. How do you think the pulp you made differs from the pulp used to make brand-new paper? How are they similar? *Brand-new pulp is made directly from wood; recycled pulp is made from paper, and is thus indirectly made from wood. They are similar in that both are wood products.*

2. How do the characteristics of the paper you made differ from the original paper you recycled? *Answers will vary but may include differences in texture, color, thickness, and size.*

3. How might the process of recycling paper on a large scale cause pollution? *Answers will vary. One potential problem is that pulp not filtered from the water could pollute water supplies.*

4. What recycled paper products have you seen in use? *Answers will vary but will generally include paper items such as bags, cardboard boxes, and envelopes. Students may also mention construction materials such as insulation and certain types of wood substitutes.*

Going beyond

When making the pulp, include pieces of other materials in the mix. Onion skins, short threads, and crumbled leaves make good additions.

Supplemental reading

"How to Make Homemade Paper," *Mother Earth News,* December 1993/January 1994, p. 30.

Name ______________________
Date ____________ Hour ______________

24–Support and Movement of the Body

Ideas 24a

Human Skin

Direction: Complete the words missing in the following statements by filling in the necessary letters. The circled letters form a phrase that tells one of the most important functions of the skin.

1. The fluid secreted by the sweat glands is called P E R S (P) I R A T I O N.
2. The E P I D E (R) M I S is the outer layer of skin, which continuously sheds dead cells.
3. The body adjusts the amount of B L (O) O D in the skin to help control the body temperature.
4. The water in a B L I S (T) E R helps to protect the deeper layer of the skin.
5. The D (E) R M I S is the inner, thicker layer of the skin.
6. A (C) A L L U S is an area of thick, tough epidermis that protects the skin.
7. A yellowish pigment found in the skin is C A R O (T) E N E.
8. M E L A N (I) N is the dark brown pigment that colors the skin.
9. A layer of loosely arranged fat cells and fibers below the skin is the S U B C U T A N E (O) U S layer.
10. A T A (N) is a darkening of the skin and is caused by a buildup of melanin.
11. Blood vessels in the skin contract and the pores of the sweat glands close when the body is C (O) L D.
12. Hair develops from cells in the hair (F) O L L I C L E S.
13. D A C T Y L O G R A P H (Y) is the study of fingerprints.
14. The hair and skin are kept soft, flexible, and water-resistant by the (O) I L made by glands in the skin.
15. Overexposure to ultraviolet rays results in a S (U) N B U R N.

A major function of the skin is

P	R	O	T	E	C	T	I	O	N	O	F	Y	O	U
1	2	3	4	5	6	7	8	9	10	11	12	13	14	15

Ideas 24b

The Skeletal System

Directions: On the skeleton diagram below, label the following bones.

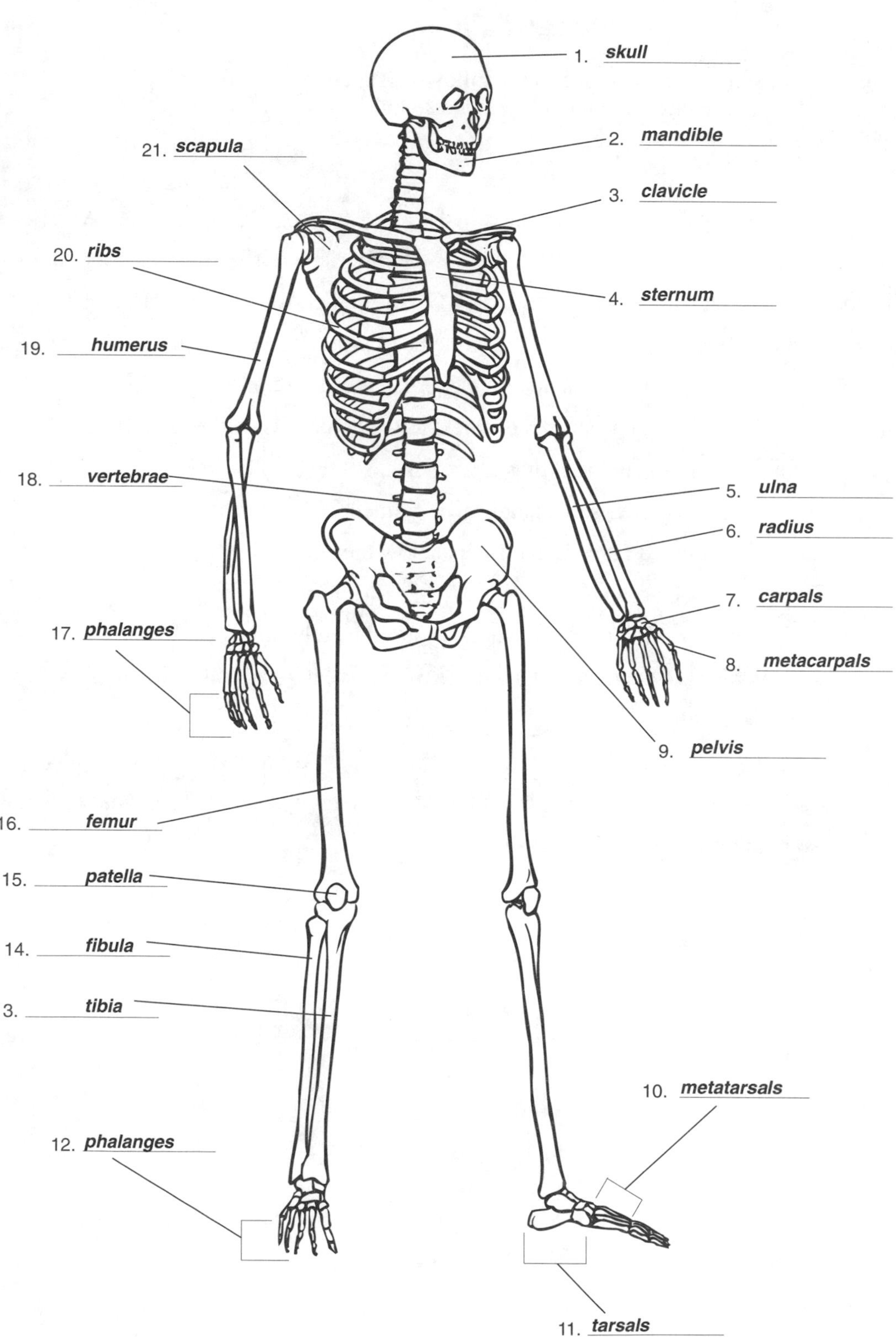

Name ______________________
Date __________ Hour ______________

Ideas 24c

Joints

Directions: Below is a series of diagrams of various actions. In the space provided, tell what type of joint is responsible for each action and which bones form the joint responsible for the action.

	Type of Joint	Bones Forming the Joint
1.	*Hinge*	*Femur and tibia*
2.	*Pivot*	*Vertebrae (first two)*
3.	*Gliding*	*Carpals*
4.	*Ball-and-socket*	*Femur and pelvic bone*
5.	*Pivot*	*Radius and humerus*
6.	*hinge*	*phalanges*

Students may give skull as an answer, but the first two vertebrae are the only bones actually involved.

Ideas 24d

The Muscular System

Directions: Below is a series of diagrams of actions and a list of muscles. Match the action with the muscles most responsible for the action by writing the muscle name in the space provided. In the diagram, color the area where the muscle would be.

biceps	latissimus dorsi	sternocleidomastoid
deltoid	pectoralis	tibialis anterior
gastrocnemius	rectus abdominis	trapezius
gluteus	rectus femoris	triceps
external oblique	sartorius	

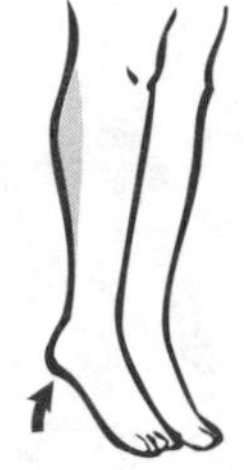

1. *gastrocnemius*

2. *deltoid*

3. *sartorius*

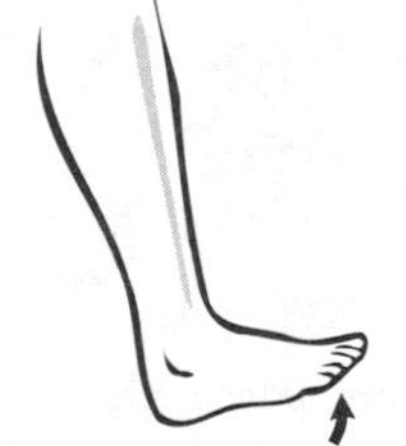

4. *tibialis anterior*

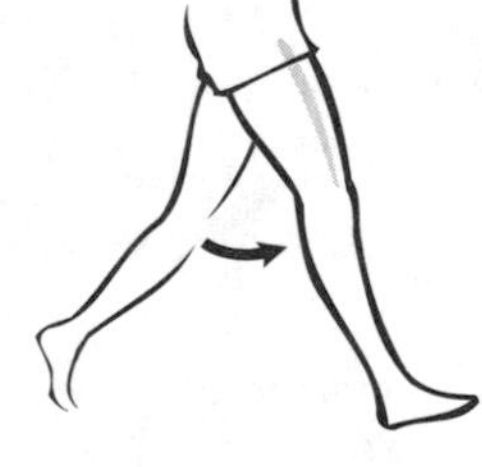

5. *rectus femoris*

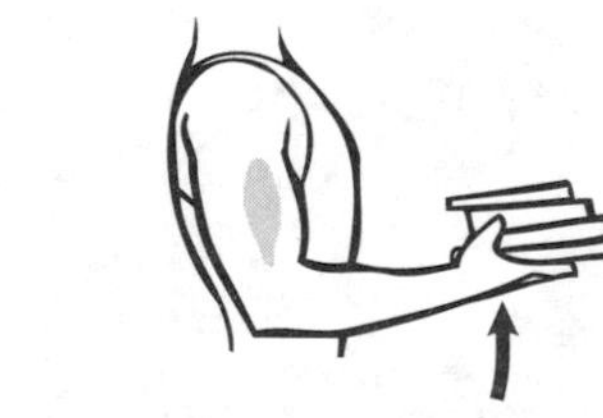

6. *biceps*

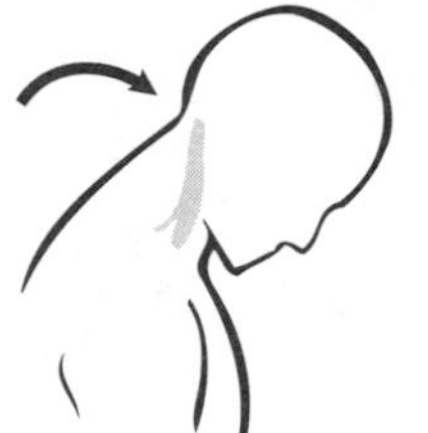

7. *sternocleidomastoid*

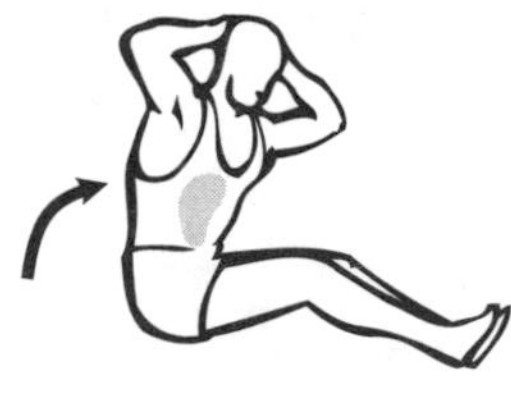

8. *rectus abdominis*

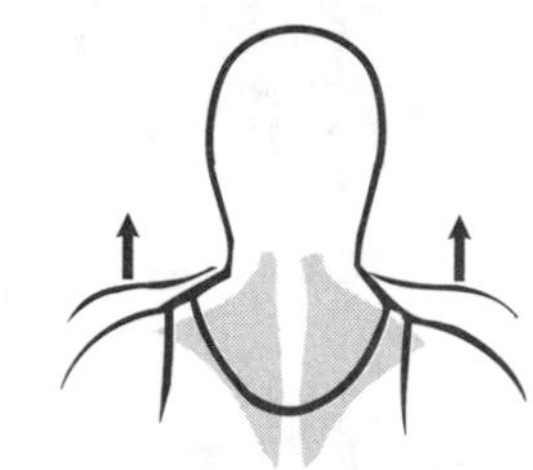

9. *trapezius*

10. *pectoralis*

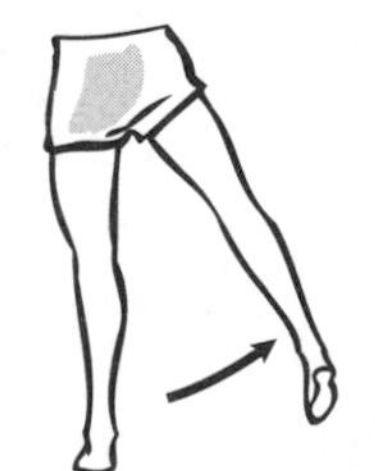

11. *gluteus*

12. *latissimus dorsi*

Name ______________________

Date ____________ Hour ____________

Ideas 24e

Review 1

Directions: Unscramble the terms and write them in the blanks. For some of the words, a definition has been supplied. For those that lack a definition, you must write one in the space provided.

1.	muetpreios	*periosteum*	The tissue that covers bones
2.	lsitgnaem	*ligaments*	*Tough, flexible bands that connect bones to bones*
3.	tsondne	*tendons*	*The structures that connect muscles to bones*
4.	worarm	*marrow*	Substance found in the cavities of bones
5.	netsoso	*osteons*	*Tiny units that make up bone*
6.	ratcigale	*cartilage*	*A supporting tissue that is more flexible than bone*
7.	eusdf	*fused*	*Completely formed; allowing no movement*
8.	sypgno	*spongy*	Type of bone that has many irregular spaces in it
9.	vtbererea	*vertebrae*	*Bones of the back*
10.	tcarligea aestlp	*cartilage plates*	Structures that permit long bones to grow in length
11.	ssniotriat	*striations*	*The stripes seen in some muscle tissue*
12.	ouepstr	*posture*	*One of the functions of muscles*
13.	revshi	*shiver*	Muscle movement that creates heat for the body
14.	nocratct	*contract*	*What muscles do when nerves stimulate them*
15.	aictlc daci	*lactic acid*	Substance produced when muscles do not receive enough oxygen
16.	ouayvlntr	*voluntary*	Muscle actions that you have control over
17.	eeoslktn	*skeleton*	*All the bones of the body*
18.	iouanvlntry	*involuntary*	*Muscle actions that you have no control over*
19.	osomht	*smooth*	*Muscle tissue that lacks striations*
20.	areht	*heart*	An organ that is involuntary but is made of striated muscle tissue

Ideas 24f

Review 2

Directions: In the spaces provided describe the difference between the terms given.

Answers will vary.

1. dermis / epidermis *The dermis is the thick, inner layer of the skin. The epidermis is the thin, outer layer.*

2. endoskeleton / exoskeleton *An endoskeleton is an internal support system made of bone and/or cartilage. An exoskeleton is a hard, external support.*

3. ligament / tendon *Ligaments attach bones to bones. Tendons attach muscles to bones.*

4. cartilage / bone *Cartilage is a supporting material that is softer than bone. Cartilage covers bones at movable joints.*

5. voluntary muscle / involuntary muscle *Voluntary muscles are muscles that a person can consciously control. Involuntary muscles are automatically controlled by the nervous system and cannot be consciously controlled by a person.*

6. striated muscle / nonstriated muscle *Striated muscle shows tiny stripes formed by layers of protein. Nonstriated muscles do not have these stripes.*

7. triceps / biceps *The biceps bends the elbow, and the triceps straightens it.*

8. aerobic cellular respiration in muscles / anaerobic cellular respiration in muscles *Aerobic cellular respiration requires oxygen in the breakdown of glucose and releases energy and carbon dioxide. Anaerobic cellular respiration breaks down glucose without using oxygen, and it produces lactic acid.*

Name ____________________

Date ____________ Hour ____________

Class Investigation 24a

Structure of the Skin

Good prepared slides are the secret to success with this investigation.

You may want to have the microscopes already set up.

You can combine this investigation with Investigation 24b and/or Investigation 24d.

If you have a microprojector, you can do this investigation as a class demonstration.

Goal

- Observe and learn about the structures of the skin.

Materials

microscope, prepared slide of a cross section of human skin

Procedures and observations

Obtain and set up your microscope

Focus your microscope on the slide of human skin. The epidermis should be toward the top, and the subcutaneous layer toward the bottom.

1. Find and observe the epidermis. Which layer is the epidermis? *It is the top or outermost layer.*

2. Describe the epidermis. *Answers will vary. It is a multiple-layered tissue of variable thickness.*

3. Find and observe the dermis. Where is the dermis? *It is under the epidermis.*

4. Look for the following structures in the dermis. If you can find them, describe what they look like. Leave the lines blank for those that you cannot find.

   a. Hair *Students should find and describe hair.*

   b. Hair follicle *Students should find and describe a hair follicle.*

   c. Blood vessels *Students should find and describe blood vessels.*

   d. Oil gland *Students should find and describe an oil gland.*

e. Sweat gland *Students may not find a sweat gland, depending upon the slides you have. Normally a sweat gland will be in the subcutaneous layer with the duct passing through the dermis to the surface of the epidermis.*

f. Nerve ending *A nerve ending will be difficult to find, even with the best slides.*

g. Muscle *Muscle tissue is easy to find on some slides, impossible on others.*

5. Where are the oil glands located in relation to the hair follicles? What is the significance of this relationship? *Oil glands are located around hair follicles and open into the hair follicles. They supply oil to keep the hair and epidermis soft.*

6. Describe the shape of a hair inside the follicle. *Answers will vary. The hair is thicker in the lower part of the hair follicle. The end of it wraps around blood vessels.*

7. Pull a hair out of your scalp. Does the end of the hair from your scalp resemble the end of the hair you observed through the microscope?
☐ Yes ☐ No If not, how does if differ? *It should appear about the same. The "roots" are actually what was wrapped around the blood vessels.*

8. Find and observe the subcutaneous layer. Where is the subcutaneous layer? *It is below the dermis.*

9. Describe the subcutaneous layer in comparison to the dermis and epidermis. *The subcutaneous layer appears less structured and less "full" than the dermis and epidermis.*

10. What structures can you find in the subcutaneous layer? *Answers will depend upon your slides. Sweat glands, blood vessels, and muscles are common. Most of the subcutaneous layer is fat, which will appear as open, empty areas.*

Name ______________________

Date __________ Hour __________

Class Investigation 24b

Observing a Beef Bone

Goal

• Observe and learn the structures of a bone.

Material

fresh beef bone

Observations

Carefully observe a beef bone. Locate all the structures described in the illustration on page 396 of your text.

On the lines below, list the structures you can find on your section of bone. Describe them. Tell their colors, shapes, and textures; whether they are hard, soft, or firm; and anything else you can observe.

Answers will vary.

You may want to do this investigation as a class demonstration.

You can obtain fresh bones from a butcher. Contact him several days in advance. Often a butcher can supply large bones only on certain days of the week. Some smaller supermarkets or meat markets do not do their own butchering and may not have large beef bones. Some butchers will charge you for bones; others, if they know that the bone will be used for educational purposes, may not charge you.

The bones of any large animal will do. A hunter may be willing to give you a bone of his butchered deer. Wear latex gloves if you use bones from a wild game animal. Some diseases (e.g., Lyme disease) can be transmitted when cuts in the skin contact infected blood.

If possible, obtain several sections of bone. You should have one section of bone for every four or five students. In this way, they can all make their observations at once rather than one after another.

Be sure you get a longitudinal section of the bone. If you get only a cross section, you may not be able to see the bone marrow or the spongy bone well. If possible, get a cross section of a joint. This will allow you to see easily all the structures and the articular cartilage. Fresh bones can be kept in the refrigerator for several weeks without problems. You can also freeze the bones and keep them for future years. After a few years, however, you will need to replace them. You will also need a beef (or other animal's) heart for Investigation 25a. You may want to make arrangements for the heart at the same time that you arrange for the bone. The heart will also keep in a refrigerator or freezer. Observation of a cow eyeball is a suggested activity used in Chapter 27. These are best used fresh. Make arrangements to obtain fresh ones when you cover Chapter 27. Not all butchers can provide these.

Name ______________________

Date __________ Hour __________

Class Investigation 24c

Heat from Muscles

Choose a weight for the student that is neither too light to not be tiring nor so heavy that the student tires quickly.

Goal

- Demonstrate that muscle contractions produce heat.

Materials

dumbbell or similar weight, two strip thermometers

Procedures and observations

1. Choose a student to sit where everyone can see him. He should wear a short-sleeved shirt or roll up his sleeves.
2. Put one strip thermometer on each of his biceps muscles. Allow about 15 seconds for the thermometers to indicate the correct temperature. Record these temperatures as the starting temperatures in the table below.
3. Choose one arm to be the exercised arm. With this arm the student should lift and lower the weight at a constant rate of about once every second. The other arm should remain motionless.
4. After thirty seconds, record the temperature of each arm. It is not necessary to stop the lifting and lowering to record the temperature.
5. Continue taking temperature readings for several minutes or until the student's arm is too tired for him to continue.

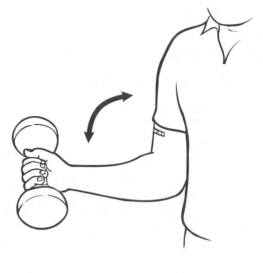

Home School Tip
With a single student, the student should be the experimenter and a family member should be the weight lifter.

	Arm Temperature	
Time (sec)	**Exercised Arm**	**Nonexercised Arm**
Start		
1		
2		
3		
4		
5		

The temperature recorded is not necessarily normal body temperature.

Alternatively you could have the student hold the weight motionless in a position that requires the biceps to be contracted.

Summing up

1. Did the temperature of the exercised arm increase in this investigation? Why do you think this did or did not happen? ***Yes, muscles produce heat when they contract.***
2. Did the temperature of the nonexercised bicep increase? Why do you think this did or did not happen? ***No, the muscle in that arm was not contracted.***

In our test with a junior high student, 36 repetitions with an 8 lb. weight within 30 seconds had no effect on the arm surface temperature. An additional 30 repetitions made the student strain and raised the arm surface temperature 1.8° F. The temperature of the unexercised arm was unchanged.

Name ______________________

Date ____________ Hour ____________

Class Investigation 24d

The Structure of Bones and Muscles

Goal

- Observe the microscopic structures of muscles and bones.

Materials

microscope; prepared slide of a cross section of dry, ground human bone; prepared slide of striated human muscle

Procedures and observations

1. Obtain and set up your microscope.
2. Focus your microscope on the prepared slide of human bone.
   - Before the bone was made into a slide, all the cell cytoplasm and blood vessels were removed. All that you will see are the hard, "bony" structures.
   - Examine the slide and compare it to the material on page 398 of your text. You may need to use high power in order to see some of the structures clearly.
   - Name and describe the various structures that you see. *Students should see osteons, the canal for blood vessels, layers of nonliving material, and the chambers where the bone cells would have been.*
3. Focus your microscope on a prepared slide of human muscle.
   - Examine the slide and compare it to material on page 399 of your text. You may need to use high power in order to see some of the structures clearly.
   - What type of muscle are you observing? Check the proper box in each pair. ☒ voluntary or ☐ involuntary ☒ striated or ☐ smooth
   - Name and describe the various structures that you see. *Students should see nuclei, cell membranes, and the striation (stripes) of the cells.*

Good slides are the key to success with this investigation.

Be sure that the students describe the structures they see from their microscopic view, not from their text's description.

You may wish to have the microscopes set up before the students come to class.

You may wish to combine this investigation with Investigation 24b.

If you have a microprojector, you can do this investigation as a class activity.

Name ______________________
Date ____________ Hour ____________

25–Internal Balance of the Body

Ideas 25a

The Heart and Blood Vessels

Directions: Fill in the missing words in the following statements. The circled letters will form a word that describes the internal balance of the body.

1. Blood is pumped by the (H) E A R T.
2. The B L (O) O D carries substances through the body.
3. A heart M U R (M) U R is an unusual heart sound.
4. An artificial P A C (E) M A K E R may be used to keep a damaged heart beating.
5. The blood entering the right atrium is D E (O) X Y G E N A T E D.
6. The K I D N E Y (S) filter wastes from the blood.
7. An A R R H Y (T) H M I A is an unusual heart rhythm.
8. O X Y G E N (A) T E D blood enters the left atrium.
9. Arteries, veins, and capillaries are V E S (S) E L S.
10. The sac around the heart is the P E R I C A R D (I) U M.
11. Doctors use a S T E T H O (S) C O P E to listen to the heart.

Maintaining the internal balance of the body is

H	O	M	E	O	S	T	A	S	I	S
1	2	3	4	5	6	7	8	9	10	11

Ideas 25b

The Structure of the Heart

Directions: Label the following drawing by supplying the missing terms; then draw a line from each term to the proper structure in the drawing.

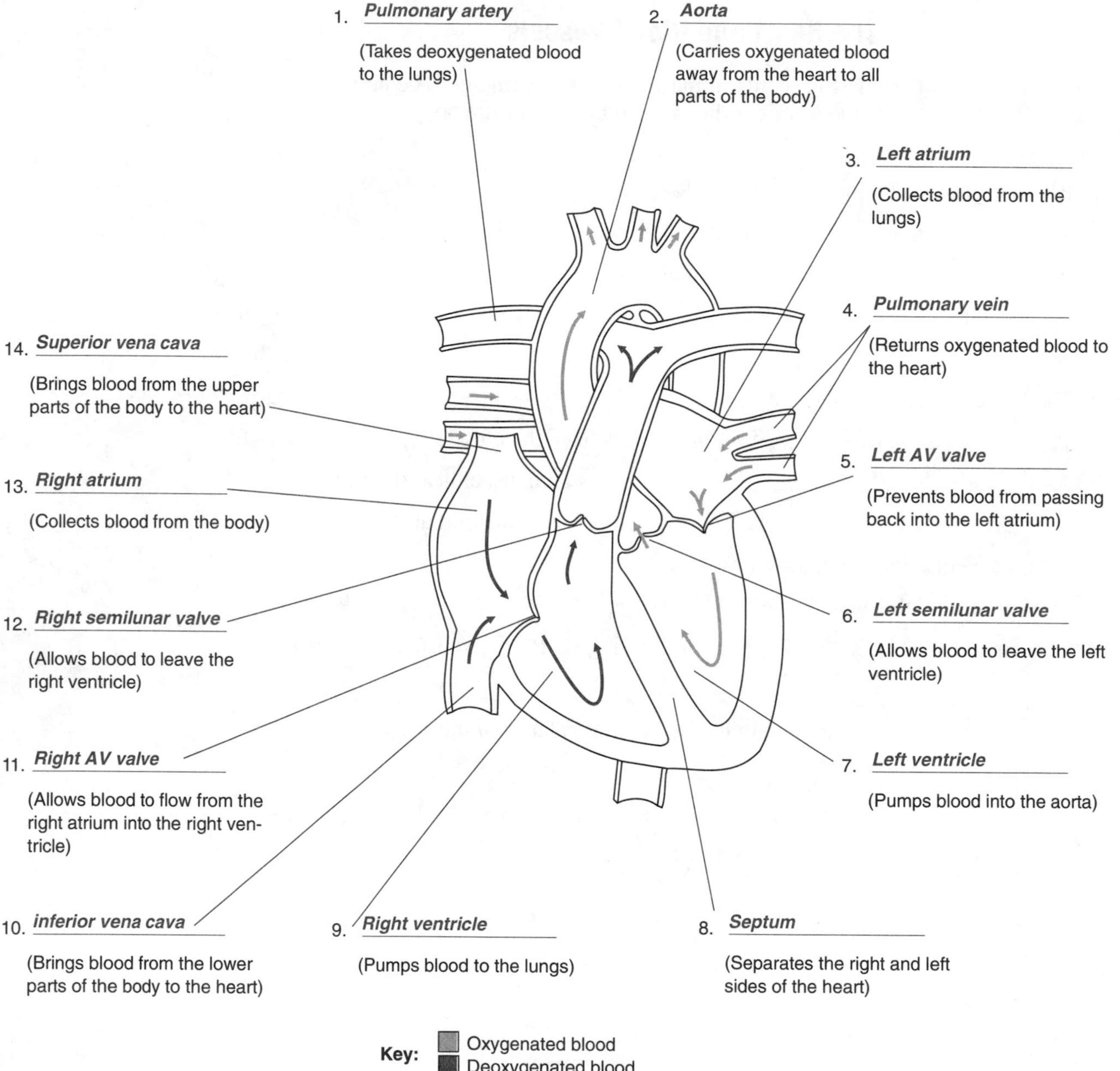

Ideas 25c

The Path of Blood

Directions: On the diagram of the heart above, draw arrows indicating the flow of blood through the heart. Use one color for oxygenated blood and another color for deoxygenated blood. On the key, indicate which color you used for each type of blood. Wherever an arrow enters the heart or leaves the heart, indicate where the blood is going or where it is coming from.

Name ______________________

Date ____________ Hour ______________

Ideas 25d

The Blood

Directions: Read the following statements. In the space provided, write *True* if the statement is true and *False* if the statement is false and draw a line through the word or words that make the statement false. In the space in the margin, write the word or words necessary to make the statement true.

There may be more than one way to correct some false statements.

True 1. Erythrocytes are shaped like discs that have been pressed in on both sides.

False 2. Leukocytes are ~~smaller~~ than erythrocytes. *larger*

True 3. If a coronary artery is blocked by a floating blood clot, a coronary thrombosis will result.

True 4. Blood plasma is a straw-colored fluid that contains dissolved foods, hormones, minerals, and other materials.

False 5. Another name for ~~leukocytes~~ is red blood cells. *erythrocytes*

True 6. If a person's blood cannot carry enough oxygen, the person has anemia.

True 7. The body forms antibodies, which attack disease-causing agents.

False 8. Carbon ~~dioxide~~ easily combines with hemoglobin at the same place that oxygen combines with hemoglobin. *monoxide*

False 9. Infections in the body cause the number of ~~erythrocytes~~ to increase. *leucocytes*

True 10. Hemoglobin carries oxygen.

True 11. Coronary atherosclerosis is the development of fatty tissues inside the walls of the coronary artery.

False 12. If a person's diet lacks ~~lead~~, he may develop anemia. *iron*

True 13. Erythrocytes lack nuclei, but leukocytes have nuclei.

True 14. Some types of leukocytes engulf and digest foreign matter.

False 15. There are ~~many more~~ leukocytes in the blood than there are erythrocytes. *fewer*

True 16. An arrhythmia in which the heart quivers and does not pump blood is called fibrillation.

True 17. Platelets are irregular cell fragments that are needed to form blood clots.

True 18. Blood pressure is the push that blood has against artery walls.

True 19. The septum separates the right side of the heart from the left.

True 20. If a person's heart is beating irregularly, that person has an arrhythmia.

cavities False 21. The heart is divided into four chambers called ~~atria~~.

True 22. Blood pressure normally increases as you exercise vigorously.

pulse False 23. Using your finger to push an artery against a bone will permit you to count your ~~blood pressure~~.

True 24. A major cause of high blood pressure is tension.

arteries False 25. Blood moving away from the heart travels in the ~~veins~~.

3-5 False 26. A human body normally contains about ~~8-10~~ quarts of blood.

True 27. Blood becomes oxygenated in the lungs and deoxygenated in other body tissues.

True 28. Hemoglobin is an iron-containing pigment that makes the blood appear red.

True 29. Platelets are produced in the bone marrow.

90 False 30. Blood plasma is about ~~50~~ percent water.

Name ______________________________
Date ______________ Hour ______________

Ideas 25e

The Excretory System

Directions: Write the proper terms next to the following definitions. Then eliminate the letters used in your answers from the letter list. The remaining letters will form a bonus word that involves the main function of the excretory system.

ureters 1. Tubes that carry urine from the kidneys to the urinary bladder

nephron 2. Microscopic structure that filters the blood inside a kidney

urinary bladder 3. A muscular sac that stores urine

kidney 4. The filtering organ of the excretory system

urethra 5. Tube that leads from the urinary bladder to the outside of the body

blood 6. Substance that is filtered as it passes through the kidney

urine 7. Substance that is excreted by the nephron after all of the useful products have been reabsorbed into the blood

urea 8. A substance that is a waste product of protein digestion and is normally found in urine

diabetes mellitus 9. Condition indicated by too much sugar in the blood and urine

dialysis 10. Proper name for an artificial kidney: __________ machine

analysis 11. What a physician does to urine in order to determine certain physical conditions

excretion 12. The primary function of the kidneys

Bonus: The main function of the excretory system involves *wastes*.

Letter List

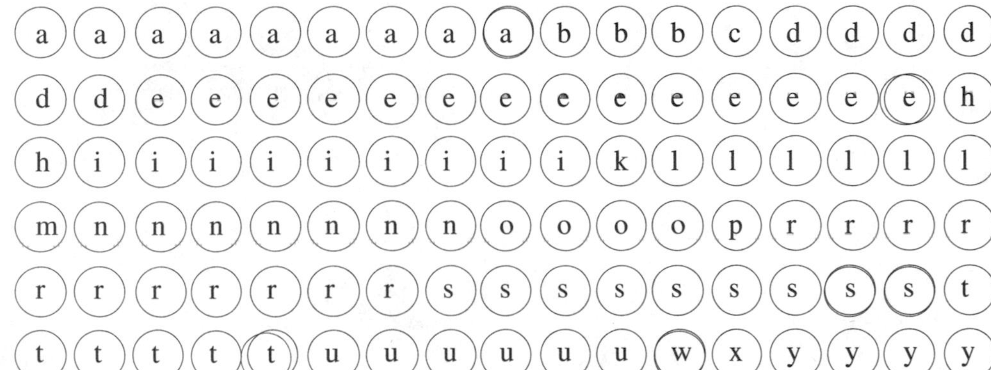

You can obtain beef or other large animal (pig, lamb) hearts from a butcher. See the teacher's notes for Investigation 24b regarding obtaining materials from a butcher.

When you obtain the heart, ask the butcher to include an inch or more of as many blood vessels that lead into the heart as possible. Sometimes this is not possible if the heart was prepared elsewhere. Unless you have a very sharp knife, you may want to ask the butcher to make a transverse cut through the heart so that you have a top and a bottom section.

Having one heart for every four or five students is ideal.

You can do this investigation as a demonstration. Only a small group of students can easily view the heart at a time. You may wish to divide your class into several groups and give them an assignment to work on (one of the other investigations). Then do this investigation as a demonstration for each group while the other groups work on the assignment.

Class Investigation 25a

Observing a Beef Heart

Goal

- Observe and identify the structures of the heart.

Materials

a dissected beef heart, large forceps, glass or wooden rods, red and blue yarn

Procedures and observations

1. A beef heart is larger than, but similar to, a human heart. Examine the outside of the heart. Then remove the top section of the heart to see its chambers.
2. Use a blunt rod to probe into the blood vessels and see where they go. Find the heart structures and trace the path in which the blood flows through the heart.
3. Find all the heart structures illustrated on page 408 of your text. Using a small piece of paper, label the parts of the heart.
4. Using a blue piece of yarn, trace the path of deoxygenated blood through the heart.
5. Using a red piece of yarn, trace the path of oxygenated blood through the heart.
6. Have your teacher inspect your work.

Name ____________________

Date __________ Hour __________

Class Investigation 25b

Using a Stethoscope

Goals

- Learn how to correctly use a stethoscope.
- Listen to the sounds of your heart.
- Compare your pulse rate to your heart rate.

Materials

alcohol, stopwatch or clock with a second hand, stethoscope, tissues

You can do this investigation as a class demonstration with only one or two students actually doing the activity. It is exciting, however, for students to hear their own heartbeats. If at all possible, permit students to find and hear their own hearts.

Setting up

Using alcohol and a tissue, clean the earplugs of the stethoscope. The earplugs should always be cleaned with alcohol and a tissue before they are put into the ears of another person.

Whenever you put the earplugs of the stethoscope into your ears, be sure the diaphragm of the stethoscope does not tap against any hard object. The sound made by tapping a button or a table top can be very loud and can damage your ears.

Using a stethoscope to listen to a person chewing gum is also interesting.

Procedures and observations

Place the ear plugs of the stethoscope into your ears. Place the diaphragm of the stethoscope on a friend's cheek. Ask the friend to chew. Describe what you hear. *Answers will vary.* ____________________

____

Listen to the sounds of your heart

1. Place the diaphragm of the stethoscope onto the center of your chest. Listen carefully.
2. Move the diaphragm of the stethoscope to the left of the center of your chest so that it is no longer over your sternum.
3. Move the diaphragm of the stethoscope slightly up and down to be sure that you do not have it directly over a rib.
4. Once you have found a good place where you can hear your heart, listen carefully. What does it sound like? *Answers will vary.* ____________________

____

Determine how fast your heart beats while you are sitting quietly

1. After you have sat quietly for about five minutes, continue this exercise.
2. Count the number of times your heart beats in fifteen seconds. Recall that your heart makes two sounds for each beat. In other words, each "lup-dup" is a single beat.
3. Multiply by four the number of times your heart beats in fifteen seconds. This number will tell you how many times your heart beats per minute. Record this amount in the space below.
4. Repeat counting the number of times your heart beats in fifteen seconds three times. Convert the numbers to the number of beats per minute and record them in the spaces on the next page. Average your results.

Heartbeat rate per minute

1. ____________ 2. ____________ 3. ____________ 4. ____________

Average: ________

Determine how fast your pulse throbs while you are sitting quietly

1. You can feel your pulse by putting light pressure against a blood vessel that flows past a bone. Find the pulse in your neck or in your wrist by placing your fingers as illustrated in the diagrams.
2. Count your pulse for fifteen seconds and then multiply the number by four. This number tells you your pulse rate for one minute. Record this number in the space below.
3. Repeat counting your pulse rate for fifteen seconds three times. Convert the numbers to the number of beats per minute and then record them in the spaces provided. Average your results.

Pulse rate per minute

1. ____________ 2. ____________ 3. ____________ 4. ____________

Average: ________

Summing up

1. What is the difference between your average heartbeat rate per minute and your average pulse rate per minute? ***Answers will vary. The number should be the same, but it may vary by a couple of beats.***
2. Should there be a difference between your heartbeat rate and your pulse rate? ☐ Yes ☒ No Why? ***Since both of these rates are a measure of the heart's pumping, they should both be the same.***

Name ______________________

Date __________ Hour ______________

Class Investigation 25c

Heart Rate Increases

Goals

- Determine whether heart rate is proportional to amount of exercise.
- Identify how much time the heart takes to return to its normal rate after exercise.

Materials

stopwatch or clock with a second hand

Setting up

1. Be able to find your pulse quickly and to take it accurately. (See Investigation 25b for instructions on taking a pulse.)
2. Map out an area where you and your classmates can walk and run. This area should be about 134 meters (1/12 mi.) and should start and end near your classroom.
3. Divide your class into teams of two people each. In each team, one person should do the activities, and the other person should take the pulse rate and keep the records. Both people should do the Summing Up section at the end.
4. Each time you take a pulse rate for this exercise, do so for fifteen seconds and then multiply your answer by four to obtain the pulse rate for one minute.

Procedures and observations

1. Lie quietly for three minutes. What is the pulse rate? ________ bpm (beats per minute)
2. Sit quietly for three minutes. What is the pulse rate? ________ bpm
3. While seated, move your arms above your head for three minutes. What is the pulse rate? ______ bpm
4. Sit quietly to allow the pulse rate to return to normal. How long did you have to rest until the pulse rate became the same as the "sitting quietly" rate? ______ min. ______ sec.
5. Walk slowly around the mapped area. What is the pulse rate? ________ bpm
6. Rest until the pulse is the same as the "sitting quietly" rate. How long did you have to rest? ______ min. ______ sec.
7. Walk briskly around the mapped area. What is the pulse rate? ________ bpm
8. Rest until the pulse is the same as the "sitting quietly" rate. How long did you have to rest? ______ min. ______ sec.
9. Jog around the mapped area. What is the pulse rate? ________ bpm
10. Rest until the pulse is the same as the "sitting quietly" rate. How long did you have to rest? ______ min. ________ sec.
11. Run rapidly around the mapped area. What is the pulse rate? ________ bpm
12. Rest until the pulse is the same as the "sitting quietly" rate. How long did you have to rest? ______ min. ______ sec.

This investigation may require a great amount of time. You may want to do the investigation as an out-of-class project. Consider having a few volunteers conduct the exercises after school or during their lunch hour. Another reason to use this as an out-of-class project is the likelihood that your subject will not find lying down truly relaxing in a classroom situation; especially with junior-high students nearby. Results charts from your volunteers could be duplicated for distribution to the class or posted on a bulletin board. Instruct the entire class to do the Summing Up section.

Home School Tip

If you have only one student, it is best that you or another family member be the exerciser and the student be the one who takes the pulse rate and keeps the records.

Be on guard for modesty when having the students lie down. Provide a cot for comfort and convenience.

Students with health problems could participate in this investigation as "pulse takers."

Summing up

Fill out the charts below by shading in the bars of the charts (up to the highest number for each catagory) with the data you have obtained.

Chart A—Pulse Rate Per Minute

Pulse Rate

176, 174, 172, 170, 168, 166, 164, 162, 160, 158, 156, 154, 152, 150, 148, 146, 144, 142, 140, 138, 136, 134, 132, 130, 128, 126, 124, 122, 120, 118, 116, 114, 112, 110, 108, 106, 104, 102, 100, 98, 96, 94, 92, 90, 88, 86, 84, 82, 80, 78, 76, 74, 72, 70, 68, 66, 64, 62, 60, 58, 56, 54, 52, 50

Lying	Sitting	Sitting with Motion	Walking Slowly	Walking Briskly	Jogging	Running

Name ______________________

Date ____________ Hour ____________

Chart B—Time Required to Return Pulse Rate to Normal

Minutes	After Sitting with Motion	After Walking Slowly	After Walking Briskly	After Jogging	After Running
10					
9.5					
9					
8.5					
8					
7.5					
7					
6.5					
6					
5.5					
5					
4.5					
4					
3.5					
3					
2.5					
2					
1.5					
1					
.5					

1. By comparing the charts, what are you able to determine about the relationship between pulse rate and length of time needed to return pulse to normal rate? ***Answers will vary. Normally, higher pulse rates will take longer to return to normal than lower ones will.***

2. Compare your chart to the charts of other people. Are they about the same? ☐ Yes ☐ No Does any person in your class have an unusual chart? ☐ Yes ☐ No What could explain the difference? ***Answers will vary. A person who is in unusually poor or unusually good physical condition may have a chart with unusually long or short recovery times and usually fast or slow pulse rates.***

You may wish to do the Summing Up section orally in class. By doing so, you can direct the students' thinking and point out the differences in the various charts. If all the students in your class are in about the same physical condition, there may be little or no variation in the pulse rates and recovery times. You should explain what certain variations would mean even if they are not present in your class's results.

Name ______________________________

Date ____________ Hour ______________

Class Investigation 25d

Blood

Goals

- Observe blood cells.
- See some of the effects that certain diseases have on the blood.

Materials

microscope, prepared slide of human blood, prepared slides of the blood of people who had various blood diseases

Procedures and observations

Obtain and set up your microscope. Focus your microscope on a prepared slide of normal human blood. You will need to use high power in order to observe the blood cells clearly.

1. Locate and observe the erythrocytes. Describe their appearance. *Answers will vary, depending upon the slides you have. Erythrocytes usually appear as clear or pink disks.*

2. Are there different types of erythrocytes? ☐ Yes ☐ No If so, tell the differences between the types you see. *Students will often notice differences in shapes or numbers. These are usually the results of the slide manufacture, not of the cells themselves.*

3. What is the primary function of erythrocytes? *Their primary function is transporting oxygen.*

4. Locate and observe several leukocytes. Describe their appearance and compare them to the erythrocytes. *Answers will vary, depending upon the slides you have. Leukocytes are usually round, contain nuclei, and are larger than erythrocytes.*

5. Compare the number of leukocytes to the number of erythrocytes. *There are many more erythrocytes than there are leukocytes.*

You may wish to eliminate the observation of blood disorders. However, you may want to set up one or two slides of them for the students to observe. If you have a microprojector, you can do this section orally.

Some blood disorders do not show abnormal cells or other unusual structures. Blood disorders such as sickle cell anemia, African sleeping sickness, and certain types of leukemia do show abnormal structures (depending upon the slide preparation).

Home School Tip

It is possible to make a slide using a drop of fresh blood from a skin prick made with a sterile lancet on a fingertip. However, the only cells that can be clearly seen in such a slide are erythrocytes. White blood cells must be specially stained with Wright's stain. Additionally, materials with human blood on them should be treated as hazardous waste. It is simpler, easier, and safer to purchase one prepared slide of normal human blood. Diseased blood slides are optional.

6. Are there different kinds of leukocytes? ☐ Yes ☐ No If so, tell the differences between the kinds you see. *Answers will vary. The shape of the nuclei, whether or not the cytoplasm contains colored material, and the fact that their shapes are often different are the primary things that students will see.*

7. What is the primary function of leukocytes? *The primary function is to protect the body.*

8. Observe several slides of the blood of humans who had blood disorders. Compare them to what you have seen in normal blood. In the spaces below, record the name of the blood disease you observed and describe the differences between this blood and normal blood. *Answers will vary, depending upon the slides you have and their quality.*

9. In the space below draw and label an erythrocyte, a leukocyte, and a blood cell, illustrating one of the blood disorders you observed.

Name ____________________
Date __________ Hour __________

26–Energy of the Body

Ideas 26a

Metabolism

Directions: Below is a list of terms and a series of examples. Decide which term is being described in the example and write its letter in the space. You may use each term twice.

a. Basal metabolic rate
b. Digestive system
c. Metabolic rate
d. Metabolism
e. Respiratory system

d 1. All of the processes your body carries on to keep you alive

c 2. How quickly your body uses energy

e 3. The structures responsible for supplying oxygen to the body

a 4. The rate at which your body uses energy when you are sleeping quietly

b 5. The structures responsible for supplying food for the body to use

a 6. Takes place more quickly in babies than in eighteen-year-old people and will begin to decrease as a person reaches old age

e 7. The structures that exchange carbon dioxide and oxygen

c 8. Increases as you engage in strenuous physical activity

a 9. Measurement of body activity at rest

b 10. The structures that supply the glucose for aerobic cellular respiration

Ideas 26b

Structures of the Respiratory System

Directions: In the spaces provided, describe the difference between the terms given.

Answers will vary.

1. bronchi / bronchioles *Both carry air into the lungs, but the bronchioles are smaller and branch off from the bronchi.*

2. pharynx / larynx *The pharynx is the throat. From the pharynx, the larynx (or voice box) opens to the trachea.*

3. glottis / epiglottis *The glottis is a space between the folds of the larynx. The epiglottis is a flap that prevents substances from entering the larynx.*

4. bronchi / alveoli *The bronchi are tubes that carry air to the lungs. Alveoli are tiny air sacs in the lungs.*

5. thorax / diaphragm *The thorax is the chest cavity. The diaphragm is the muscle that forms the lower wall of the thorax.*

6. trachea / esophagus *The trachea carries air to the lungs. The esophagus carries food to the stomach.*

Ideas 26c

The Respiratory System

Directions: Write the proper terms next to the following definitions, then find and circle the terms in the word puzzle on the next page. In the word puzzle the words may appear horizontally, vertically, or diagonally and may be forward or backward.

lungs 1. Main organs of the respiratory system

mucus 2. Thick, sticky substance that coats the membranes of the respiratory system

larynx 3. The voice box

glottis 4. Opening between the vocal folds

bronchi 5. Branches of the trachea that lead into the lungs

alveoli 6. Small, thin sacs in the lungs

inhale 7. To breathe in

bronchioles 8. Tiny tubes that allow air to pass into the alveoli

pharynx 9. Chamber that is located at the back of the mouth and nose and that leads into the esophagus and larynx

epiglottis 10. Structure that covers the larynx during swallowing

collapsed 11. Condition of a lung that cannot expand because of a hole in the thorax (chest)

Name ______________________

Date ____________ Hour ____________

pneumonia 12. A disease in which the alveoli become filled with fluid

esophagus 13. Structure that carries food from the pharynx to the stomach

diaphragm 14. Major muscle responsible for inhaling

trachea 15. Structure that leads from the pharynx to the lungs

tuberculosis 16. Disease caused by bacteria growing in the alveoli

virus 17. A tiny piece of DNA or RNA with protein; causes various diseases

immune 18. Having antibodies and other factors that can fight off an infection before it affects the body

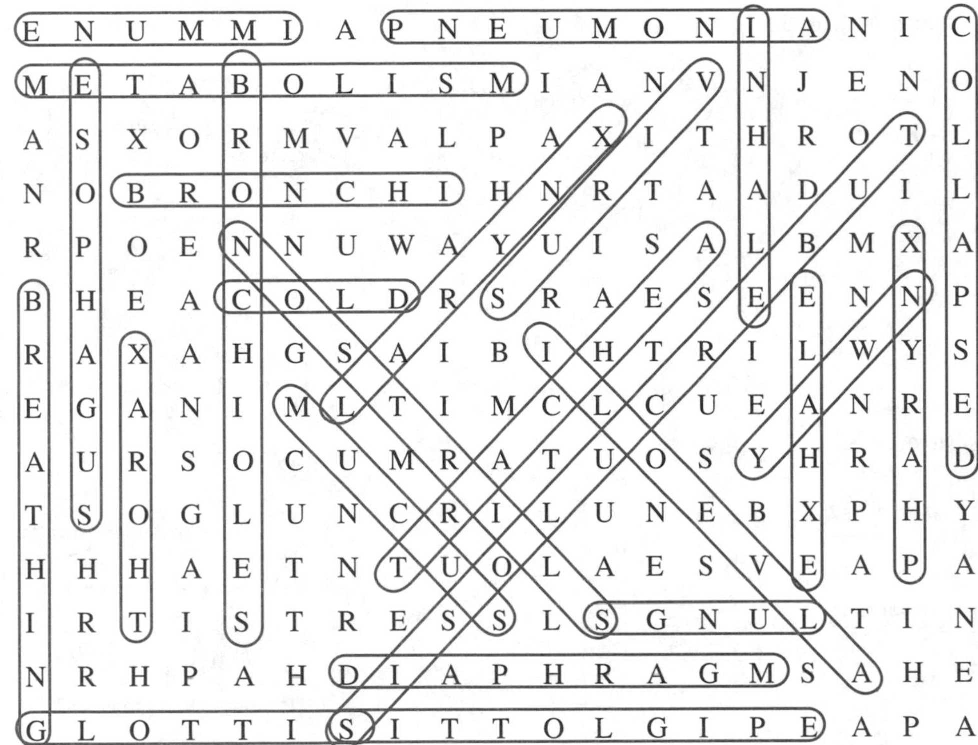

In the word puzzle, there are at least seven other words that deal with the respiratory system. Find and define at least five of them.

metabolism 19. *Total of all the body processes*

breathing 20. *Forcing air into and out of the lungs*

thorax 21. *The chest area*

cold 22. *A viral infection affecting the respiratory system*

nostrils 23. *Openings in the nose*

exhale 24. *To breathe out*

yawn 25. *Exchange of a large amount of air in the lungs (not in text)*

Ideas 26d

The Digestive System

Directions: Below are drawings of the human digestive system. Label the drawings by supplying the missing terms. Then draw a line from each term to the proper structure in the drawing. Some of the label lines have been drawn for you.

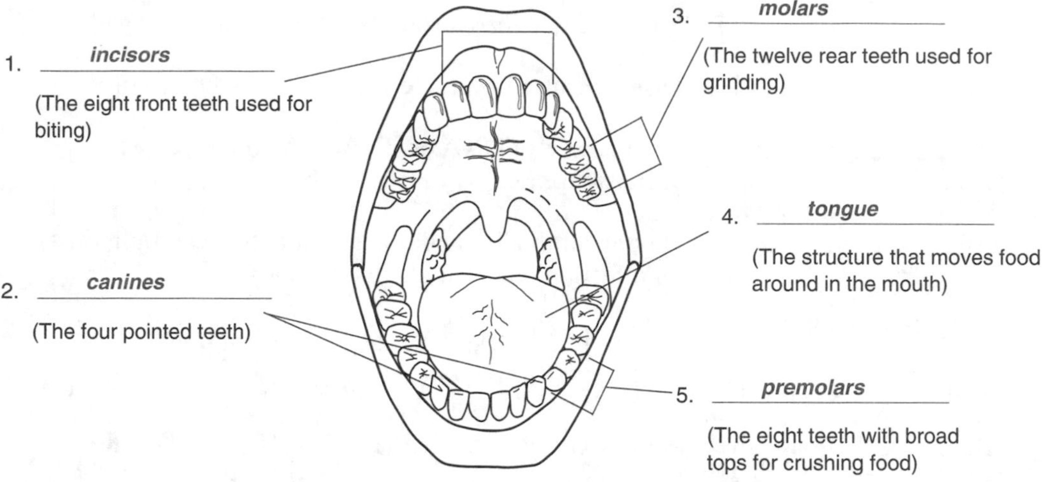

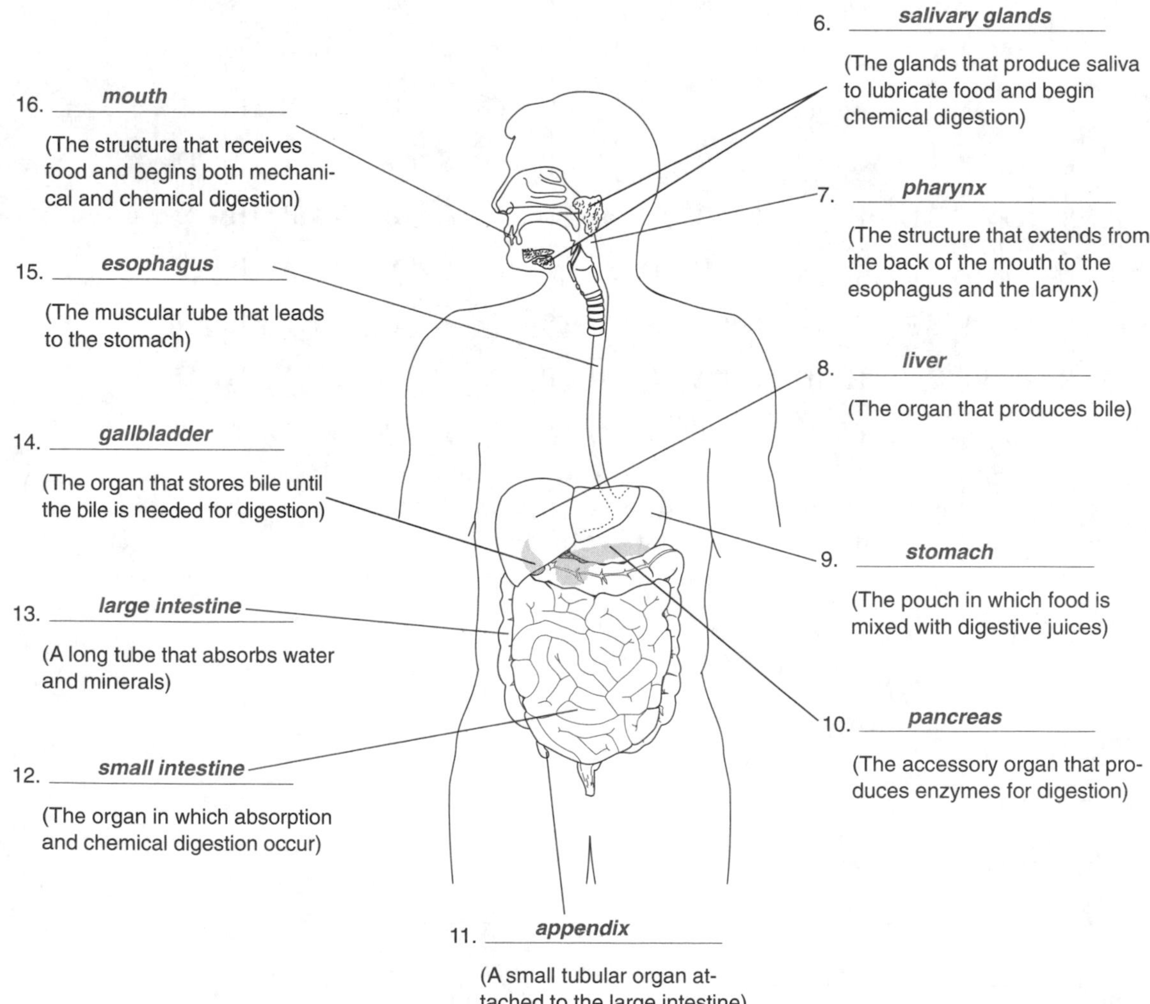

Name ____________________
Date __________ Hour __________

Ideas 26e

Digestion

Directions: Below is a list of scrambled words. Unscramble the words and write them on the lines to the right of the words. Then match them to the definitions given below by putting the proper letters in the blanks by the definitions.

a. stucd *ducts*

b. iavlas *saliva*

c. anbosiotrp *absorption*

d. laptro nvie *portal vein*

e. snimvtai *vitamins*

f. allgrbeladd *gallbladder*

g. lorcaie *calorie*

h. cerlu *ulcer*

i. loacloh *alcohol*

j. pndxpaei *appendix*

c 1. Process that takes place primarily in the small intestine

d 2. Structure that carries blood from the digestive organs to the liver

a 3. Tiny tubes that carry the secretions of glands to the areas that need them

f 4. Organ that stores bile

g 5. A measure of energy

e 6. Essential substances required by some living things

i 7. A substance that the liver tries to filter out of the blood

h 8. An open sore that discharges a fluid and does not heal normally

j 9. A small tubular organ attached to the large intestine

b 10. The enzyme-containing fluid secreted in the mouth

Review

Directions: Record your responses in the spaces provided.

1. Suppose that a person's BMR (basal metabolic rate) causes him to use 1,500 calories per day, and his additional metabolism causes him to use an additional 1,800 calories per day.

   If the person consumes 4,000 calories per day, what will probably happen? *This person will probably store the extra energy as fat and will gain weight.*

   If the same person consumed 3,000 calories per day, what would probably happen? *This person would use stored energy (fat) that he already had and would lose weight.*

2. Why is mucus important in both the respiratory system and the digestive system? *Mucus protects both of these systems.*

3. List as many functions of the liver as you can. *The liver produces bile, filters out and breaks down harmful substances, adjusts blood sugar, filters out and breaks down red blood cells, and secretes substances used in blood clotting.*

4. Why is it important that blood from the digestive system pass through the liver before entering the rest of the body? *The liver removes excess sugar from the blood and stores it. If the sugar level in the blood is too low, the liver adds sugar to the blood. The liver also filters out and breaks down a certain amount of harmful substances that have been absorbed into the blood from the digestive system.*

5. Describe the immune system of the body. In your description be sure to use and define the following words: *immune, antibodies,* and *vaccines.* For extra credit also use the word *leukocyte*. (See Chapter 25.) *The immune system helps the body fight infections caused by viruses, bacteria, and other harmful substances. Leukocytes help protect the body by attacking various disease-causing agents. The body also produces antibodies to fight specific types of harmful substances. A person is immune to a particular disease if his body has antibodies to fight off the disease-causing substance before it affects the body. Vaccines can cause the body to produce certain antibodies, thus immunizing the body.*

Name ______________________

Date ____________ Hour ______________

Class Investigation 26a

Digestive Enzymes

Goal

- Observe starch being broken down into sugar by digestive enzymes.

Materials

Benedict's solution, Bunsen burner or butane lab burner, graduated cylinder, marking pencil, plain saltine crackers, test tubes, test-tube rack, test-tube tongs

Procedures

Use a marking pencil to label five test tubes *A* through *E*.

Test A

- In test tube *A* place a crushed piece of cracker. Add enough water to moisten the cracker.
- Add 5 ml (1 tsp.) of Benedict's solution and heat the contents until it boils. Then set it aside.

Test B

- Rinse out your mouth with water. Then collect in test tube *B* about 5 ml of your saliva.
- Add 5 ml of Benedict's solution and heat the contents to a boil. Then set it aside.

Test C

- Place a cracker on your tongue. Do not chew it. Hold it there for five seconds.
- Break the cracker into small pieces and place it into test tube *C*.
- Add 5 ml of Benedict's solution and heat the contents to a boil. Then set it aside.

Test D

- Chew a cracker only five chews. Place the chewed cracker into test tube *D*.
- Add 5 ml of Benedict's solution and heat the contents to a boil. Then set it aside.

Test E

- Chew a cracker thoroughly. It should be a soft mass. Place the chewed cracker into test tube *E*.
- Add 5 ml of Benedict's solution and heat the contents to a boil. Then set it aside.

You may wish to do this investigation as a demonstration. You could then have one student contribute the saliva, another lay the cracker on his tongue, another chew, and so on. Another student can add the Benedict's solution and another can heat the test tubes.

You can add water to the crackers in the test tubes so that they will react properly to the Benedict's solution and the heat. A few tries the night before should show you what you need to do.

Use about a third of a plain saltine for each of these experiments. Do not use other types of crackers since these may have sugar in them and will give erroneous results.

Home School Tip

Butane lab burners are generally better for the home school than Bunsen burners because the butane lab burners are self-contained. A propane torch could be used as well, but it must be held securely since they tend to be top-heavy. In this investigation you could substitute a hot water bath for the heat source (place or hold the test tubes upright in a pan of boiling water).

Benedict's solution can be purchased ready-made less expensively than its ingredients can be purchased individually.

Observations

When heated, Benedict's solution will change color if sugar is present.

- If there is no sugar present, it will remain blue.
- If there is little sugar present, it will appear yellow.
- If there is more sugar present, it will turn orange.
- If there is a large amount of sugar present, it will turn brick red.

Compare the color of the five test tubes. Record your responses below.

Test tube	Color	Amount of sugar present
A	*blue*	*none*
B	*blue*	*none*
C	*yellow*	*little*
D	*orange*	*some*
E	*red*	*much*

Summing up

1. In which test tube(s) is there the most sugar? *E*
2. In which test tube(s) is there the least sugar? *A, B*
3. Crackers are predominantly starches (carbohydrates). When starches are digested, what are they broken down into? *They are broken down into sugars.*
4. Does there seem to be more sugar when the cracker is chewed more?

   ☒ Yes ☐ No If so, explain why. *The saliva digests the starch of the cracker to sugars. The more the saliva works on the crackers, the more sugar there is.*

Name ______________________

Date __________ Hour __________

Field Investigation 26b

Counting Calories

Goals

- Determine how many calories you consume in a day.
- Recognize the problems encountered in gathering accurate data, analyzing the data properly, and drawing correct conclusions.

Materials

measuring cups, measuring spoons, scales or balance (optional)

Procedures

1. For one 24-hour day, carefully measure and record each food item you eat. Include all meals, snacks, and beverages except water. During this activity, try not to alter your food intake from what it would normally be when you are not being surveyed.
   - Be sure to record food items in the units in which they are given on the calorie table.
   - Your teacher will demonstrate how to accurately measure foods with measuring cups and measuring spoons.
   - Record or calculate the number of calories that are in each food item you eat and indicate this information on the chart.
   - Calculate the total calories you consume during this day and enter this total as the "Daily total."
2. Bring your data sheets to school on the day your teacher indicates.
3. Your teacher will collect your data sheets during class and will prepare a summary of the data. The summary will then be given to you.
4. Use the data on the summary charts to analyze your class data.

Home School Tip

It is best if you can share data with several other home educators doing this same investigation. If this is not possible, either "create" sample data based on your knowledge of the eating habits of junior high students or omit this investigation. Kitchen scales can be used.

Give the students oral instructions for measuring foods and estimating calories. Try not to be burdensome with exactness, but do stress the need for accuracy.

Name ______________________

Data Chart for Counting Calories			
Time	Food Item	Amount eaten	Calories
	1. 2. 3. 4.		
	1. 2. 3. 4.		
	1. 2. 3. 4.		
	1. 2. 3. 4.		
	1. 2. 3. 4.		
	1. 2. 3. 4.		
		Daily total :	______________

By assigning the students numbers, you will avoid possible embarrassment to them.

Name ______________________

Date __________ Hour __________

Summary Chart #1 (from teacher)

Hour of the day	Total calories consumed by the class	Average calories consumed per person each hour	Percent of the day's total calories
midnight - 1 A.M.			
1-2 A.M.			
2-3 A.M.			
3-4 A.M.			
4-5 A.M.			
5-6 A.M.			
6-7 A.M.			
7-8 A.M.			
8-9 A.M.			
9-10 A.M.			
10-11 A.M.			
11 A.M. - noon			
noon-1 P.M.			
1-2 P.M.			
2-3 P.M.			
3-4 P.M.			
4-5 P.M.			
5-6 P.M.			
6-7 P.M.			
7-8 P.M.			
8-9 P.M.			
9-10 P.M.			
10-11 P.M.			
11 P.M. - midnight			

The teacher should compile the class data for Summary Charts #1 and #2.

Duplicate the charts and hand them out. Students can then do the rest of the investigation based on the data you have supplied on the charts.

Boys age 11-14 typically require 2500 calories per day. Girls the same age typically require 2200 calories per day. There are many variables, thus your averages may not agree with these averages.

Summary Chart #2 (from teacher)

	Total daily calories	Number of individuals surveyed	Average daily calories per individual
Males:			
Females:			

Analysis 1 (use Summary Chart #1)

Determine *when* the calories your class consumes are consumed each day.

Below are six statements interpreting the information in Summary Chart #1. In the blank in each statement write the hour in which your class consumed the most calories. (Use the same hour of the day for all the blanks.) Darken the box in front of the statement if the data support the statement.

- ☒ A typical member of your class usually consumes more calories at ________ than at any other time.
- ☐ People around the world consume more calories at ________ than at any other time.
- ☐ Your class as a group always consumes more calories at ________ than at any other time.
- ☐ A typical member of your class is hungrier at ________ than at any other time during the survey.
- ☐ The human body needs more calories at ________ than at any other time.
- ☐ More tests should be given at ________, since people eat more food at that time and therefore have more energy.

Analysis 2 (use Summary Chart #2)

Compare the caloric intakes of the boys and girls in your class. Below are six statements interpreting the information in Summary Chart #2. Darken the box in front of the statement if the data support the statement.

- ☐ All boys in your class ate something during this survey.
- ☐ The girls in your class consumed more calories at lunch than the boys did.
- ☐ The average number of calories that the boys in your class consumed during the survey is greater than the average number of calories that the girls consumed.

Name ______________________

Date ____________ Hour ______________

☐ The average number of calories that the girls in your class consumed during the survey is greater than the average number of calories that the boys consumed.

☐ The difference in calorie consumption between boys and girls also occurs between adult men and women.

According to the data obtained in this survey, do the boys or the girls in your class usually consume more calories? ☐ boys ☐ girls

- If your answer was *boys,* complete the questions in box B below.
- If your answer was *girls,* complete the questions in box G below.

Box B

Darken in the boxes to the left of the statements that could be supported with the data from this survey.

☐ All boys consume more calories than girls do.

☐ All boys eat more for breakfast than girls do.

☐ Boys need more calories than girls do.

☐ Boys are late to school more often than girls because they take longer to eat their larger breakfasts.

☐ Boys in junior high school are generally taller than girls their age because they consume more calories than girls do.

☐ In order to be healthy, boys should consume at least as many calories per day as the average amount consumed by a boy per day in this survey.

None are supported.

Box G

Darken in the boxes to the left of the statements that could be supported with the data from this survey.

☐ All girls consume more calories than boys do.

☐ All girls eat more for breakfast than boys do.

☐ Girls need more calories than boys do.

☐ Girls are late to school more often than boys because they take longer to eat their larger breakfasts.

☐ Girls in junior high school are generally taller than boys their age because they consume more calories than boys do.

☐ In order to be healthy, girls should consume at least as many calories as the average amount consumed by a girl in this survey.

None are supported.

Often subjects of a survey alter their habits during the survey because they are reporting on themselves.

- Darken the proper box. During this survey did you eat
  - ☐ more than usual,
  - ☐ less than usual, or
  - ☐ about the same as usual?
- Do you think that many other people who took this survey changed their eating habits during the survey? ☐ Yes ☐ No How could this affect the accuracy of the survey? ***If people alter the amounts they eat, the survey will not reflect what really happens under normal circumstances, and the survey will not be valid.***

List several ways your class could have made your survey more accurate.

Answers will vary. Taking the survey for a longer period of time could make it more accurate. Measuring food more accurately could improve the survey's accuracy.

Based on the analysis and your own careful thoughts, list several conclusions that you feel are accurate concerning the survey that your class conducted. ***Answers will vary. Students should conclude that the survey reveals very little information and that the validity of the survey is questionable.***

Name ____________________

Date ____________ Hour ____________

Calorie Table

The following table lists some common foods. Listed on the packages of many foods are the size of one serving and the number of calories contained. If this information is available, use it rather than the approximate figures given in this table.

Helpful Conversion

8 fluid ounces = 1 cup

16 tablespoons = 1 cup

3 teaspoons = 1 tablespoon

Item	Approx. cal
Apple, 1 (with peel)	125
Applesauce, sweetened, ½ cup	100
Bacon, 3 slices	110
Bacon, Canadian, 1 slice	40
Banana, 1 (without peel)	105
Beef (best to check)	
gravy, 1 cup	125
ground beef, 3 oz.	245
lean, 3 oz.	230
roast, 3 oz.	215
sirloin, lean, broiled, 3 oz.	170
Bread (best to check)	
corn, 2" x 2" x 1"	140
French/Vienna, 3" x 2" x 1"	55
raisin, 1 slice	60
rye, white, whole wheat, 1 slice	60
Burrito, bean, 1	322
Butter, 1 tbsp.	100
Cantaloupe, ½ of a 5" diameter	60
Carrot, 1 raw	30
Cereal (best to check the box)	
flake type, unsweetened, 1¼ cup	110
puffed type, unsweetened, 1¼ cup	90
oatmeal, cooked, ½ cup	75
shredded wheat, 2 biscuits	125
Cheese	
American, 1 oz. (1 slice)	105
cheddar, 1 oz.	115
cottage, small curd 1 cup	215
mozzarella, from whole milk, 1 oz.	80
Swiss 1 oz.	105
Cheeseburger, 4 oz.	525
Cherries, fresh 1 cup	75

Item	Approx. cal
Chicken	
fried, batter dipped, 1 thigh	240
fried, floured, 1 thigh	160
gizzards, 3 simmered,	100
gravy, 1 cup	190
patty sandwich, 1	440
roasted, 1 thigh	150
Cocoa, 1 cup	235
Coffee, black, 1 cup	2
Corn chips, 1 oz	155
Corn on cob or 1/2 cup cooked	70
Corn oil, 1 tbsp.	125
Doughnuts	
cake type, 1	210
yeast type, 1	235
Egg	
boiled, 1	80
fried, 1	90
scrambled, 1	100
Enchilada, cheese, 1	320
English muffin, 1	140
Fish (best to check)	
baked, 3 oz.	100
broiled, 3 oz.	140
fried, 3 oz.	175
sandwich with cheese, 1	420
Gatorade, 1 cup	40
Grapefruit, 1 without peel	38
Grapes, 10	155
Green beans, 1 cup	40
Grilled cheese sandwich, 1	400
Grits, 1 cup	120

Item	Approx. cal
Ham	
broiled, 3 oz.	275
cured, roasted, 3 oz.	140
Honey, 1 tbsp.	65
Honeydew melon, 1 (without rind)	45
Hot dog and bun, 1	260
Ice Cream, vanilla, 1 cup	350
Ice Milk, vanilla, 1 cup	185
Jams, jellies, preserves, 1 tbsp.	55
Juice	
apple juice, 1 cup	116
grapefruit juice, sweetened, 1 cup	115
grapefruit juice, unsweetened, 1 cup	100
grape juice, 1 cup	155
orange drink, 1 cup	105
orange juice, 1 cup	110
pineapple juice, 1 cup	135
prune juice, 1 cup	170
Ketchup, 1 tbsp.	15
Lima beans, ½ cup cooked	90
Liver, fried, 4 oz.	245
Mango, 1 (without skin)	135
Maple syrup, 1 tbsp.	55
Margarine, 1 tbsp.	100
Mayonnaise, 1 tbsp.	100
Milk	
whole, 1 cup	150
2%, 1 cup	120
skim, 1 cup	85
buttermilk, 1 cup	120
chocolate, lowfat, 1 cup	150
chocolate milk shake, 10 oz.	360
vanilla milk shake, 10 oz.	315
Muffin, 1	180
Mustard, 1 tsp.	5
Nectarine, 1 raw	67
Noodles	
egg noodles, cooked, 1 cup	210
chow mein, dry, 1 cup	240
Octopus, raw, 1 cup	80
Orange, 1 (without peel)	62
Pancake, 4" in diameter,	160
Peach, 1 (without skin)	37
Peanut butter, 1 tbsp.	70
Peanut butter and jelly sandwich, 1	350
Peanuts	
oil roasted, 1 oz.	160
dry roasted, 1 oz.	160
Pear, 1 (with skin)	100
Peas	
edible pod 1 cup	67
green, ½ cup	60
Peppers, green, 1	20
Pie	
apple, slice (1/6 pie)	405

Item	Approx. cal
banana cream, slice (1/6 pie)	310
cherry, slice (1/6 pie)	410
lemon meringue (1/6 pie)	355
pumpkin (1/6 pie)	370
Pineapple	
raw, 1 cup	75
sweetened (canned), 1 cup	170
Pinto beans, 1 cup	235
Pizza, cheese, 1/8 of 15" round	290
Plum, 1 (with skin)	36
Popcorn	
air popped, plain, 1 cup	30
popped in oil	55
Potatoes	
baked, 1	220
fried, 10 strips	160
hash browns, 1 cup	340
mashed, 1 cup	220
Prune, dried, 10 large	200
Radish, red, 10	10
Raisins, ¼ cup	100
Rice, cooked, 1 cup	260
Safflower oil, 1 tbsp	125
Salsa, 1 cup	90
Salt, 1 tsp.	0
Sausage, 4 oz.	540
Sherbet, 1 cup	270
Shrimp, boiled, 2 large	85
Soft drinks, 1 cup (best to check)	95
Spaghetti in tomato sauce w/ cheese	
canned, 1 cup	190
homemade, 1 cup	260
Spinach, cooked, 1 cup	45
Strawberries	
fresh, 1/2 cup	25
sweetened, 1/2 cup	125
Sugar	
brown, 1 tbsp.	50
white, granulated, 1 tbsp.	45
Taco shell, 1	60
Tangerine, 1 (without peel)	37
Tea, unsweetened, 1 cup	2
Tomato	
raw, 1 (with skin)	35
cooked, 1 cup	65
Tortilla chips, 1 oz.	140
Tuna, water pack, 3 oz.	110
Turkey	
dark, 3 oz.	160
light, 3 oz.	130
Vegetable juice, 1 cup	50
Vegetable shortening, 1 tbsp.	15
Watermelon, wedge, 4" x 8"	110
Yogurt, low fat (best to check)	
Plain, 1 cup	145
with fruit, 1 cup	230

Name ______________________
Date ____________ Hour ____________

27–Control of the Body

Ideas 27a

Neurons, Nerve Impulses, and Reflexes

Directions: Match the terms with the definitions by writing each term next to its definition.

axons	interneuron
brain	motor neuron
cell body	nervous
central	neurons
coordination	peripheral
dendrites	reflex
endocrine	sense organs
eye	sensory neuron
hormones	spinal cord
impulse	synapse

coordination ______ 1. Organization of the systems and processes of the body

endocrine ______ 2. The system that produces hormones to control and coordinate the body

cell body ______ 3. The part of the neuron that contains the nucleus

neurons ______ 4. Cells of the nervous system that are capable of transmitting impulses

brain ______ 5. The part of the central nervous system that is found in the skull

nervous ______ 6. The system of the body that includes the brain, eyes, ears, and nerves

axons ______ 7. Extensions of a neuron that carry impulses away from the cell body

eye ______ 8. The sense organ responsible for sensing light

hormones ______ 9. Chemicals produced by the glands of the endocrine system

impulse ______ 10. That which travels along a neuron

sense organs ______ 11. Structures, such as the eye and ear, that receive various kinds of stimuli

central ______ 12. The division of the nervous system that is composed of the brain and spinal cord

interneuron ______ 13. A neuron that is in a reflex arc and serves as a go-between for the other cells in the reflex arc

synapse 14. The space that impulses jump across by means of a transmitting chemical

peripheral 15. The division of the nervous system that is composed of the nerves and the sense organs

reflex 16. An immediate, inborn reaction to a stimulus

spinal cord 17. The part of the central nervous system not found in the skull

sensory neuron 18. In a reflex arc, the neuron that receives the stimulus from outside the body

dendrites 19. Extensions of a neuron that carry impulses toward the cell body

motor neuron 20. In a reflex arc, the neuron that carries an impulse to a muscle

Ideas 27b

Bob Uses His Brain

Directions: Below is a list of the divisions of the brain and a list of statements describing Bob's actions. For each statement, choose the one brain division that is involved the most with Bob's action. Write the proper letter choice in the space by the number.

a. brain stem
b. cerebellum
c. cerebrum, frontal lobe
d. cerebrum, occipital lobe
e. cerebrum, parietal lobe
f. cerebrum, temporal lobe

c 1. Bob decided to play catch with Bill.

b 2. Bob starts to walk to Bill's house.

e 3. On the way Bob smells something.

c 4. Bob recognizes the smell as being that of hot tar.

d 5. Bob sees something.

c 6. Bob realizes that it is a sign that says "Road Construction."

c 7. Bob understands why he smelled tar.

f 8. Bob hears something behind him.

b/c 9. It frightens Bob, and he jumps.

a 10. Bob takes a deep breath.

c 11. Bob recognizes that someone was yelling "Watch out, sonny!"

c 12. Bob decides to turn around and see who spoke to him.

Name ____________________

Date ______________ Hour ______________

b 13. Bob turns around.

c 14. Bob recognizes a truck used for laying asphalt.

c 15. Bob realizes the truck is coming at him.

a 16. Bob's heart begins to beat faster. His blood pressure goes up.

c 17. Bob decides that he should move.

b 18. Bob turns and walks onto the lawn.

e 19. Bob feels heat as the truck passes.

f 20. Bob hears something.

c/f 21. Bob recognizes Bill's voice.

c 22. Bob realizes Bill has called his name.

c 23. Bob realizes that Bill is coming toward him.

c 24. Bob smiles and decides to go toward Bill.

b 25. Bob goes toward Bill.

Ideas 27c

The Eye

Directions: Label the eye drawing by supplying the missing definitions; then draw a line from the terms to the proper structures in the drawing.

Definitions may vary.

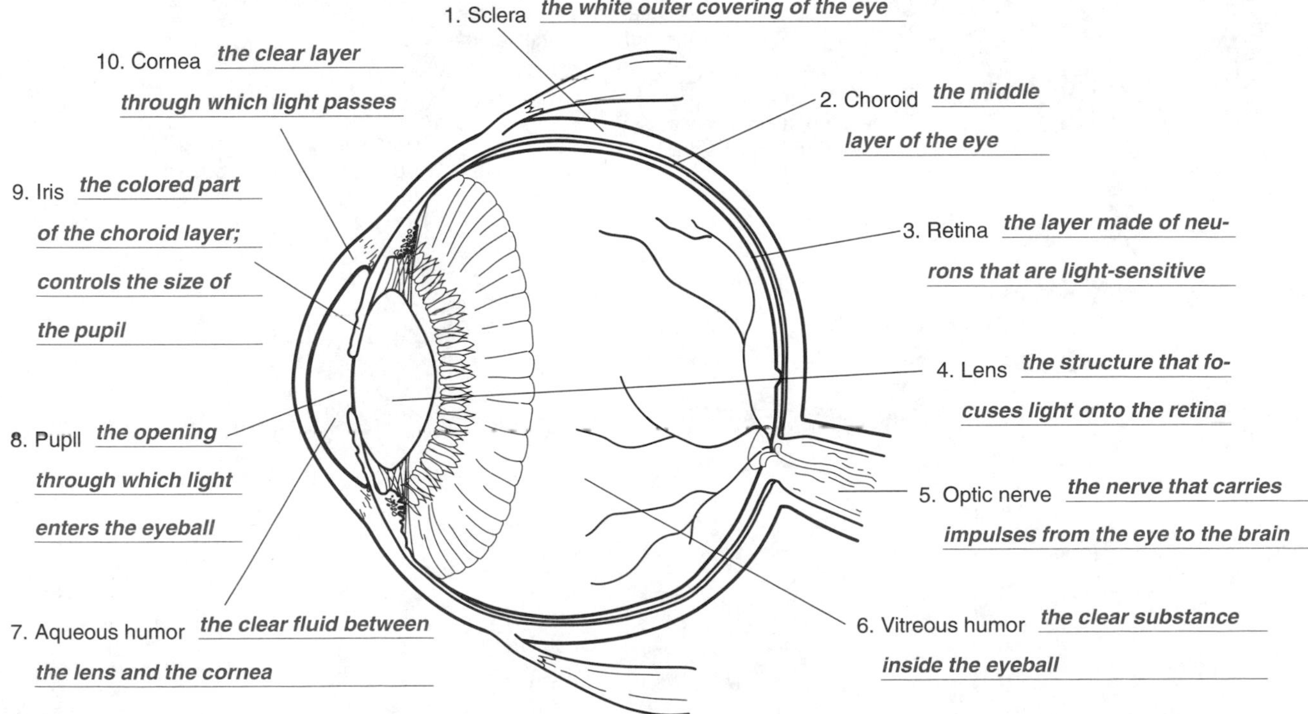

Ideas 27d

The Ear

Directions: Label the ear drawing by supplying the missing terms; then draw a line from the terms to the proper structures in the drawing. Some label lines have been provided for you.

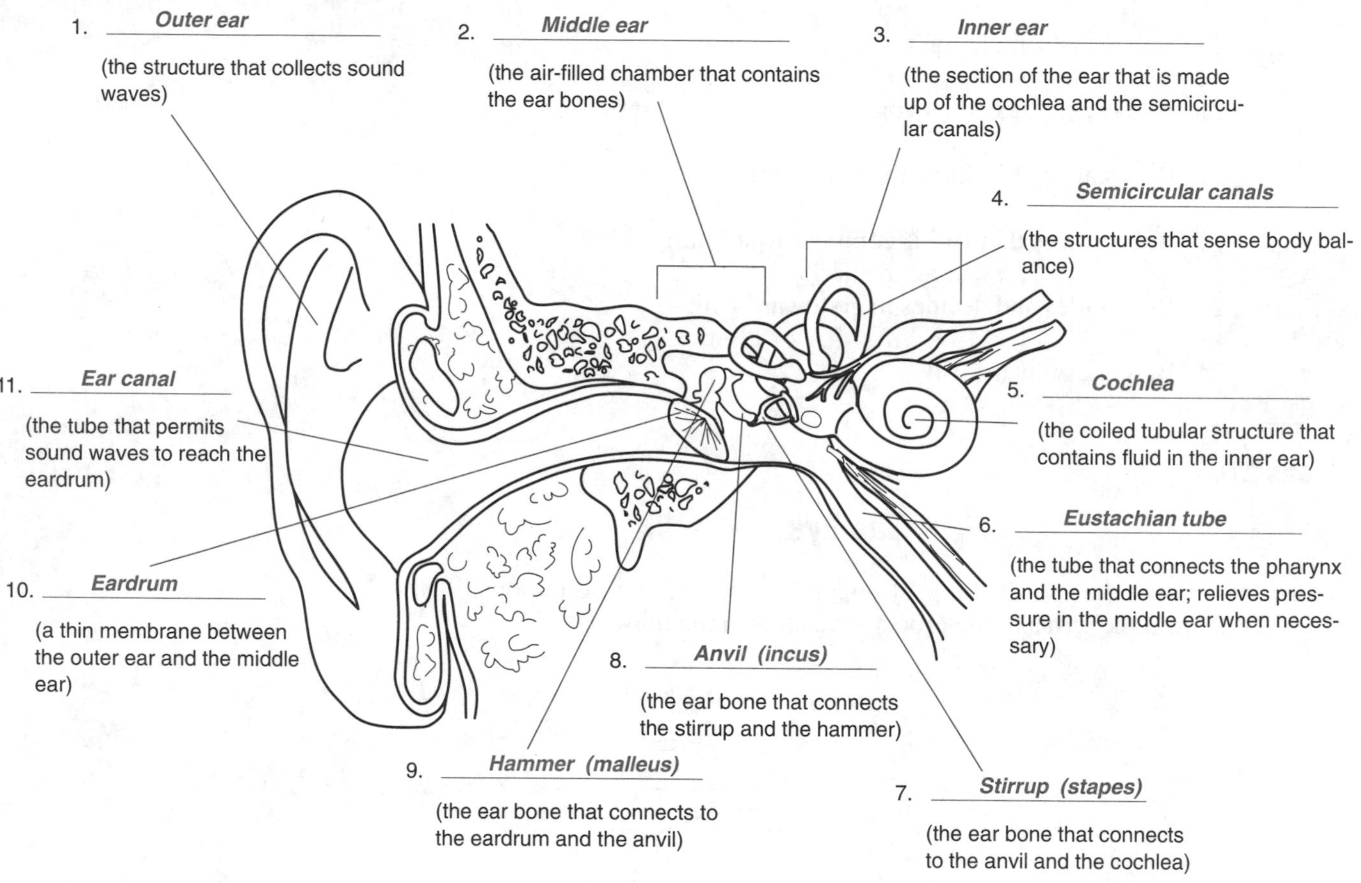

Name ______________________
Date ____________ Hour ____________

Ideas 27e

The Endocrine System

Directions: Fill in the chart by selecting the correct descriptions from the lists below the chart. All the blanks on the chart will have at least one entry; some will have several.

Locations (Use only five of these.)

Behind the stomach
Under the stomach
On top of the kidneys
In the chest
Below the brain
In the lower abdomen
In the neck
Under the sternum

Hormones (Use all of these.)

Growth hormone
Insulin
Reproductive hormones
Thyroxin
Epinephrine

Notes (Use all of these.)

Called the glands of emergency
Also produces digestive enzymes
Responsible for diabetes mellitus
Produces hormones that cause puberty
Cause an increased supply of oxygen and food to be carried to body tissues
Also produce gametes (ova or sperm)
Controls the body's metabolic rate
Master gland of the body
A goiter indicates malfunction
Produces more hormones than any other gland in the body.

Gland	Location	Hormones produced	Notes
Pituitary gland	*Below the brain*	*Growth hormone*	*Master gland of the body; produces more hormones than any other gland in the body*
Pancreas	*Behind the stomach*	*Insulin*	*Also produces digestive enzymes; responsible for diabetes mellitus*
Adrenal glands	*On top of the kidneys*	*Epinephrine*	*Called the glands of emergency; cause an increased supply of oxygen and food to be carried to body tissues*
Thyroid gland	*In the neck*	*Thyroxin*	*A goiter indicates malfunction; controls the body's metabolic rate*
Ovaries or testes	*In the lower abdomen*	*Reproductive hormones*	*Also produce gametes (ova or sperm); produce hormones that cause puberty*

Review 1

The answers given here are the most logical. Students, however, may devise other good sentences that involve three of the four words in each group. The day after assigning this exercise, you may wish to work half of it in class and then grade the rest when you collect the assignment.

Directions: Below are several groups of words. In each group, three of the four words (or phrases) are related to one another. Draw a line through the unrelated word and write a sentence using the remaining words. Your sentence should show how the words are related. You may slightly change the form of the word in your sentence (for example, *neuron* to *neurons, smell* to *smelled*).

1. internal coordination / ~~synapse~~ / nervous system / endocrine system *The systems of internal coordination are the nervous system and the endocrine system.*

2. dendrite / axon / cell body / ~~cerebellum~~ *The dendrites and axon extend from the cell body.*

3. ~~peripheral nervous system~~ / nerve impulse / transmitting chemical / synapse *Nerve impulses jump across synapses by using transmitting chemicals.*

4. interneuron / motor neuron / ~~neuron~~ / sensory neuron *The reflex arc is made up of a sensory neuron, an interneuron, and a motor neuron.*

5. hemispheres / lobes / cerebrum / ~~brain stem~~ *The cerebrum is divided into two hemispheres, and the hemispheres are each divided into four lobes.*

6. ~~Spinal cord~~ / cerebrum / brain stem / cerebellum *The brain consists of the cerebrum, the cerebellum, and the brain stem.*

7. sclera / ~~synapse~~ / choroid / retina *The three layers of the eye are the sclera, the choroid, and the retina.*

8. choroid / ~~retina~~ / iris / pupil *The iris is the colored part of the choroid, and the pupil is the opening in the iris.*

9. aqueous humor / vitreous humor / lens / ~~iris~~ *The aqueous humor is in front of the lens, and the vitreous humor is behind the lens.*

Name ______________________

Date ____________ Hour ____________

10. ~~lens~~ / rods / cones / retina *The retina contains rods, which are sensitive in dim light, and cones, which are sensitive in bright light.*

11. outer ear / ~~ear bones~~ / eardrum / ear canal *The outer ear consists of an outer flap, the ear canal, and the eardrum.*

12. Eustachian tube / ~~cochlea~~ / pharynx / middle ear *The Eustachian tube connects the middle ear and the pharynx.*

13. ~~smell~~ / pain / cold / touch *Pain, touch, and cold are senses of the skin.*

14. ~~stirrup~~ / cochlea / inner ear / semicircular canals *The inner ear consists of the cochlea and semicircular canals.*

15. eardrum / ear bones / cochlea / ~~semicircular canals~~ *The ear bones transfer sound vibrations from the eardrum to the cochlea.*

16. pancreas / ~~insulin~~ / pituitary / thyroid *The pancreas, pituitary gland, and thyroid are endocrine glands.*

17. endocrine / ~~sugar~~ / hormones / ductless *The endocrine glands are ductless glands that produce hormones.*

18. ~~diabetes~~ / thyroid / goiter / thyroxine *A condition called "goiter" may result if the thyroid gland cannot produce enough thyroxine.*

19. ~~dwarfs~~ / insulin / pancreas / sugar *The pancreas produces insulin to help regulate the amount of sugar in the blood.*

20. growth hormone / pituitary / dwarf / ~~ductless~~ *A person may be a dwarf if the pituitary does not produce enough growth hormone.*

Review 2

Directions: Record your responses in the spaces provided.

1. Why is internal coordination of the body essential? *If a person's internal body processes were not coordinated, substances and processes would soon be out of balance, and the person would die.*

2. Name three significant differences between the type of control the nervous system has over the body and the type of control the endocrine system has over the body. *Nervous control is rapid, short-lived, and directed to a single, specific area. Hormonal control is slower, longer-lived, and directed to tissues found in various parts of the body.*

3. What is a hormone? What do hormones do? List several hormones and tell their functions. *A hormone is a chemical messenger. Hormones cause various body processes to operate. Lists of hormones will vary.*

4. In what two systems does the pancreas function? What are its functions in each system? *The pancreas functions in the endocrine and digestive systems. As part of the endocrine system, it produces a hormone. As part of the digestive system, it produces digestive enzymes.*

5. The ovaries and testes do not begin producing their hormones until the early teenage years. What happens to a person of your sex when these hormones begin to be produced? What name is given for the time period when these changes occur? *Puberty is the time when a young person's body matures. Characteristics will vary, depending on sex. (See pages 464-65 of the text.)*

6. What is a reflex arc? Explain why reflexes are important. *A reflex arc is a series of neurons that receive a stimulus and cause the body to react to the stimulus. Reflexes, which are immediate and involuntary, help prevent serious injuries by allowing a person to react quickly to a harmful stimulus.*

Name ______________________
Date __________ Hour ______________

Class Investigation 27a

Skin's Sensation of Temperature

You may want to do this investigation as a demonstration.

Goals

- Demonstrate the skin's ability to detect differences in temperature.
- Observe the fallibility of the senses.

Home School Tip
If you have only a single student, he or she should be the experimenter. Use family members or friends as the subject and assistant.

Materials

large cups or glasses, hot water, cold water, thermometer

Large Styrofoam cups are best. The larger water volume and insulating nature of Styrofoam will limit temperature changes.

Setting up

1. Put warm water into a glass. Have a person place two fingers into the water. Add hot or cold water to make the water feel lukewarm (neither cool nor warm).
2. When the water temperature is lukewarm, use a thermometer to find out what temperature the water is.
3. Prepare seven glasses of water of different temperatures. The middle temperature should be the one at which the water feels lukewarm.
4. One of the glasses should be five degrees hotter, another ten degrees hotter, and a third fifteen degrees hotter than the lukewarm temperature. One of the glasses should be five degrees colder, another ten degrees colder, and another fifteen degrees colder than the lukewarm temperature.
5. Label all the glasses as follows: hot, very warm, warm, lukewarm, cool, very cool, cold.
6. Prepare twenty-one small pieces of paper. On three of them write *hot,* on three write *very warm,* on three write *warm,* and so on. Fold these pieces of paper and place them in a dish.

For this experiment, use the Fahrenheit temperature scale. If you use the Celsius scale, the temperature difference between successive glasses of water should be about 3 degrees.

Procedures and observations

During the experiment frequently test the temperatures of the various glasses of water. If necessary, add hot or cold water to them so that they maintain their original temperatures throughout the entire experiment. Have a person place his fingers in each of the glasses of water to feel the temperatures. The person should briefly dry his fingers before placing them in each glass. While the person looks away (or blindfold him), dip his fingers into the various glasses and have him tell you which of the glasses his fingers are in.

Tell students not to put a student's fingers into another glass until he has responded. Instruct them not to put the fingers back into a glass to give the person a second chance to describe the temperature of the water.

1. Determine the sequence of glasses you dip his fingers into by drawing pieces of paper randomly out of the dish.
2. Dip his fingers into the glass for five seconds; then remove them.
3. Put a check in the box of the water temperatures that were used and put an *X* in the box of the temperature that the person says it is. If the response is correct, darken in the entire square.

Try to have the person's fingers out of the water for only a few seconds. To do this, several people will have to work together to do the experiment (one recording data, one dipping the fingers, one marking temperatures, one lining up the glasses, and one occasionally checking the water temperatures).

Responses

	Hot	Very Warm	Warm	Luke-warm	Cool	Very Cool	Cold
1.							
2.							
3.							
4.							
5.							
6.							
7.							
8.							
9.							
10.							
11.							
12.							
13.							
14.							
15.							
16.							
17.							
18.							
19.							
20.							

Summing up

Question 4 may cause some students difficulty. To figure out the answer, they will need to tell whether the temperature of the water was higher or lower than the temperature that was previously tested and whether the person's response indicated that the water temperature was higher or lower.

1. How often was the person incorrect? __________

   How often was he correct? __________

2. How often was the person only one temperature off? __________

3. How often was the person only two temperatures off? __________

4. How often was the person correct about a temperature being higher or lower than the previous temperature tested? __________

   How often was he incorrect? __________

5. Compare your group's results with those of other groups. Are they about the same? ☐ Yes ☐ No If your answer is no, what do you think accounts for the difference? ***Answers will vary. Poorly conducted experiments or a person with unusual ability or lack of ability to determine temperatures can cause the difference.***

6. What are your conclusions about the skin's ability to determine temperatures? ***Answers will vary. Most people are sensitive to changes and can tell whether temperatures increase or decrease, but they frequently are unable to determine the difference between temperatures that are close together.***

Name ______________________________
Date ____________ Hour ______________

Class Investigation 27b

Pupil Reflex

Goals

- Demonstrate a reflex.
- Understand the purposes of reflexes.

Materials

darkened room, penlight (small flashlight)

Setting up

The iris (colored portion) of the eye controls the size of the pupil (black spot). The pupil is actually an opening into the eye. When the pupil is large, a great amount of light is let into the eye. When the pupil is small, very little light enters the eye. The size of the pupil is controlled by a reflex. This reflex is stimulated by the amount (intensity) of light available to the eye.

Procedures and observations

You will need to perform the following procedures with a partner.

Often just turning off the lights and closing the blinds will darken the room enough for students to conduct this investigation.

1. Sit in a darkened area for several minutes. This should cause your pupils to become large. If they do not, go to a darker area.
2. Shine a penlight into the right eye of your partner, being careful not to shine it into his left eye.
   - What happens to the pupil of the right eye? *It becomes smaller.*
   - What happens to the pupil of the left eye? *It also becomes smaller.*
   - How fast does the reflex take place? *It takes place rapidly.*
3. Turn off the penlight and allow the eyes to readjust to the dim light.
4. Repeat the above experiment but shine the penlight into the left eye. Does the same thing happen? ☒ Yes ☐ No If not, what does happen? ______

Summing up

1. Why is the pupil reflex necessary? *Too much light could damage the eye. In dim light a person cannot see unless the pupils are opened widely.*
2. Why must the reflex happen quickly? *It must occur quickly so that a person can see quickly when moving from bright to dim light and so that a person's eyes will not be damaged when moving from dim to bright light.*

Name ____________________

Date __________ Hour __________

Class Investigation 27c

AfterImages

Goals

- Demonstrate afterimages.
- Evaluate the functioning of the cones of the eye.

Supply only dark, solid colors of construction paper. Deep blue, red, purple, green, orange, and black are good colors to use. These colors will permit students to see opposite colors easily.

Materials

colored construction paper (dark, bright colors), bright light, glue or tape, white paper, scissors

Setting up

You may also try these colors on a black background for variety.

1. Cut circles, triangles, squares, and other simple shapes from colored construction paper.
   - You should have at least four different colors of each shape.
   - Each figure should be about 5 centimeters (2 in.) square.
2. Glue or tape each of these shapes in the center of a sheet of white paper (one shape per sheet of paper). If you use tape, use tiny rolls of tape behind the shape so that none of the tape shows.
3. Using a pencil, place a tiny dot in the center of each shape.

Procedures and observations

You may want to put students into groups and then distribute a different color to each group. Have every student in the group try the experiment and then combine results. Once all the groups have done the experiment, you can ask the various groups for their results and have all the students record them on the chart.

1. Place a sheet of white paper with a colored shape on it in a brightly lighted area about ½ meter (18-20 in.) away from your face.
2. Stare at the dot in the center of the shape for twenty seconds. Keep your eyes on the dot for the entire time.
3. Look at some light-colored area in the distance (the ceiling is good) and close your eyes.
   - What you see immediately after you close your eyes is called an afterimage.
   - Describe the afterimage you saw. (Be sure to describe its shape and its color in relation to the shape and color you stared at.) ***The afterimage's color should be opposite on the color wheel (complimentary colors) from the color that caused it. The shape and size should be the same as the one stared at.***

You may need to use a lamp near the paper at which students are staring in order to obtain a good afterimage.

Opposite (complementary) colors are red/green, blue/orange, and yellow/violet.

4. After you have performed this experiment and have seen an afterimage, you should wait until you no longer can see that afterimage before you do the experiment again.
5. Try obtaining other afterimages using different colors and shapes. Record your findings on the chart below. In the "Notes" column, record anything unusual you observe about the afterimage.

6. If time permits, you may want to form some afterimages by using colored shapes on pieces of colored paper. What are the results? ______

	Shape	Color of Shape	Color of Afterimage	Notes
1.				
2.				
3.				
4.				
5.				
6.				
7.				
8.				

Summing up

The cones in your eyes have different chemicals that break down when exposed to different colors. Thus when you are looking at something blue, a certain chemical breaks down. When you are looking at something red, a different chemical breaks down, and so on. Different shades of color are seen when different amounts and combinations of these chemicals breakdown.

Afterimages result when you break down a large amount of a particular color's chemical and then look away. The temporary lack of a chemical in the area causes the afterimages.

1. About how long did the afterimages last? *a few seconds*

2. What observations can you make about different colors of afterimages? *Answers will vary. Students should note that the afterimages are always colors that are opposite the ones at which they stared.*

3. List normal, everyday situations in which afterimages occur. *Answers will vary. If a person glances at a light source, he will often see afterimages. When one has watched television in a darkened room for a period of time, he will see afterimages. Glare can cause afterimages and can even result in accidents when one is driving.*

Year-end Review

Directions: Complete the crossword puzzle.

Across

1. Biblical ________ is the belief that God created all things.
6. The ________ theory claims non-recorded events between Gen 1:1 and 1:2.
10. the science of heredity
13. common preposition
14. Atomic Energy Commission
15. special luxury edition
16. grows on bread, has hyphae, and produces spores
17. A plant cell ________ contains cellulose.
18. short for evolution
20. marine arthropod
22. how Jill got up the hill
23. French "me"
24. personal pronoun
26. All cells have this boundary.
29. ocular organ
30. photosynthetic pigment

Down

2. sharp as a razor's ________
3. regulates the pupil of the eye
4. Genetic ________ involves transferring individual genes.
5. type of behavior that involves reasoning
7. small particle of matter
8. 3.14
9. not brand new
11. has an axon and dendrites
12. unit of energy
13. everyone
15. first digestive fluid in your digestive system
19. large tub or barrel
20. honeybees' storage facility
21. what an embryo is
25. smallest living unit
27. not you
28. We must ________ on the Lord.

	1 C	R	2 E	A	T	I	O	N	3 I	S	M	
4 E			D						R			5 I
N			6 G	7 A	8 P		9 U		I			N
10 G	E	11 N	E	T	I	12 C	S		S		13 A	T
I		E		O		14 A	E	C		15 S	L	E
N		U		16 M	O	L	D		17 W	A	L	L
E		R				O				L		L
18 E	19 V	O	L		20 C	R	A	21 B		I		I
22 R	A	N		23 M	O	I		A		V		G
24 I	T		25 C		26 M	E	27 M	B	28 R	A	N	E
N			E		B		29 E	Y	E			N
G			L						L			T
	30 C	H	L	O	R	O	P	H	Y	L	L	

Appendix A

Laboratory Equipment

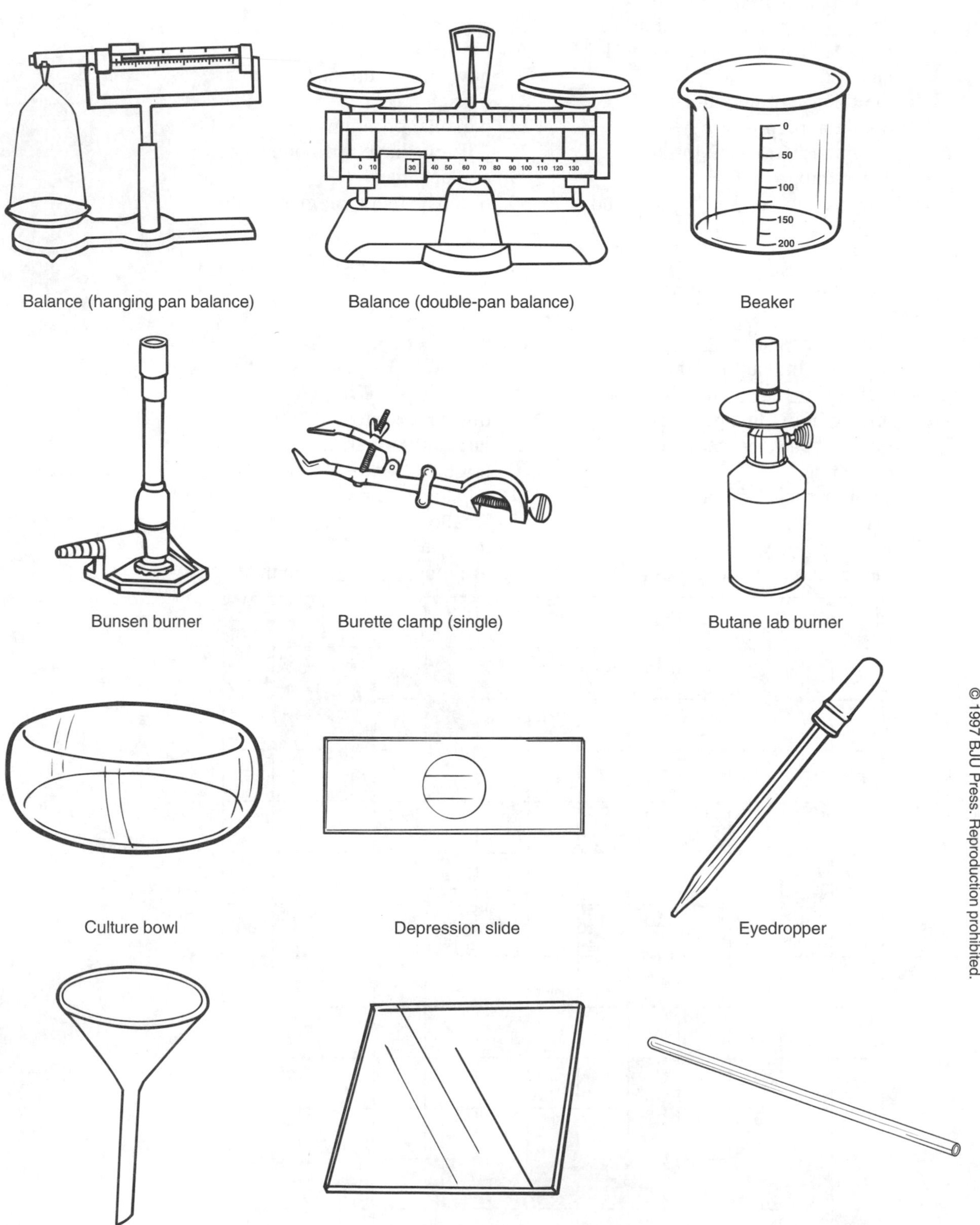

Balance (hanging pan balance)

Balance (double-pan balance)

Beaker

Bunsen burner

Burette clamp (single)

Butane lab burner

Culture bowl

Depression slide

Eyedropper

Funnel

Glass plate

Glass tubing

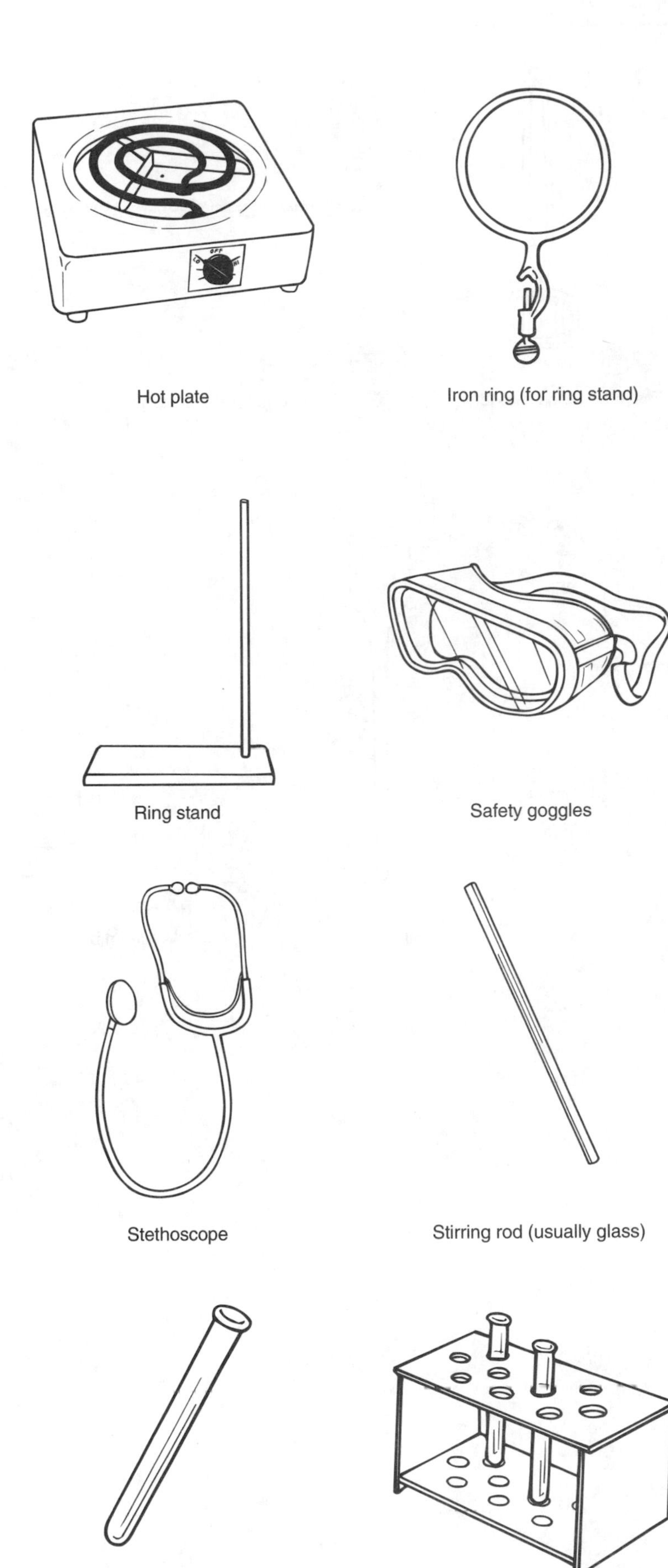

Graduated cylinder

Hot plate

Iron ring (for ring stand)

Petri dish

Ring stand

Safety goggles

Scalpel, probe, dissection pins, forceps

Stethoscope

Stirring rod (usually glass)

Stoppers

Test tube

Test tube rack

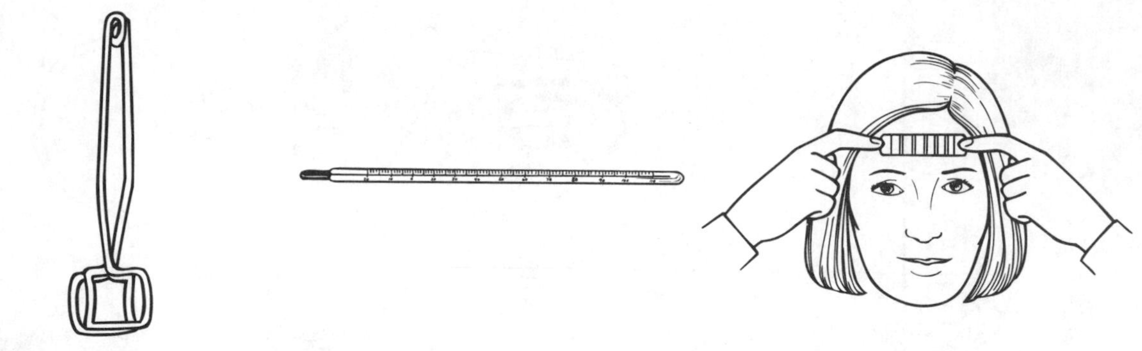

Test tube tongs (Stoddard)

Thermometer (laboratory)

Thermometer (strip)

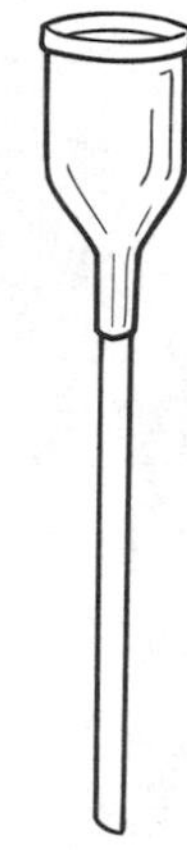

Thistle tube

Vacuum bottle (Thermos bottle)

Appendix B

Chromosomes for Class Investigation 7B

Photocopy this page as many times as necessary and cut out individual chromosomes. Sort them by length and put a pair of each length into each bag, resulting in eight different length pairs per bag. You will need two bags for each spudoodle to be constructed. It is not necessary for each pair of chromosomes to be homozygous or heterozygous (i.e., some bags can have chromosome pairs which consist of uppercase lettered chromosomes, some can be both lowercase, and some can be mixed).

H	
h	
A	n
a	N
E	g
e	G
B	r
b	R
D	d
d	D
R	b
r	B
G	e
g	E
N	a
n	A
h	
H	

Material	Source	Activity	Notes
alcohol	L or SH	2C 5C 21B 25B	70% ethanol or 70% isopropyl 70% ethanol or 70% isopropyl 70% isopropyl 70% ethanol or 70% isopropyl
aluminum foil	L	5C	
ant food	L	19A	corn flakes, wheat or barley seed, potato
ant microcosm chamber	L or SH	19A	
ants	L or SH	19A	
apple juice	L	5B	Any sugary fruit juice should work.
aquarium, small	L	17A	
bags	L	7B	small paper or plastic bags
bags, plastic	L	13A	small trash can size
		7A	half-pint to pint size
balance or scales	SH	1A 11A 13A 23C 26B	 Kitchen scales may be used. Kitchen scales may be used. Kitchen or bathroom scales may be used. Kitchen scales may be used.
balloons	L	5B	
beaker, 500 ml	SH	4B	
beaker, 250 ml	SH	4A 5C 21B	Two are needed. Glass container can be used.
Benedict's solution	SH	26A	
Biuret solution	SH	3B	
blender	L	23D	
bone, fresh beef	L	24B	
box (shoebox)	L	2C 13F	
box, cardboard	L	13B 13D	
bread, one slice	L	21B	
Bunsen burner or butane lab burner	SH	26A	
cabinet	L	5C	or other dark area
celery stalks with leaves	L	13B	
clamp (burette clamp)	SH	4B 13D	 Three are needed.
cloth	L	23D	or blotting paper
coins	L	7B	penny, nickel, or quarter
containers (cups or glasses)	L	18A 27A	Cups from fast-food restaurants work well.
contour feather	L or SH	18B	
cork	L or SH	4D	
corn syrup (clear)	L	4B	
cotton	L	13F	
cover slips	SH	4C 4D 13C 22D	
crackers, saltine	L	26A	
culture bowls	L or SH	11B	clear glass bowls
dishes	L or SH	5A	

Material	Source	Activity	Notes
dishes	L or SH	13D	large, clear, and flat
dishpan, large	L	23D	
dissection pan	SH	15A 17B 17C	A dissection pan is included in the dissection kit available from BJU Press.
dissection pins	SH	15A 17B	Dissection pins are included in the dissection kit available from BJU Press.
down feathers	L or SH	18A 18B	enough to fill a cup Only a few are needed.
dumbbell	L	24C	or similar weight
egg cartons	L	13F	plastic or Styrofoam
electric fan	L	13B	
elodea	L or SH	4D 13D	Elodea is available from aquarium hobby shops.
encyclopedia or other reference book	L	9A 9B 10B 10C 15B 16A 20B 21A 22A 23A	land animal books dinosaur books animal books animal books
ethyl acetate	L or SH	2C	Use non-acetone type fingernail polish remover.
eyedropper	L or SH	4C, D 3C, F 19A 22D	An eyedropper is included in the dissection kit available from BJU Press.
fern fronds with spores	L	12B	
fingernail polish	L	2C	clear
fish, live	L	17A	Use an inexpensive goldfish.
flower	L	4D 14A	 Provide several different kinds of flowers.
flowerpots	L	8A 12B 13E 22C	 clay with saucer base two, identical
folder	L	12A	
food coloring	L	13B	red or blue
forceps	SH	17B 17C	A pair of forceps is included in the dissection kit available from BJU Press.
forceps, large	SH	25A	
freezer	L	18A	
funnel, large	L or SH	21B	
geranium or coleus	L	5C 13A	Geranium is the better choice.
glass plates (panes)	L or SH	13F	
glass or wooden rods	L or SH	25A	
glass tubing	SH	5B	
gloves	L	11A	ordinary work gloves
gloves	L or SH	17B 17C	plastic or latex gloves plastic or latex gloves
goggles, safety	L or SH	3B	
graduated cylinder (10 ml)	SH	3B 26A	

Material	Source	Activity	Notes
graduated cylinder (100 ml)	SH	3B	
hand lens	L or SH	2C 18B 21B	A hand lens is included in the dissection kit available from BJU Press.
heart, beef	L	25A	
hot plate	L or SH	1B 3C 5C	Do not use an open-flame heat source.
household trash and garbage	L	11A 23C	
ice	L	17A	
ink	L	4A	or dark food coloring
iron (clothes iron)	L	23D	
iodine solution	L or SH	4D 5C	Or make from iodine and potassium iodine.
jars, wide-mouth	L	13B	
insect killing jar	L or SH	2C	
knife	L	5A 11C 13B	
labels	L	14B	
leaf (geranium)	L	4D	
leaves	L	12A	Students should collect.
leaves	L	13C	geranium, lettuce, or philodendron
lichen specimens	L	22D	
light/lamp	L	13D 27C 21B 27A	fairly bright, like a sun lamp Bright room light is sufficient. incandescent, 60-100 watt small flashlight or penlight
litter of kittens or puppies	L	20A	with at least one parent, better with both
marshmallows, mini	L	7B	several colors; Use highlighters to color.
measuring cups	L	3C 26B	
measuring spoons	L	3C 4A 26B	
meter stick	L	1A	or yardstick
methylene blue	L	4D	
microscope, compound	SH	4D 6A 11B, C 13C 18B 22D 24A, D 25D	
microscope, stereoscopic	SH	11B	
microscope slides	SH		
depression slides			
concave	SH	11B	
plain	SH	4C, D 13C 22D	
prepared slides			
various cells	SH	4D	available
root tips	SH	6A	onion, lily, or hyacinth (for mitosis)
mushroom	SH	11C	
leaf, c.s.	SH	13C	
prepared slides (cont.)			
animal hairs, w.m.	SH	18B	
lichens	SH	22D	
human skin, c.s.	SH	24A	
human bone, c.s.	SH	24D	dry, ground human bones, c.s.
striated muscle	SH	24D	striated human muscle
human blood	SH	25D	normal human blood
blood diseases	SH	25D	various blood diseases
milk	L	3C	
mixing bowls	L	3C	
moth balls	L	2C	
mushrooms, fresh	L	11C	wild or cultivated
nails	L	13D	
number spinner	L	10A	
nutrient agar plate	SH	21B	
onion	L	4D	
painted lady butterfly larvae	SH	16B	butterfly garden
paper	L	1A 2A 4C 6B 10A 11C 12A 12B 23D 27C	13 cm or 5 in. square newspaper or other printed material construction paper black and white newspaper newspaper white paper and bright construction paper
paper clips	L	5C	
paper towels	L	13F	
pencils, colored	L	6B	or crayons
pencil, glass marking	L	26A	
petri dish	SH	5C	
pH meter	SH	3A	
pH paper	SH	3A	
pipe cleaner	L	7B	
plant food	L	11B	soluble fertilizer
plants	L	13E	violet, begonia, tomato, willow, holly
plastic wrap	L	12B	
popcorn, unpopped	L	1B	various colors
popcorn, popped	L	7B	
popcorn popper	L	1B	
potato	L	4D 5A 7B	 must be fresh
potting soil	L	8A 12B 13E 14B 22C	
potting trays	L	14B	
preserved earthworm	SH	15A	
preserved frog	SH	17B, C	
probes	L	14A 15A 17B	
protozoan culture	SH	4D	

Material	Source	Activity	Notes
puffed wheat	L	7B	breakfast cereal
pushpins	L	7B	several colors
putty or modeling clay	L or SH	13A	
rennet tablets	L or SH	3C	
rice	L	11B	
ring stand	SH	4B 13D 21B	
iron ring	SH	21	for use with ring stand
rooting hormone	L or SH	13E	
rubber bands or string	L	4B 12B 13F	
ruler	L	1A 8B 9A 13B 17B	
sand	L	1A 12B 19A	
scalpel or single-edged razor blade	L or SH	4D 14A 15A 17B 17C	
scissors	L	6B 8B 13C, F 15A 17B, C 27C	A pair of scissors is included in the dissection kit available from BJU Press.
screen, mesh	L	23D	window screen
seeds, bean	L	13F 14B 22C	
seeds, irradiated	SH	8A	available from Carolina Biological Supply
selectively permeable membrane	SH	4B	dialysis tubing
shellac, spray	L	11C	
shovel	L	11A	
sponge, large	L	23D	
spoons	L	3C	
staple gun	L	23D	
stethoscope	L or SH	25B	
stirring rod or spoon	L or SH	4A	
stones, small	L	12B	or pieces of broken clay pottery
stopper, two-hole, rubber	SH	5B	
stopwatch or a clock	L	4A 25B 25C	or clock with a second hand
straight pins	L	2C	
straw, thin	L	17B	
string	L	5B	
sugar	L	3C 5B	table sugar table sugar
sunny window	L	5C 8A 11B 13E	or other warm, bright area
tablespoon	L	1A	
tape	L	5B 6B 8B 12A 27C	
test tubes	SH	3B 13D 26A	large or small large large or small
test tube rack	SH	3B 26A	
test tube tongs	SH	26A	Stoddard tongs
thermometers, lab	SH	3C 5B 17A 18A 27A	 Three are needed.
thermometers, strip	L	24C	
vacuum flask	L	5B	Thermos bottle
thistle tube	SH	4B	
thread	L	13D	
thumb tacks	L	7B	
tissues	L	25B	
toothpicks	L	4D 7B 13C	
topsoil	L	21B	collected locally and recently
twist tie (or tape)	L	13A	
vanilla	L	3C	
water	L	4A 4B 5A 5C 11B 12B 17A 23D 27A	hot and cold tap water tap water tap water and salt water tap water pond water boiling hot tap water tap water hot and cold tap water
wire screen	L	21B	quarter-inch mesh
wood and nails	L	11A	to build a compost bin
wood frame	L	23D	
woody stem cross section	L	1A	Cut tree limb clearly showing annual rings.
wool	L	18A	
yarn	L	1A 25A	 red and blue
yeast	L	5B	dry active yeast

Ribosome Pattern for Investigation 6b   Each square equals ½ inch.

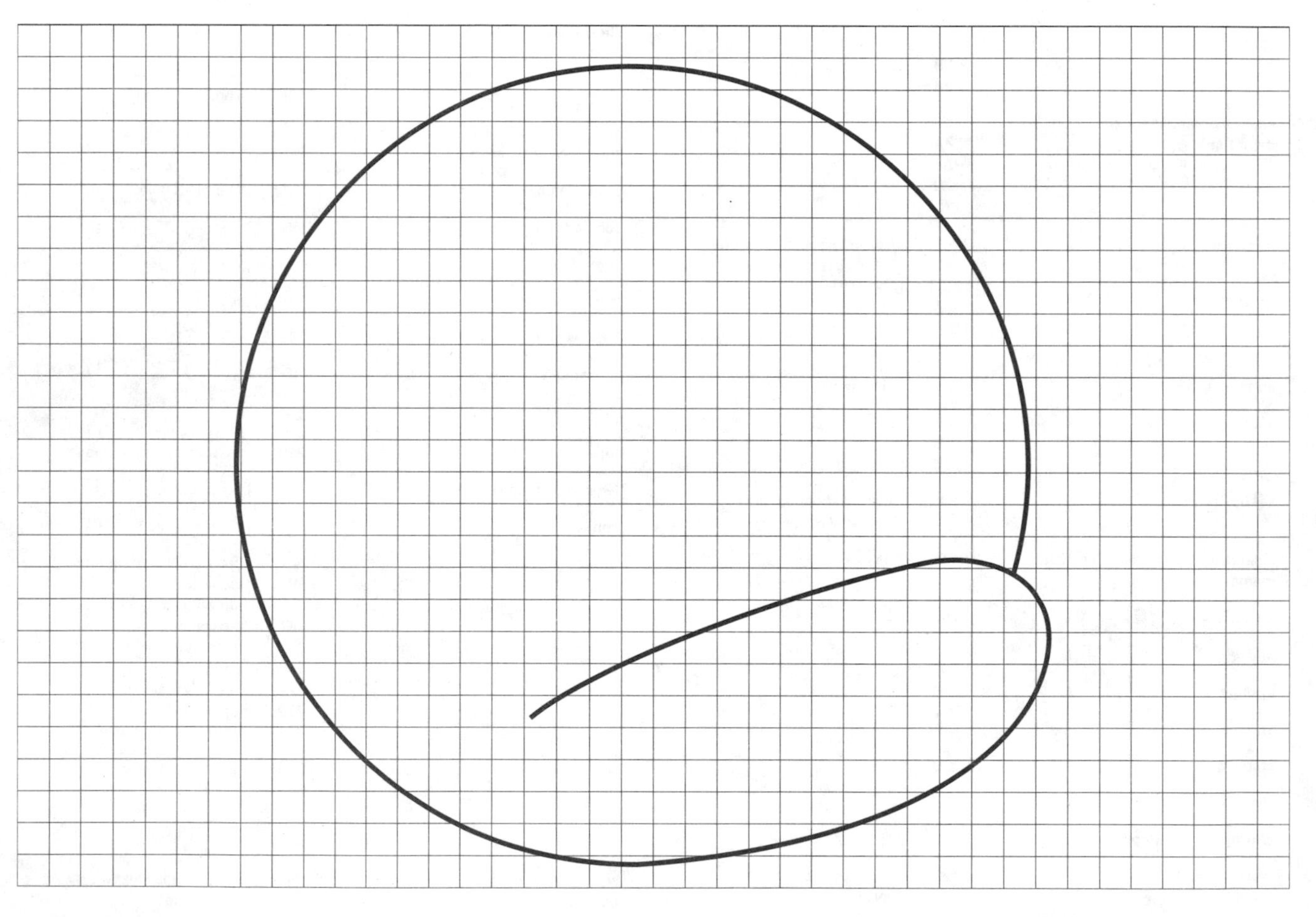